THE CONSTRUCTION LAW LIBRARY FROM ASPEN LAW & BUSINESS

ALTERNATIVE CLAUSES TO STANDARD CONSTRUCTION CONTRACTS
James E. Stephenson, Editor

ALTERNATIVE DISPUTE RESOLUTION IN THE CONSTRUCTION INDUSTRY
Robert F. Cushman, G. Christian Hedemann, and Avram S. Tucker, Editors

ARBITRATION OF CONSTRUCTION DISPUTES
Michael T. Callahan, Barry B. Bramble, and Paul M. Lurie

ARCHITECT AND ENGINEER LIABILITY: CLAIMS AGAINST DESIGN PROFESSIONALS
Robert F. Cushman and Thomas G. Bottum, Editors

CALCULATING CONSTRUCTION DAMAGES
William Schwartzkopf, John J. McNamara, and Julian F. Hoffar

CALIFORNIA CONSTRUCTION LAW (FIFTEENTH EDITION)
Kenneth C. Gibbs and Gordon Hunt

CONSTRUCTION AND ENVIRONMENTAL INSURANCE CASE DIGESTS
Wiley Law Publications, Editors

CONSTRUCTION BIDDING LAW
Robert F. Cushman and William J. Doyle, Editors

CONSTRUCTION CLAIMS AND LIABILITY
Michael S. Simon

CONSTRUCTION CONTRACTOR'S HANDBOOK OF BUSINESS AND LAW
Robert F. Cushman, G. Christian Hedemann, and Peter J. King, Editors

CONSTRUCTION DEFAULTS: RIGHTS, DUTIES, AND LIABILITIES
Robert F. Cushman and Charles A. Meeker, Editors

CONSTRUCTION DELAY CLAIMS (SECOND EDITION)
Barry B. Bramble and Michael T. Callahan

CONSTRUCTION ENGINEERING EVIDENCE
Loren W. Peters

CONSTRUCTION FAILURES
Robert F. Cushman, Irvin E. Richter, and Lester E. Rivelis, Editors

CONSTRUCTION INDUSTRY CONTRACTS: LEGAL CITATOR AND CASE DIGEST
Wiley Law Publications Editorial Staff

CONSTRUCTION INDUSTRY FORMS (TWO VOLUMES)
Robert F. Cushman and George L. Blick, Editors

CONSTRUCTION INDUSTRY INSURANCE HANDBOOK
Deutsch, Kerrigan & Stiles

CALCULATING CONSTRUCTION DAMAGES

SUBSCRIPTION NOTICE

This Aspen Law & Business product is updated on a periodic basis with supplements to reflect important changes in the subject matter. If you purchased this product directly from Aspen Law & Business, we have already recorded your subscription for the update service.

If, however, you purchased this product from a bookstore and wish to receive future updates and revised or related volumes billed separately with a 30-day examination review, please contact our Customer Service Department at 1-800-234-1660, or send your name, company name (if applicable), address, and the title of the product to:

ASPEN LAW & BUSINESS
A Division of Aspen Publishers, Inc.
7201 McKinney Circle
Frederick, MD 21701

CALCULATING CONSTRUCTION DAMAGES

WILLIAM SCHWARTZKOPF

Forcon International Corp.
Denver, CO

JOHN J. McNAMARA

Gadsby & Hannah
Boston, MA

JULIAN F. HOFFAR

Watt, Tieder, Killian & Hoffar
McLean, VA

ASPEN LAW & BUSINESS

Library of Congress Cataloging-in-Publication Data

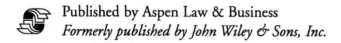
Published by Aspen Law & Business
Formerly published by John Wiley & Sons, Inc.

ISBN 0-471-54703-4

Printed in the United States of America

10 9 8

PREFACE

The pursuit of construction claims can be a very expensive process. Although collecting damages is the ultimate goal of a construction claim, it is often treated as an afterthought in the preparation of a claim. Many claims are submitted in which 90 percent or more of the presentation is devoted to entitlement. To further compound this problem, the damages are often assembled and presented in a confusing manner. Approaching damages in this way undermines the entitlement and basis of the claim.

The primary purpose of this book is to provide practical guidelines for the calculation and preparation of damages. We have endeavored to set forth methods of damage calculation that are easily explained, understood, and related to most construction cost accounting systems. In addition to outlining the methods and calculations, we have provided the legal support for recovery, although a legal treatise on damages is *not* the primary focus of this text.

This book is organized by type of damages rather than type of claim. It provides a detailed treatment of each type of damage, such as labor loss, material costs, and so on, rather than focusing on types of entitlement. Numerous examples and sample calculations are provided, all taken from actual claims.

This book is intended to be used not only by attorneys but by contractors, owners, accountants, subcontractors, and anyone involved in a construction claim. It is our intent to provide a better understanding of damages, both from the practical standpoint of how to compute them and the legal standpoint of how to support the recoverability of the claimed damages.

Although concisely calculated damages which reference cost accounting data can aid in the early and amicable resolution of construction claims, this book is presented as though the analysis is being done in anticipation of litigation. However, it is the hope of the authors that by doing a thorough, careful analysis, litigation can be avoided.

Two appendixes are included as examples. **Appendix A** contains three sets of sample cost accounting reports that have been adapted from actual reports. These are included to demonstrate the source material from which damage amounts are developed. **Appendix B** is an example of a damage presentation. It contains damage calculations adapted from a number of different claims and is included merely as an example, not an endorsement, because there is no single way to prepare damages.

iii

This book provides a starting point for the calculation of damages in construction claims. It should not be viewed as a stopping point because damage calculations are unique to each case and must be carefully considered each time damages are calculated. There is no one method, formula, or format which is applicable to every situation.

The authors wish to thank our editors at Wiley Law Publications, particularly Mary Hope, for all their patience, support, and assistance. We also want to thank Helen Smagh, Carla Oswalt, and Victoria Perry of Watt, Tieder, Killian & Hoffar; Kathryn Young, LaVina Betts, and Johnna Weirich with Forcon International; and Joan M. Palmer with Gadsby & Hannah for their able assistance in preparing this book.

February 1992

WILLIAM SCHWARTZKOPF
Denver, Colorado

JOHN J. MCNAMARA
Boston, Massachusetts

JULIAN F. HOFFAR
McLean, Virginia

ABOUT THE AUTHORS

William Schwartzkopf is treasurer and general counsel for Forcon International Corp., a national consulting firm specializing in construction claims and contract surety defaults. He was formerly vice president and general manager of an *Engineering News Record* 150-building contractor, and vice president and general counsel of an *Engineering News Record* top-10 specialty contractor. A registered professional engineer, Mr. Schwartzkopf is a member of the National Society of Professional Engineers as well as the American Bar Association and its Public Contract Law Section and Forum Committee of the Construction Industry. He received both a B.S. in electrical engineering and a J.D. from the University of Nebraska.

John J. McNamara is an attorney with the Boston, Massachusetts, Washington, D.C., law firm of Gadsby & Hannah, where he specializes in the litigation and arbitration of construction disputes. He graduated summa cum laude from Worcester State College, and earned his law degree from the Catholic University of America, Columbus School of Law, where he was an editor of the *Law Review*. He is admitted to practice before state and federal courts in the Commonwealths of Massachusetts and Virginia, and is a member of the American Bar Association's Public Contract Law Section and its Forum on the Construction Industry. He is the author of legal articles and seminar materials on international trade law, construction law, and public works contracts.

Julian F. Hoffar, a senior partner in the Washington, D.C., law firm of Watt, Tieder, Killian & Hoffar, specializes in national and international contract law. Mr. Hoffar earned his undergraduate degree from Wittenburg University and is an honor graduate of the National Law Center, George Washington University, where he was a member of the *Law Review*. Mr. Hoffar has written several articles on construction contracting, and has lectured before several industry groups on the subject of construction law.

SUMMARY CONTENTS

DETAILED CONTENTS

CHAPTER 1

OVERVIEW OF DAMAGE CALCULATION

§ 1.1 Introduction

A construction claim consists of two major parts: (1) the entitlement section, which typically includes a detailed description of the actions or inactions of the party from whom relief is sought, entitling the claimant to compensation; and (2) the damages section, which sets forth the calculations and support for the compensation claimed. The two parts are equally important because without entitlement, damages cannot be recovered, and without damages, proving entitlement is of little value. Despite this duality, most of the published literature focuses on entitlement. Based on the authors' review, most claim documents devote 80 to 90 percent of their presentation to entitlement facts and issues. The damages section of most claims is often given inadequate explanation, cursory analysis, and sketchy presentation and backup.

As a result of poor or inadequate damage analysis, otherwise valid construction claims are often rejected during the negotiation phase of the dispute or are substantially undervalued. Moreover, detailed damage analysis should not be limited to those preparing claims. When defending against a construction claim, it is necessary to focus on damage issues as well as entitlement. It is possible that entitlement exists but that damages have been substantially overstated. A failure to focus on damages to at least an extent equal with entitlement results in half the battlefield being overlooked. Ultimately, it leaves the trier of fact with only the claimant's presentation and analysis, without the benefit of either an alternative damage calculation or detailed analysis of the appropriateness of the damages claimed.

A damage analysis, rather than coming at the end of the claim process, should proceed concurrently with the entitlement analysis. Construction claims frequently have multiple theories of entitlement that fit the fact situation. By preparing damage analyses early, the entitlement aspects of a claim can be subject to further meaningful scrutiny. In other words, the determination of damages under the various theories of entitlement can identify more appropriate entitlement theories. When defending a construction claim, performing damage analyses early can result in finding alternative explanations for increased costs by examining the contractor's own cost records. Such alternative theories frequently identify contractor- or subcontractor-caused damages.

Perhaps the most important reason for a detailed and thorough damage analysis early in the process is that the clients are most interested in recovering (or avoiding) money damages. For a claimant ultimately to prove entitlement but not recover damages is particularly disappointing. The claimant has won the battle but lost the war. Early damage analysis focuses efforts on the bottom line, which should drive most claim decisions. When defending claims, it is equally important to understand damages. If significant damages exist and the client appears to have liability, the client should consider resolving the matter prior to incurring extensive litigation costs. Conversely, if damages do not appear to be present, a party should look to settle only for litigation costs and defend vigorously even if entitlement appears to exist. Ultimately, the parties are not interested in legal theories of entitlement; they are interested in either receiving or avoiding the payment of money damages.

Frequently, damage analysis is left to the client or the client's accountants. This is probably because attorneys are generally more comfortable with legal and factual theories of entitlement rather than the tedious process of establishing credible pricing data. Leaving the damage analysis in the client's hands can be a serious error. Contractors and owners are not necessarily good analysts of construction damages. They frequently use shorthand approaches to calculate damages, resulting in answers which are correct but not readily presentable to the triers of fact. Additionally, they frequently choose estimating-based methods, which also may be accurate but are not appropriate in the courtroom. A detailed analysis of the source documents is required rather than using summary documents and short-hand analyses.

Careful attention should be given to the calculation of damages early in the process. Either owner or contractor personnel are qualified to do this, but they need direction and guidance. The purpose of this book is to provide that direction by setting forth examples and detailed information on the calculation of damages. This book does not focus on entitlement theories or how to prove entitlement. There are ample texts in the field that discuss entitlement.

§ 1.2 Preliminary Damage Analysis

Early in the claims process, relatively quick calculations can be done to determine where damages exist and their approximate amounts. It is important to do this early so that if damages do not appear to exist in sufficient amount to justify the claims process, the process can be abandoned or re-oriented. Further, these short-form analyses may suggest additional areas of entitlement. When defending against a construction claim, perhaps the first course of action after reading the claim is to perform an immediate survey of the cost records supporting the claimed damages. The approach to defending the claim can vary significantly, depending on the nature of the cost records supporting the damages.

The basic source document of damage analysis is the contractor's cost accounting system and reports. Cost accounting reports vary widely in sophistication and detail from contractor to contractor. They range from extremely sophisticated reports that allow tracking of trends and costs in several different ways to rudimentary summations of costs incurred to date. Any damage analysis must focus on the variance from estimated costs of actual costs incurred or committed. When there are significant deviations in either direction, that is, costs over or under budget, the reason for that variance must be determined. The reason may be that after the project started, or after it was bid, the contractor changed the method of performance. For example, if significant segments of the work, which at bid time had been intended to be subcontracted, are actually performed by contractor personnel, the contractor could show a large increase in total labor cost from its original estimate. In this example, this should be offset by an equally large decrease in estimated subcontract costs. The apparent enormous overrun in estimated labor does not necessarily indicate a problem with the estimate. In this example it merely demonstrates a change in work method and a shift in performance of the work from subcontractor to contractor. Similarly, a contractor may shift from labor-intensive methods of performing the work to equipment-intensive methods. The mere fact that there are significant variations between actual and estimated costs does not necessarily lead to the conclusion that a basis for a damages claim exists. It does mean that an explanation is needed.

Once it is determined that the shifts in costs are not due to changes in method or performance of work, a more careful analysis must be done to determine the cost differential. Changes may have occurred because of differing site conditions. If they resulted from bad weather, they may or may not be compensable. Other causes for changes may involve the owner/engineer's failure to provide constructable drawings; the late delivery of material from the owner or contractor; or the failure of the contractor to have adequate supervision, equipment, or material. It is extremely important to determine the cause of the overruns rather than simply focus on the magnitude of the overruns and assume that a basis for a compensable claim exists. Even worse is the practice of preparing damages based on assumptions of what should have occurred, in other words, assuming the entitlement theories are correct and estimating the damages based on those assumptions. Such a superficial damages preparation can be detected in many cases by looking at the actual cost data.

The more detailed cost accounting data that exists, the better the potential for analysis. It is not sufficient merely to focus on the last or final cost accounting report. It is necessary to look at the interim cost accounting reports to determine trends. Were the items in question consistently over budget or did they start out over budget and then as a learning curve was experienced become under budget as the project progressed? Were costs consistently under budget until the claim events occurred? These trends can be extremely useful in proving entitlement and damages. Further, damages may exist even if actual costs underran the estimates if it can be shown that but for the claimed event the cost savings would have been greater.

If sophisticated cost accounting data is not available, it may be necessary to re-create the data from such source documents as time sheets, inspector's logs, or similar secondary documents. Frequently, when certain crews do only certain types of work, the cost of performing that work can be isolated and identified. Similarly, the quantity of work can sometimes be determined from secondary sources. For example, if concrete-related items are being analyzed, delivery tickets for concrete can provide a useful measure of the quantity of work performed during specific periods of time.

In reviewing contractor cost reports, there are generally two types of reports to examine. One is an overall project cost report, frequently called a job cost report, work-in-progress report, or job status report. Such a report will show all costs on a job, such as labor, material, and equipment, arranged by cost code and type of cost. The cost codes usually delineate units or phases of the work, such as conduit, wire, concrete footings, steel erection, or similar items. The second type of report normally used is a labor report that focuses only on labor expenditures by cost code. Such reports frequently give both manhour as well as hourly cost data. Worker-hour data is extremely useful because it allows a ready analysis of whether labor costs are over budget because the number of man-hours has increased or because the cost per manhour has increased due to overtime, higher wage rates, or other factors.

Cost analysis can be performed using these reports on a cost code or line item basis to determine in what areas labor, material, equipment, and subcontract cost overruns have been incurred. Further, by analyzing reports over time, the period in which the overruns occurred can be identified. In the case of material contracts and subcontracts, the overruns may have resulted at the start of the project because the amount of purchase orders or subcontracts exceeding the estimated cost. The overruns may have occurred later in the project because of wage escalation, acceleration, delay, or additional work. Determining when the increase occurred is invariably useful in determining why it occurred.

The type of cost overrun often provides a clue to the entitlement puzzle. When the overruns are concentrated in general conditions items such as project management or cleanup of job office expense, it is frequently a sign that the project has been delayed. As a result, initial entitlement analysis should focus on delay items. When the cost overruns occur in productive work items, such as installation of concrete, pipe, or fixtures, there is likely either a productivity-related problem such as acceleration, disruption, or inadequate plans and specifications, or an estimating problem. Additionally, apparent overruns can occur if the contractor has received substantial change orders but has not updated the estimated costs to reflect the change orders. It is extremely important when doing this kind of rudimentary analysis to be sure that the estimated costs have been updated for changes. If they have not been updated, what appear to be major overruns may in fact be changes for which the contractor has been compensated by change orders.

When reviewing cost overruns, be careful not to confuse symptoms with causation. For example, added work may result in extended job duration and apparent job delays. In fact, however, there may be no job delays when the effect of time extensions and additional job overhead contained in the change orders are considered. The sophistication of the contractor's recordkeeping will have a significant impact on the ability to determine damages. Good recordkeeping generally means that detailed, tightly defined damages can be prepared. Poor recordkeeping means either that damages are likely to be poorly linked to causation or that cost records will need to be re-created from source documents to prove the nature and extent of cost overruns.

§ 1.3   General Methods of Damage Calculation

The claimant always has the burden of proving both the existence and the amount of damages incurred. However, the inability to calculate the amount of damage with absolute precision does not preclude recovery of damages. Because of the nature of construction damages, precise measures are often not possible in construction claims. This is not to say that having once established entitlement, damages will automatically result. The claimant is obligated to provide the best evidence of damages that is possible under the circumstances. A good, detailed presentation of damages will frequently result in a greater recovery of damages. Conversely, a detailed analysis of damages by a defendant can frequently result in a dramatic reduction in damages awarded.

Damages are frequently broken down into *general damages,* which are the damages arising directly from the claim event, and *consequential damages,* which are damages not directly caused by the claim event but that may have been a result of the event. This distinction has become less clear over the years. This discussion focuses on the calculation of damages, not on the somewhat artificial distinction between general and consequential damages.

§ 1.4   —Actual Cost Method

Courts have shown a strong preference for the actual damage method of calculation. In this method, the actual cost records of the contractor are used to calculate the damages. This method is also referred to as the segregated or discrete cost method. If the existence of the claim is known prior to the completion of the job, it may be possible to arrange the contractor's cost accounting system to allow for the immediate identification of damages. Certainly, whenever there is any thought of a construction claim during a project, every effort should be made to facilitate the recordkeeping of the damages items. Many times, however, this is not possible. For example, when work is both added and deleted by a change, no actual cost record will exist for the deleted work. When dealing with labor productivity loss, the "inefficient" component of the labor is commingled with the "efficient" portion.

When detailed cost records exist, whether they are segregated for the claim or not, a line-by-line analysis of the cost records must be performed. During the first review of the records, every item with a significant overrun or underrun should be identified and the causes of these overruns and underruns determined. Do not make the mistake of only focusing on overruns. Sometimes underruns can be equally telling. Examining the reasons for underruns can avoid making unjustified claims for large labor overruns, which result from the contractor's performing rather than subcontracting certain items. In that situation, a correspondingly large underrun may exist in the subcontractor category. Additionally, costs should be explored to determine if certain linkages exist. As an example, if an excavation contractor has significant labor overruns, there should be corresponding overruns in equipment costs. If those overruns do not exist, closer scrutiny is required because the equipment and the labor costs should be parallel. Another example would be a concrete contractor who alleges a significant labor overrun but also has a significant quantity overrun in concrete. This may be a sign that there have been changes in the project requiring more concrete, or it could be evidence of an estimating error. Not understanding the reasons for cost overruns can be fatal to an otherwise valid claim.

How detailed and elaborate the cost accounting records are is a function both of the size of the project and the size of the contractor. However, the greater the detail and the greater the accuracy of the records, the greater the chances of recovery by the contractor on legitimate claims. Examples of several cost accounting systems used by general contractors appear in **Appendix A**. As these examples show, the level of sophistication of contractors' cost accounting records varies significantly. All three of these examples relate to general building contractors of approximately the same dollar volume doing approximately the same type of work.

To the extent possible, the actual cost method should be used. Even if actual cost analysis is not applicable to all elements of the claim, the more elements to which it is applied, the better the overall analysis. Providing many different line item calculations rather than a single damage calculation improves the presentation of the claim and also allows for a more detailed analysis of cause and affect.

§ 1.5 —Estimated Cost Method

One approach often used in construction claims is to estimate the amount of the damages. Contractors are often able to estimate damages with some degree of accuracy. Requiring such estimation is not unreasonable because contractors survive economically by being able to estimate the cost of projects with reasonable accuracy. If enough items are known so that reasonable assumptions can be made, estimates of damage costs can be calculated with reasonable accuracy.

Under the estimated cost method, the claimant furnishes a wide variety of data, including estimates by contractor personnel, expert witnesses, cost data, and accounting records, in an attempt to provide a reasonable value for the damage. It is important that the assumptions used to estimate the damages be carefully examined. Frequently, slight variations in assumptions can produce significant variations in the outcome. When using estimates, the assumptions are critical and must be carefully examined. It is frequently useful to vary the assumptions to see the effect on the calculations. This can avoid surprises later, such as discovering that a slight change in the assumptions eliminates all damages.

It is also necessary when using this method to be cognizant of other projects performed by the contractor that had similar problems or were similar in design or use so that comparisons can be made. Many contractors maintain histories of their projects that allow cost comparisons. It is important that such histories on prior projects be examined so that the validity of the contractor's estimates can be analyzed accordingly. Most contractors would testify that they base their estimates largely on their prior history on similar types of work. As a result, their cost performance on earlier projects is often relevant and extremely useful in either verifying or attacking the accuracy of the estimate.

§ 1.6   —Total Cost Method

The use of the total cost method is often discouraged. The total cost method, however, has great appeal to contractors because it allows them to recover what they invariably feel are their damages: all costs expended in excess of the estimate. The courts have often disfavored the total cost method because of the implicit assumption that the contractor did everything right and all cost overruns must be the result of owner actions. In something as complex as a construction project, such a simplistic analysis is subject to attack. The objects of the attack are (1) the validity and accuracy of the original estimate; (2) errors and deviations from the work plan by the contractor that result in added costs; and (3) actions increasing cost (such as weather) that are not the fault of the owner. If the total cost method is used, these points must be addressed by the claimant in any claim presentation as part of its burden of proof.

§ 1.7   —Modified Total Cost Method

As a result of the deficiencies in the total cost method, the modified total cost method developed. This is effectively the same as a total cost method except the contractor provides an allowance for bid errors, costs arising from contractor actions, and costs arising from actions of parties other than the owner. The estimates of value for these other factors, of course, bring in new areas on which attacks can be based.

Even when using the modified total cost or total cost approaches, it is frequently possible to estimate some elements of damages using actual costs. Any damage elements that can be calculated using methods other than total cost should be broken out from the claim and independently calculated.

Further, to the extent possible, total cost calculations can be made on separate items or areas of the work, allowing further refinements of the calculation, rather than taking all costs as a lump sum. This also allows a more careful estimate of other actions than the modified total cost method allows. The use of independent experts to estimate the costs of actions not related to the owner is facilitated by this method because different experts can estimate different cost items more easily if they are segregated.

§ 1.8   Linking Causation and Damages

Damages that are calculated even to the smallest degree of detail are of no value if the damages are not causally linked to the entitlement claimed. When preparing damage claims it is necessary to look back continually at the entitlement claim to make sure that the damages claimed actually flow from the entitlement event asserted. Damage claims should contain explanations of how they are linked to the entitlement claimed.

When defending against a claim, the causal link or lack thereof between damages claimed and entitlement asserted provides a basis upon which to attack the claim.

§ 1.9   —Attacking Causal Connection

In analyzing an affirmative claim, there are usually alternate or additional explanations for the contractor's damages besides the one asserted. It is often more effective to defend by providing the alternative explanations, rather than directly attacking the asserted causation.

When the contractor is asserting a delay claim, one owner defense would be to assert that there was a concurrent delay that was the contractor's responsibility. *Concurrent delays* occur when both parties have caused delays, either of which would, by itself, have resulted in delaying the project. Some sources of concurrent delay are:

1. Weather (either the weather was anticipated or the contractor assumed the weather risk contractually)
2. Failure of contractor-furnished material to arrive on time
3. Contractor's failure to submit promptly and adequately shop drawings and other required submittals
4. Failure to have the appropriate equipment and machinery for the project on-site
5. Contractor's installation of improper or defective work
6. Lack of progress by the contractor because of poor planning or financial difficulties.

The damages resulting from any of these items are identical to the damages that result when an owner or an owner's agent delays the job. As a result, when analyzing damages, it is necessary to examine the causation carefully to be sure that the proper link has been asserted.

§ 1.10   —Bid and Estimating Errors

Contractors may incur cost overruns because of actions of owners or other third parties. Cost overruns also occur because of errors in the contractor's original bid. Such errors can include:

1. Underestimating the difficulty of the work and hence the labor and equipment hours required to perform it
2. Miscalculating the volume of the work required
3. Miscalculating the length of time required to perform the work
4. Making assumptions about the method and manner of work that are not appropriate for the work required.

Any of these errors, whether the result of judgment or calculation, can lead to overruns from the contractor's bid. Such overruns are not the fault of the owner, although they are similar to cost overruns from errors or omissions of an owner. It is necessary to analyze the causal linkages carefully to be sure that the causation asserted results in the damages claimed. This is particularly true when the total cost or modified total cost method is used because these methods rely upon the accuracy of the original bid.

§ 1.11   —Productivity Claims

Linkage between causation and damages is particularly important in productivity claims. The essence of a productivity claim is that the labor expended to perform each unit of work was substantially greater (that is, productivity was lower) than anticipated because of acts of the owner or other parties. If the contractor makes an error in its bid, has poor management on-site, or makes errors in the work that cause rework to occur, the same type of cost overruns will appear. When linking the entitlement—the actions asserted to cause the productivity loss—to the damage, it is important to determine if the actions would have affected the entire project or just certain portions of the project. If only specific portions of the project would have been affected, these portions should be isolated and shown to be either the only ones affected by the actions asserted, or the ones most affected. Other areas may have been affected, but to a lesser degree. The affected portions can be identified either by time period or by type or phase of work. If the productivity on the project was uniformly poor, that is, the labor costs exceeded the budget fairly consistently throughout the entire project, but the asserted acts occurred long after the project had started, the causal linkages can be challenged.

When performing such evaluations, it is important to make the comparisons correctly. For instance, if the initial portion of the project involved substantial start-up labor but only small pieces of work, it would not be surprising to find poor productivity. By contrast, if the productivity was low during the major portion of the project when the "production" work was ongoing and the asserted acts occurred, it would support the productivity loss theory.

§ 1.12 —Equipment and Small Tool Costs

When additional equipment and small tool charges are asserted, it is important to verify that the additional equipment and small tools were required either because of additional work or because additional labor was required. Further, if additional equipment was added to the project, it should be verified that the type of equipment added was appropriate for the type of work being performed and was not added because of equipment problems or other reasons. As with labor productivity claims, the estimate should be carefully examined to verify that it was reasonable and that the overruns and equipment costs were not due to a bid error or an overly optimistic estimate.

CHAPTER 2

LABOR COSTS

§ 2.1   Introduction

Labor is a major cost item on any construction project, and labor costs often comprise a major portion of construction claims. Increased labor costs may result from a variety of events, including owner-caused delay,[1]

---

[1] *See* Luria Bros. & Co. v. United States, 369 F.2d 701 (Ct. Cl. 1966) (lost productivity damages from owner-caused delay recoverable despite the presence of a no damages for delay clause).

owner-directed changes, and defective specifications. Labor costs are recognized elements of construction claims.[2]

Increased labor costs may be divided into three main groups: direct labor overrun, escalated wages, and decreased labor productivity. Increased labor costs may be calculated through a variety of methods. Particular attention should be paid to labor calculations because increased labor costs are frequently overstated and labor calculations are often thoroughly examined by a reviewing party or tribunal.

§ 2.2 Direct Labor Overrun

Direct labor overrun is the additional labor hours expended in performance of the contract which exceed the labor hours originally estimated for performance. Direct labor overrun may result from owner-caused delay, acceleration, or directives to perform work outside the scope of the contract. The following information is necessary to calculate direct labor overrun: the applicable hourly wage rate, the amount of additional labor hours performed, and the labor burdens.

§ 2.3 —Determination of Additional Hours

The determination of additional hours worked is virtually compulsory if precise records are available. The amount of additional labor hours actually worked may be established by payroll records, daily labor reports, or other supporting data. Often, a precise accounting and allocation of additional hours is difficult, if not impossible, due to multiple change orders or numerous delays. In these cases, courts and boards of contract appeals may permit contractors to recover the estimated excess labor costs based on a total cost calculation.[3] Total cost calculations seek to recover the difference between the contractor's actual labor costs and the contractor's anticipated labor costs.[4] Total cost calculations are generally disfavored and are not accorded the presumption of reasonableness as are calculations which establish costs through actual proof. Total cost calculations may be used to determine

---

[2] United States Steel Corp. v. Missouri Pac. R.R., Co., 668 F.2d 435 (8th Cir.), *cert. denied,* 459 U.S. 836 (1982); E.C. Ernst, Inc. v. Koppers Co., 520 F. Supp. 830, 833 (W.D. Pa. 1981); J.D. Hedin Constr. Co. v. United States, 347 F.2d 235 (Ct. Cl. 1965); McDevitt & Street Co. v. Department of Gen. Servs., 377 So. 2d 191 (Fla. Dist. Ct. App. 1979); Pebble Bldg. Co. v. G.J. Hopkins, 288 S.E.2d 437 (Va. 1982).

[3] H. John Homan Co. v. United States, 418 F.2d 522 (Ct. Cl. 1969); McDevitt & Street Co. v. Department of Gen. Servs., 377 So. 2d 191 (Fla. Dist. Ct. App. 1979); Pebble Bldg. Co. v. G.J. Hopkins, 288 S.E.2d 437 (Va. 1982).

[4] *See* H. John Homan Co. v. United States, 418 F.2d 522 (Ct. Cl. 1969).

direct labor overrun when it is virtually impossible to calculate direct labor costs by any other method.[5]

§ 2.4   —Determination of Wage Rates

The applicable wage rate can be easily determined when the additional labor hours have been carefully segregated by date and class or craft. If such records are present, the union contracts in existence during the period of overrun will determine the applicable wage rate. On nonunion projects, however, the contractor's average wage rate in effect for the particular craft at the time of delay may be used to establish the applicable wage rate.

Often, however, precise accounting records have not been maintained for the period when additional labor hours were expended. In these cases, the additional hours must be allocated to the periods in which the delay or change occurred.[6] These types of estimated allocations are necessarily imprecise and are usually reviewed carefully.[7]

An example of this type of imprecise allocation is found in *E.C. Ernst, Inc. v. Koppers Co.*[8] The plaintiff, a subcontractor, sought compensation for an increase in labor hours due to the prime contractor's inefficiency, revised schedule, delay, and acceleration. The plaintiff proposed to allocate the additional labor hours to the years in which revised project drawings were issued.[9] The percentage of labor hours allocated to each year was based on the number of revised drawings issued during that year.[10] The United States District Court for the Western District of Pennsylvania rejected this approach for lack of a causal connection between the issuance of revised drawings and the additional hours.[11] Instead, the court determined that the impact of the prime contractor's acts or omissions was felt primarily during 1975.[12] Therefore, the entire labor overrun, 87,010 labor hours,

---

[5] Generally, total cost calculations are permitted when (1) no alternative calculation is feasible, (2) the original bid is found to be reasonable, (3) the actual costs incurred are reasonable, and (4) the contractor is not responsible for the excess costs. For further judicial discourse on the use of the total cost method, see Skip Kirchdorfer, Inc. v. United States, 14 Cl. Ct. 594 (1988); *In re* Meyertech Corp., 831 F.2d 410 (3d Cir. 1981); Huber, Hunt & Nichols, Inc. v. Moore, 67 Cal. App. 3d 278, 136 Cal. Rptr. 603 (1977); Seattle W. Indus. v. David A. Mowat Co., 750 P.2d 245 (Wash. 1988).

[6] E.C. Ernst, Inc. v. Koppers Co., 520 F. Supp. 830 (W.D. Pa. 1981).

[7] *Id.*

[8] *Id.*

[9] *Id.* at 834.

[10] *Id.*

[11] E. C. Ernst v. Koppers, 520 F. Supp. 830, 837 (W.D. Pa. 1981).

[12] *Id.* at 838.

was multiplied by the wage rate in existence during that year.[13] *E.C. Ernst* illustrates that a causal connection must exist between the period in which the additional labor hours are allocated and the events which caused the need for the additional hours.

§ 2.5 Labor Burdens

Labor burden is a cost directly related to the employment of individuals but not reflected in the employees' wages. Common labor burdens are taxes, workers' compensation and other insurance, benefits, and supervisory costs. Labor burdens have been increasing constantly during the past 25 years and can represent a major cost in construction claims.[14] Labor burdens are almost always recoverable unless such costs are specifically precluded by contract.[15]

§ 2.6 —Common Labor Burdens

Payroll taxes are almost always recoverable as direct labor costs.[16] Federal payroll taxes, such as the Social Security tax (FICA), are constant throughout the country. Recently, FICA costs have increased rapidly; on projects performed over several years, effective FICA rates may double due to increases in both percentage and base. State and local taxes, however, vary according to the rate set by the particular state or county. State and local taxes have also increased rapidly during the past 25 years, and such costs represent a significant portion of labor burden costs.

The cost of workers' compensation insurance is also recoverable as a direct labor cost. A contractor's workers' compensation rate is determined by multiplying the manual rate, which is set on a statewide basis, by the contractor's modification rate, which is based on the contractor's safety record and experience. For example, a contractor with an above-average safety record could have a modifier of .8 or 80 percent of the manual rate. Contractors should be aware that workers' compensation increases often exceed wages increases over the same period of time.[17]

---

[13] *Id.*

[14] *See* Fidelity Constr. Co., DOT CAB No. 1113, 81-2 BCA (CCH) ¶ 15,345 (1981) (labor burden markup was 28.4% of direct wages).

[15] Racquette River Constr. Inc., ASBCA No. 26,486, 82-1 BCA (CCH) ¶ 15,769 (1982); Fidelity Constr. Co., DOT CAB No. 1113, 81-2 BCA (CCH) ¶ 15,345 (1981).

[16] Clarke Baridon, Inc. v. Merritt-Chapman & Scott Corp., 311 F.2d 389 (4th Cir. 1962); Racquette River Constr. Inc., ASBCA No. 26,486, 82-1 BCA (CCH) ¶ 15,769 (1982).

[17] In Colorado, for example, the manual rate for iron workers exceeds 100% of wages.

Fringe benefits on union contracts are also recoverable as direct labor costs.[18] Fringe benefits include vacation pay, holiday pay, and sick pay. On large, labor-intensive contracts, fringe benefit costs can be considerable. Fringe benefit costs may also be recoverable as an element of the contractor's overhead costs. In calculating labor burdens, contractors should ensure that they have not duplicated such costs elsewhere in the claim.[19] Duplication of costs in the final calculation of damages, if discovered, detracts from the validity of the entire calculation.

Supervisory costs are recoverable only for those employees assigned to the project on a day-to-day basis.[20] In damage calculations, however, contractors often attempt to recover the costs of all supervisory personnel, regardless of whether they worked at the project. The cost of home office personnel such as engineers and project managers is not recoverable as a direct project expense, however, and should not be included in a labor burden calculation.

To determine whether a contractor has incurred additional supervisory costs, the anticipated ratio of supervisors to laborers must be compared to the ratio on the project. For example, if it was estimated that one foreman was needed to supervise five craft laborers, the supervision ratio would be one to five. If a total of 150,000 labor hours were actually expended on the project, one-sixth of those hours, or 25,000 labor hours, would be expected to be attributable to craft supervision. But if the project conditions actually required one foreman to supervise four craft laborers, then one-fifth of the total labor hours, or 30,000 hours, would be attributable to craft supervision. The additional 5,000 supervisory hours represent a direct labor cost and a possible element of damages.

A decrease in the supervisory ratio is not necessarily a good sign, however. On troubled projects, a decrease in the supervisory ratio might be viewed by the owner or claim reviewer as evidence that the contractor was responsible for any problems because supervision was lacking. In any event,

---

[18] J.D. Hedin Constr. Co. v. United States, 347 F.2d 235 (Ct. Cl. 1965).

[19] The Corps of Engineers' *Construction Contract Negotiating Guide* specifically addresses duplication of costs in this area:

> Some [contractors] charge many items such as overtime, vacation and holiday pay . . . in the direct costs while others include most of these items in job overhead. . . . [T]he negotiator should make certain that the contractor breaks out direct costs and overhead areas to assure that each item is justified and that there is no duplication of changes.

Id. at 12.

[20] *See* Paccon, Inc., ASBCA No. 7890, 65-2 BCA (CCH) ¶ 4996 (1965).

courts and boards recognize that field supervision costs are recoverable elements in construction claims.[21]

§ 2.7   —Calculating Labor Burden

The labor burden percentage by which direct wages are marked up is determined by dividing the total labor costs by the total labor burden costs. For example, if employee-related expenses are $627,394 and total labor costs including burden are $1,575,000, then

$$\frac{\$627,394}{(\$1,575,000 - 627,394)} \times 100 = 66.21\% \text{ (labor burden percentage).}$$

On projects of long duration, labor burdens may fluctuate depending on the time period in which the work was performed. It is important to verify the time periods in which excess labor burdens were incurred because such burdens may have increased or decreased, thus affecting the amount of recovery to which a contractor is entitled.[22]

§ 2.8   Sample Direct Labor Overrun Calculation

Once the hours, wage rates, and burdens are established, calculating direct labor overrun costs is fairly straightforward. A sample calculation is as follows:

31,500 hrs. (additional labor hours) × $17.50 (applicable wage rate)
= $551,250 (direct labor overrun)

66.21% (labor burden percentage) (from example in § 2.7)

$551,250 (direct labor overrun) × 66.21% (labor burden percentage)
= $364,983

$551,250 (direct labor overrun) + $364,983 (labor burden)
= $916,233 (total direct labor overrun)

§ 2.9   Calculation of Wage Escalation

The costs of escalated wages are recognized elements of construction claims. Wage escalation is recoverable if the contractor is required to pay its

---

[21] W.G. Cornell Co. v. Ceramic Coating Co., 626 F.2d 990 (D.C. Cir. 1980); Luria Bros. & Co. v. United States, 369 F.2d 701 (Ct. Cl. 1966); Anderson Dev. Corp. v. Coastal States Crude Gathering Co., 543 S.E.2d 402 (Tex. Civ. App. 1976).

[22] The escalation calculation used for determining escalated wages discussed in § 2.9 is equally applicable to calculating escalated labor burdens.

laborers at a rate higher than anticipated due to delays, changes, or other acts of the owner which push performance of the contract into a higher wage period.[23] Contractors bear the risk of escalated wages during the original period of contract performance, however.[24] The calculation of escalated wages during one wage period is relatively simple, but the calculation of escalated wages becomes increasingly difficult when several different wage periods are involved.

In calculating wage escalation, contractors first must compare the anticipated man-loading schedule with the actual man-loading schedule in order to ascertain the periods in which labor hours were expended. Often, anticipated man-loading schedules are prepared at the time of bidding or prior to the start of work. If an anticipated man-loading schedule is not available, one must be created based on the original contract schedule. Actual man-loading schedules are prepared from daily reports, payroll records, or similar documents.

To create a man-loading schedule based on the original contract schedule after performance has taken place, the number of workers needed to complete each activity should be allocated to that activity. Next, the total labor force should be plotted on a time/labor force chart, which may be divided monthly or weekly. Once the anticipated schedule has been re-created, it should be compared with the actual man-loading schedule by plotting the actual man-loading schedule on the same time/labor force graph as the anticipated man-loading schedule. The comparison of the two schedules reveals any differences in the expenditure of labor hours and the periods in which such hours were expended.

Problems often arise in comparing anticipated and actual man-loading schedules, however. Anticipated and actual schedules often differ between the number of hours originally estimated to perform the work and the number of hours actually expended in the performance of the work. Because labor escalation calculations seek to calculate the increase in wages only for the hours actually worked, the anticipated man-loading curve must reflect actual labor hours expended in accordance with the anticipated curve. Also, it is best to prepare man-loading schedules for each trade working on the project. If it would be impossible or impractical to prepare separate schedules by trade, composite charts will usually be sufficient.

Wage rates also must be determined to calculate wage escalation. The anticipated wage rates must be compared to the actual wage rates paid to ascertain the increase in the rate. Anticipated wage rates on union projects are determined by the union wage in effect for the time period in question.

---

[23] United States Steel Corp. v. Missouri Pac. R.R., 668 F.2d 435 (8th Cir.), *cert. denied,* 459 U.S. 836 (1982); Sydney Constr. Co., ASBCA No. 21,377, 77-2 BCA (CCH) ¶ 12,719 (1977); Paccon, Inc., ASBCA No. 7890, 65-2 BCA (CCH) ¶ 4996 (1965).

[24] Clarke Baridon, Inc. v. Meritt Chapman & Scott Corp., 311 F.2d 384 (4th Cir. 1962).

On nonunion projects, it may be more difficult to determine the applicable wage rate. On nonunion projects, the anticipated wage rates may be based on the estimator's original estimate.

Actual wage rates can be determined by reference to the payroll records. On nonunion projects, wage rates may increase in a piecemeal fashion. In these cases, contractors may use the average wage rate of all workers, which is determined by dividing the amount of all labor costs for a specific time period by the total number of labor hours worked during that period. As an alternative to computing the average wage rate of the entire labor force, the average wage rates of the trades affected may be used.[25] Although average wage rates may be used in place of actual wage rates, the average rate must be reasonable in light of the surrounding circumstances.[26]

§ 2.10   —Sample Wage Escalation Calculation

Wage escalation calculations for projects anticipated to be constructed entirely in one wage period are relatively simple. The amount of labor hours expended during the higher wage period is multiplied by the difference between the anticipated and the actual wages. A sample calculation is as follows:

> 2500 hrs. (hours worked after wage increase) × $3.50
>   (difference between anticipated and actual rates) = $ 8,750

> (wage escalation) + $5,793 (labor burden at 66.21%) = $14,543 (total wage escalation costs)

In suspensions of work situations, an alternative formula to this one may be used to calculate wage escalation. In *Sydney Construction Co.,*[27] the Armed Services Board of Contract Appeals permitted the contractor to calculate the amount of escalated wages by multiplying the number of labor hours worked per day during the period of escalated wages by the total amount of wage increase, plus the number of days the contract was extended.[28]

---

[25] Paccon, Inc., ASBCA No. 7890, 65-2 BCA (CCH) ¶ 4996 (1965) (appellant permitted to use wage rates of nine trades).

[26] *Id.* at p. 23,576.

[27] ASBCA No. 21,377, 77-2 BCA (CCH) ¶ 12,719 (1977).

[28] *Id.* at 61,806.

§ 2.11   —Secondary Considerations in Calculating Escalated Wages

As with any claim calculation, it is important that costs not be duplicated. Most delay/escalation claims include additional labor hours for which the contractor may have been previously compensated. Claim calculations should not include any costs associated with labor hours for which the contractor has been directly compensated.

Escalation costs for additional labor hours expended as a result of the contractor's own inefficient performance may also be recoverable. Such costs may be recoverable if the contractor was required to perform during a higher wage period because of owner-caused delays.[29]

§ 2.12   —Calculating Wage Escalation in Varying Wage Periods

Frequently, construction projects are planned to be performed or are actually performed in several different wage periods. On these projects, wage escalation calculations become more complicated, requiring the estimated and actual percentages of labor and the estimated and actual wage rates to be segregated by time period.

Once the percentages and ratios of labor are determined, they should be arranged in a tabular form as shown in the following example:

	Period 1	Period 2	Period 3	Period 4
Original anticipated wage rate	$10.00	$10.50	$11.25	$12.25
Estimated percentage of labor expended	15%	60%	25%	0%

Thereafter, the actual labor hours and the time periods in which they were expended must be determined. A format similar to this one should be used to compare the anticipated and actual labor hours expenditure. The following example is based on a project with actual labor being 150,000 hours.

	Period 1	Period 2	Period 3	Period 4
Actual labor hours using anticipated distribution	22,500	90,000	37,500	0
Actual labor hours distribution	10,000	25,000	75,000	40,000

---

[29] *See* Keco Indus. v. United States, 364 F.2d 838 (Ct. Cl. 1966), *cert. denied,* 386 U.S. 958 (1967); Nager Elec. Co. v. United States, 442 F.2d 936 (Ct. Cl. 1971).

As can be seen, during the early and less costly time periods, less labor was expended than originally anticipated. Therefore, it is necessary to calculate the unexpended labor hours for each time period and escalate then to the next, higher wage period. A sample "carry over calculation" is as follows:

	Period 1	Period 2	Period 3	Period 4
Anticipated hours based on original schedule	22,500	90,000	37,500	40,000
Labor hours actually expended	10,000	25,000	75,000	40,000
Hours escalated from prior period	0	12,500	77,500	0
Total hours to be escalated to next period rate	12,500	77,500	40,000	
Period differential	.50	.75	1.00	
Escalated wages	$6,250	$58,125	$40,000	
Total escalated wages	$104,375			

This method uses the actual hours expended based on the anticipated distribution of hours. By using this calculation, disagreements over the number of hours originally anticipated can be minimized.

Often, contractors prefer to calculate wage escalation by using the difference between the actual average labor rate and the estimated labor rate. In periods of varying wage rates, however, these calculations are highly suspect and will be reviewed carefully.

§ 2.13   Loss of Productivity

Productivity is the measure of the quantity of work performed per labor hour.[30] Decreased productivity or efficiency may result from a variety of factors, including delays, changes, acceleration orders, deceleration orders, and weather conditions. Numerous studies have been done regarding the causes and effects of decreased productivity in the construction industry.[31] Decreased productivity, unlike direct labor, however, is difficult to document, quantify, and calculate. This fact, however, does not bar contractors

---

[30] For a practical commentary on loss of efficiency or productivity, *see* Ginsburgh & Bannon, *Loss of Efficiency,* 85-12 Construction Briefings (1985).

[31] Borcherding & Alarcon, *Quantitative Effects on Construction Productivity,* 11:1 Construction Law. (1991); National Electrical Contractors Associated, The Effect of Multistory Buildings on Productivity (1975); Grimm & Wagner, *Weather Effects on Mason Productivity,* 100 J. Construction Div. 379, ASCE, No. C03 (Sept. 1974).

from recovering costs associated with decreased productivity.[32] Because decreased productivity often results from a combination of factors, courts and boards are often more lenient in allowing contractors to recover for the total impact of all factors which have affected productivity.

§ 2.14   —Causes of Loss of Labor Productivity

Overtime is recognized to adversely effect the productivity of a project's labor force. Decreased productivity due to overtime is attributable primarily to fatigue and morale problems resulting from overtime work. Industry studies indicate that the productivity of laborers who work 50 hours per week for a period of 10 weeks can decrease by as much as 35 percent.[33] Sixty-hour work weeks performed over the same time period can result in a decrease of labor productivity of up to 45 percent.[34] Therefore, payroll records should be examined to ascertain the extent of overtime worked on a project because the project's productivity may have been adversely affected.

Weather can have a dramatic effect on productivity.[35] The risk of increased costs resulting from performing work during adverse weather is normally borne by the contractor, especially if the contractor originally anticipated performing during the winter months.[36] Contractors may usually recover for decreased productivity if owner-caused delay forces the contractor to perform work in an adverse season that was not originally anticipated.[37] The same is true if a contractor can establish that the structure would have been enclosed but for owner delays and that decreased productivity resulted from working in exposed conditions.[38]

Productivity may be adversely affected by a lack of capable laborers.[39] In most cases, however, contractors usually bear the risk of labor shortages.[40] In certain cases contractors may recover for decreased productivity due to

---

[32] Luria Bros. & Co. v. United States, 369 F.2d 701 (Ct. Cl. 1966).

[33] Business Roundtable, Scheduled Overtime Effect on Construction Projects, Construction Industry Cost Effectiveness Task Force Report (1980).

[34] *Id.*

[35] Luria Bros. & Co. v. United States, 369 F.2d 701 (Ct. Cl. 1966); Corry Bridge & Supply Co., AGBCA No. 81-149-1, 82-2 BCA (CCH) ¶ 16,008 (1982); Anderson Dev. Corp. v. Coastal States Crude Gathering Co., 543 S.W.2d 402 (Tex. Civ. App. 1976).

[36] Corry Bridge & Supply Co., AGBCA No. 81-149-1, 82-2 BCA (CCH) ¶ 16,008 (1982).

[37] Anderson Dev. Corp. v. Coastal States Crude Gathering Co., 543 S.W.2d 402 (Tex. Civ. App. 1976).

[38] J.D. Hedin Constr. Co. v. United States, 347 F.2d 235 (Ct. Cl. 1965).

[39] Arthur Painting Co., ASBCA No. 20,267, 76-1 BCA (CCH) ¶ 11,894 (1976).

[40] Clarke Baridon, Inc. v. Merritt Chapman & Scott Corp., 311 F.2d 389 (4th Cir. 1962); S&M Traylor Bros., ENGBCA No. 3942, 82-2 BCA (CCH) ¶ 15,937 (1982).

a lack of laborers, as evidenced by *Arthur Painting Co.*[41] In that case, the contractor entered into a contract with the government for painting work to be done at Wurtsmith Air Force Base in Michigan. Experienced painters were reluctant to travel to the project because the site was remotely located, and thus the contractor was consistently understaffed. The Armed Services Board of Contract Appeals permitted the contractor to recover for decreased productivity resulting from having to train new and inexperienced workers.[42] *Arthur Painting* is the exception, however, and in most cases contractors will not be able to recover for decreased productivity due to a lack of capable laborers.

Performance in a sequence different from that originally anticipated can also have a dramatic effect on productivity.[43] Contractors have the right to perform according to their original schedule and decreased productivity resulting from disruption to the anticipated schedule is a recognized element of construction claims.[44] Productivity or efficiency can be impacted in various ways as a result of performing in a sequence which differs from that originally anticipated. For example, in *Paccon, Inc.,*[45] the Armed Services Board of Contract Appeals recognized that the contractor's productivity was decreased because much time was expended in transporting employees, retraining employees, and correcting deficient work, all of which resulted from out-of-sequence performance.[46] To recover for decreased productivity resulting from out-of-sequence performance, a causal link must exist between the decreased productivity and the disrupted performance.[47]

The simultaneous operation of several trades often results in congestion and confusion, which in turn causes a decrease in labor productivity.[48] The concurrent operation or "stacking" of trades may result from a variety of factors, including owner-caused delay, acceleration orders, or change

---

[41] ASBCA No. 20,267, 76-1 BCA (CCH) ¶ 11,894 (1976).

[42] *Id.*

[43] H. John Homan Co. v. United States, 418 F.2d 522 (Ct. Cl. 1969); Luria Bros. & Co. v. United States, 369 F.2d 701 (Ct. Cl. 1966); Aetna Casualty & Sur. Co. v. Doleac Elec. Co., 471 So. 2d 325 (Miss. 1985); Anderson Dev. Corp. v. Coastal States Crude Gathering Co., 543 S.W.2d 402 (Tex. Civ. App. 1976).

[44] Louis M. McMaster, Inc., AGBCA No. 76-156, 79-1 BCA (CCH) ¶ 13,701 (1979).

[45] ASBCA No. 7890, 65-2 BCA (CCH) ¶ 4996 (1965).

[46] *Id.*

[47] Savin Bros., Inc. v. State, 405 N.Y.S.2d 516 (App. Div. 1978), *aff'd,* 393 N.E.2d 1041, 419 N.Y.S.2d 969 (N.Y. 1979).

[48] Continental Consolidation Corp., ASBCA No. 10,662, 67-1 BCA (CCH) ¶ 6127 (1967); Lew F. Stillwell, Inc., ASBCA No. 9432, 1964 BCA (CCH) ¶ 4128 (1964); Blake Constr. Co. v. C.J. Coakley, 431 A.2d 569 (D.C. 1981).

orders.[49] Decreased productivity from the stacking of trades is well recognized, and such costs often comprise a major portion of construction claims.[50]

Restricted site access may also result in decreased labor productivity.[51] Access to the site may be restricted in various ways, including actual physical obstructions or unworkable site conditions. In *Flex-Y-Plan Industries, Inc.,*[52] the General Services Board of Contract Appeals permitted a contractor to recover for decreased productivity as a result of having to renovate occupied barracks. Specifically, the Board stated:

> As a result of the occupancy of the thirty eight barracks during the period of installation Appellant had to install the panels out of sequence. Divider walls were installed first, then corridor walls were installed. This method differed from that originally intended. . . . Out of sequence installation was time consuming and costly to Appellant. . . . and credible evidence was presented that Appellant incurred $24,521.76 in added costs as a result of the work areas being occupied.[53]

In *Paccon, Inc.,*[54] restricted site access resulted in decreased productivity because laborers were found to have purposely slowed the pace of work for fear that they would be laid off if subsequent work areas were not readily accessible.[55]

Productivity may be affected by various other events including delay in the delivery of materials,[56] owner-caused changes which impact the performance of other parts of the project (ripple changes),[57] and delays attributable to other contractors.[58] As confirmed in numerous studies, lost

---

[49] *See* S. Leo Harmonay, Inc. v. Binks Mfg. Co., 597 F. Supp. 1014 (S.D.N.Y. 1984); Ginsburgh & Bannon, *Loss of Efficiency,* 85-12 Construction Briefings (1985).

[50] S. Leo Harmonay, Inc. v. Binks Mfg. Co., 597 F. Supp. 1014 (S.D.N.Y. 1984); J.D. Hedin Constr. Co. v. United States, 347 F.2d 235 (Ct. Cl. 1965); Lew F. Stillwell, Inc., ASBCA No. 9432, 1964 BCA (CCH) ¶ 4128 (1964); Ginsburgh & Bannon, *Loss of Efficiency,* 85-12 Construction Briefings (1985).

[51] Flex-Y-Plan Indus., Inc., GSBCA No. 4117, 76-1 BCA (CCH) ¶ 11,713 (1976).

[52] *Id.*

[53] *Id.* at pp. 55, 835–36.

[54] ASBCA No. 7890, 65-2 BCA (CCH) ¶ 4996 (1965).

[55] *Id.*

[56] H. John Homann Co. v. United States, 418 F.2d 522 (Ct. Cl. 1969) (contract change resulted in delay in delivery of materials, and contractor could recover disruption costs resulting from unavailability of materials).

[57] Clarke Baridon, Inc. v. Merritt Chapman & Scott Corp., 311 F.2d 389 (4th Cir. 1962) (owner-ordered change to one contractor's work disrupted work of another contractor for which disrupted contractor could recover).

[58] *See* Gasparini Excavation Co. v. Pennsylvania Turnpike Comm'n, 187 A.2d 157 (Pa. 1963).

productivity can result from many factors, and lost productivity often is attributable to a combination of events rather than a single event.[59]

§ 2.15   —Calculating Productivity Loss

Labor productivity is difficult to quantify and calculate with accuracy. Moreover, it may be difficult if not impossible to segregate the events which have impacted labor productivity. Numerous methods exist to calculate the loss of labor productivity, and although no method is generally accepted, some methods are preferred over others. Below are the major methods by which decreased productivity is calculated.

§ 2.16   —Measured Mile Calculations

The most widely accepted method of calculating lost labor productivity is known throughout the industry as the "measured mile" calculation. This calculation compares identical activities on impacted and nonimpacted sections of the project in order to ascertain the loss of productivity resulting from the impact.[60] The measured mile calculation is favored because it considers only the actual effect of the alleged impact and thereby eliminates disputes over the validity of cost estimates, or factors which may have impacted productivity due to no fault of the owner.

Measured mile calculations first require the labor productivity ratios to be calculated for a nonimpacted performance period. As discussed previously, labor productivity ratios are determined by dividing the actual amount of hours[61] by the actual quantities of work performed.[62] The productivity ratio during the nonimpacted period is the standard, or the performance mile, by which productivity is measured.

Next, the contractor must isolate the period of performance which was allegedly impacted due to one or more of the reasons discussed in § 2.14. The productivity ratio for the impacted period is calculated in the same

---

[59] For further commentary on loss of efficiency, see Clapp, *Effect of Adverse Weather Conditions on Productivity on Five Building Sites,* Construction Series Current Paper No. 21, Building Research Establishment, Watford, Eng. (Oct. 1966); Leonard, *The Effects of Change Orders on Productivity,* 6 Revay Report, No. 2 at 1 (Aug. 1987).

[60] United States Indus., Inc. v. Blake Constr. Co., 671 F.2d 539 (D.C. Cir. 1982); Flex-Y-Plan Indus., GSBCA No. 4117, 76-1 BCA (CCH) ¶ 11,713 (1976).

[61] Actual costs and labor hours may be determined by labor reports, time sheets, and other verifying data.

[62] Quantity of work performed may be determined by reference to contractor records, inspector reports, and other quantitative data.

manner as the nonimpacted period. The lost productivity is the difference in the productivity ratios between the impacted and nonimpacted periods.[63]

On highly troubled projects, however, it may be impossible to segregate one period of performance which was not impacted. Even if a nonimpacted period is available for comparison with the impacted period, it may be that wholly different types of work were performed during the two periods, making a measured mile calculation impractical or inaccurate. Therefore, on such projects an alternative method may be more appropriate to calculate labor inefficiency.

§ 2.17   —Comparison with Similar Projects

In certain cases, contractors may be required to calculate lost productivity by comparing the anticipated productivity ratio with the actual productivity ratio. The anticipated productivity rate must be supported by reference to the productivity rates on the same or a similar project.

Ideally, similar work on the same project by another contractor is the best evidence to support an estimated productivity ratio.[64] In *Robert McMullan & Sons, Inc.,*[65] a painting contractor's estimated productivity ratio was supported by the actual productivity ratio for another painting contractor working on the same project. In most cases, contractors may have to refer to the productivity on other projects to support its labor productivity estimate.

The project chosen for purposes of comparison should be similar to that upon which the contractor is seeking to recover. For example, it would be unreasonable to compare the labor productivity ratio for concrete forming at a detention facility with the productivity ratio for similar work on a hotel. The labor productivity ratio would be greater at the detention facility due to the limited access to the project, which is integral to the design of the facility.

Any calculation based on similar work at another project should reference and include supporting detail and documentation from that project. Conversely, such documentation should be closely examined in analyzing and defending against claims for decreased productivity. Any comparison without back-up documentation should be neither submitted nor accepted as evidence of the validity of the estimated labor productivity ratio.

---

[63] S. Leo Harmonay, Inc. v. Binks Mfg., 597 F. Supp. 1014 (S.D.N.Y. 1984); A.W. Burton, AGBCA No. 431, 77-1 BCA (CCH) ¶ 12,307 (1977); Flex-Y-Plan Indus., Inc., GSBCA No. 4117, 76-1 BCA (CCH) ¶ 11,713 (1976).

[64] Robert McMullan & Sons, Inc., ASBCA No. 19,129, 76-2 BCA (CCH) ¶ 12,072 (1976).

[65] *Id.*

§ 2.18 —Industry Standards

Industry manuals or standards are rarely conclusive as to the loss of productivity actually suffered by a contractor because industry manuals have no relation to the particular conditions encountered at the site. Moreover, industry manuals are sometimes regarded as self-serving publications which are promulgated to support the claims of contractors in that industry.[66]

Conversely, industry guides can be used to attack the reasonableness of a contractor's anticipated productivity ratio.[67] If a contractor asserts that its anticipated productivity ratio was normal or was the accepted productivity ratio, industry manuals may rebut such assertions. Courts and boards are more inclined to accept industry manuals as rebuttal evidence rather than direct proof of the reasonableness of an anticipated productivity ratio.[68]

§ 2.19 —Experts and Consultants

Experts or consultants are often used to establish and prove the costs incurred as a result of decreased productivity. Expert testimony must be based on project productivity studies, and such studies usually consider construction documents, cost data, correspondence, and other relevant information.

Expert opinion or analysis by itself is not sufficient to establish decreased productivity. Expert testimony must be based on the project records and such testimony must be reasonable in light of the surrounding circumstances.[69] As with all expert testimony, any opinions offered must be supported by corroborative evidence.[70]

§ 2.20 —Total Cost Method

The total cost method is the least widely accepted method to calculate decreased labor productivity.[71] Under the total cost method, decreased labor productivity is calculated by subtracting the estimated cost of performing the work from the actual cost of cost of performance.

---

[66] *Id.*

[67] Arthur Painting Co., ASBCA No. 20,267, 76-1 BCA (CCH) ¶ 11,894 (1976).

[68] *Id.*

[69] Luria Bros. & Co. v. United States, 369 F.2d 701 (Ct. Cl. 1966).

[70] *See id.;* Cosmic Constr. Co., ASBCA Nos. 24,014, 24,036, 88-2 BCA (CCH) ¶ 20,623 (1988).

[71] WRB Corp. v. United States, 183 Ct. Cl. 409 (1968); Cosmic Constr. Co., ASBCA Nos. 24,014, 24,036, 88-2 BCA (CCH) ¶ 20,623 (1988); J.D. Abrams, ENGBCA No. 4332, 89-1 BCA (CCH) ¶ 21,379 (1988).

Total cost calculations are disfavored because no attempt is made to segregate the factors which may have impacted productivity. Under the total cost method, the difference between the actual and estimated costs is presumed to be the result of a combination of factors, all attributable to the owner. Accordingly, the total cost method is viewed as a calculation of last resort.[72]

Total cost calculations are used in limited circumstances. Total cost calculations may be used only when each of the following are proven: (1) it impossible or impractical to calculate damages with a reasonable degree of accuracy;[73] (2) the contractor's bid or original estimate for the work was reasonable;[74] (3) the contractor's actual costs were reasonable;[75] (4) the contractor was not responsible for the added expenses.[76] Each of the four elements above must be present before a total cost calculation is justified.

Total cost calculations are not wholly rejected by courts and boards, however. Recently, the total cost method appears to be gaining acceptance by courts and boards, especially at the state level,[77] and by arbitrators and juries.[78]

§ 2.21   —Modified Total Cost Calculations

Total cost calculations are often modified to eliminate some of the inherent inaccuracies found in the standard total cost calculation. In modified total cost calculations, the contractor's original bid and the actual performance costs are often adjusted to ensure that the owner is not held responsible for bid inaccuracies or other increased costs over which it had no control.[79] Modified total cost calculations are accepted more often than straight total cost calculations, but all types of total cost calculations are generally disfavored.[80]

---

[72] Servidone Constr. Corp. v. United States, 19 Cl. Ct. 346 (1990); Cosmic Constr. Co., ASBCA Nos. 24,014, 24,036, 88-2 BCA (CCH) ¶ 20,623 (1988); J.D. Abrams, ENGBCA No. 4332, 89-1 BCA (CCH) ¶ 21,379 (1988).

[73] Skip Kirchdorfer, Inc. v. United States, 14 Cl. Ct. 594 (1988); J.D. Abrams, ENGBCA No. 4332, 89-1 BCA (CCH) ¶ 21,379 (1988).

[74] WRB v. United States, 183 Ct. Cl. 409 (1968); McDevitt & Street Co. v. Department of Gen. Servs., 377 So. 2d 191 (Fla. Dist. Ct. App. 1979).

[75] J.D. Abrams, ENGBCA No. 4332, 89-1 BCA (CCH) ¶ 21,379 (1988).

[76] Boyajian v. United States, 191 Ct. Cl. 233 (1970).

[77] Servidone Constr. Corp. v. United States, 19 Cl. Ct. 346 (1990); Glasgow, Inc. v. Department of Transp., 529 A.2d 576 (Pa. Commw. Ct. 1987).

[78] Prichard Bros., Inc. v. Grady Co., 436 N.W.2d 460 (Minn. Ct. App. 1989).

[79] J&T Constr. Co., DOT CAB No. 73-4, 75-2 BCA (CCH) ¶ 11,398 (1975).

[80] WRB Corp. v. United States, 183 Ct. Cl. 409 (1968).

Modified total cost calculations segregate impacted from nonimpacted work activities. By eliminating the nonimpacted periods, excess costs can be established with more accuracy. The credibility of a modified total cost calculation can be bolstered by expert opinion as to the validity of the contractor's original estimate for the cost of performing the impacted work. Further credibility may be accorded a modified total cost calculation if costs attributable to the contractor's own inefficiency are subtracted from the equation. If possible, modified total cost calculations should be chosen over the standard total cost calculation because courts and boards appear to accept the modified method more readily.[81]

---

[81] Sovereign Constr. Co., ASBCA No. 17,792, 75-1 BCA (CCH) ¶ 11,251 (1975); J&T Constr. Co., DOT CAB Nos. 73-4, 75-2 BCA (CCH) ¶ 11,398 (1975); Metropolitan Sewage Comm'n v. R.W. Constr. Co., 255 N.W.2d 293 (Wis. 1972).

CHAPTER 3

EQUIPMENT AND SMALL TOOL COSTS

ADDITIONAL EQUIPMENT COSTS

§ 3.1 Introduction

After labor, the greatest variable cost item on most construction projects is equipment. On projects involving heavy civil work, equipment costs are closely related to labor costs. If additional labor is required, additional equipment is usually required because the work is not done by bare hands alone. Moreover, equipment costs always increase when a project is extended, even in the absence of labor increases, because equipment costs are still incurred whether or not the equipment is operating.

Equipment is distinguished from small tools primarily on the basis of cost. Frequently, small tools are defined to be those items falling under a set value limit, typically under $1000. Often, small tools are accounted as a direct cost to a project, but equipment is usually capitalized. One contractor defined equipment to be "anything requiring a license or which has wheels and tracks." For that contractor, all other items may be determined to be small tools. The *Construction Dictionary*[1] defines *equipment* as "all machinery and equipment together with the necessary supplies for upkeep and maintenance; also tools and apparatus necessary for the proper construction and acceptable completion of the work."[2]

The distinction between equipment and small tools is important in claims analysis for purposes of calculating increased costs. Equipment, as a capital item, is considered to be charged to the project only for the time it is on the project. Small tools, however, are typically considered to be consumed on the project.

Increased equipment costs often are incurred due to one of the following events:

1. An extended performance period requiring the same amount of equipment to be on the project for a longer time
2. Additional work on the project requiring either the same equipment on the project for a longer time or new or additional equipment to perform the new work
3. Decreased productivity requiring more labor and hence more equipment.

In many construction claims, a combination of all three factors applies. On heavy construction projects such as roads, bridges, or earthwork,

---

[1] Greater Phoenix Chapter, National Association of Women in Construction, The Construction Dictionary (4th ed. 1980).

[2] *Id.*

equipment costs often exceed labor costs. However, even on projects which do not appear to be equipment-intensive, equipment can be a significant cost item. The claim preparer should be aware, whether the project is for the federal government[3] or private construction, that the additional cost for equipment can be recovered only if the equipment is in good working order and suitable for the project work.[4]

§ 3.2   Additional Equipment Usage

When usage of additional equipment has occurred on a project, the calculation of the additional time period for the equipment is relatively simple. The additional time period is the entire time the equipment was on the project. If the equipment was rented from an outside vendor, the cost of that equipment is the rental cost plus operating costs of that equipment. Most contractors should have a consistent method for accounting for owned equipment. However, if the equipment was owned by the contractor or an affiliate of the contractor, the appropriate rate for the equipment can be the source of significant disagreement. Both standby costs and equipment operating costs are dealt with in § 3.4.

§ 3.3   —Additional Work

If additional work results in additional use of the same equipment or if lower labor or work unit productivity results in increased equipment costs, it is necessary to calculate the additional equipment costs. If the equipment is on the project longer than scheduled in the contractor's estimate, this can be determined by comparing estimated equipment hours, weeks, or months with actual usage. This is illustrated in **Table 3–1**. In this example, the equipment was on the project far longer than anticipated. Although less dramatic than **Figure 3–1**, similar presentations can be made by presenting the data in the form shown in **Table 3–1**.

If additional equipment usage is a result of additional work, both estimated equipment costs and actual equipment costs can be used to determine the equipment costs allocable to the additional work. Ideally, the contractor will have cost accounting records showing the equipment costs for each unit of work. The cost of equipment per unit of work would be multiplied by the additional work units to obtain the added equipment costs. Even if the contractor does not maintain such records, it may be

---

[3] FAR 31.105(d)(2) (provides that payment will be allowed only for equipment in "sound workable condition").

[4] Weaver Constr. Co., ASBCA No. 12,577, 69-1 BCA (CCH) ¶ 7455 (1968).

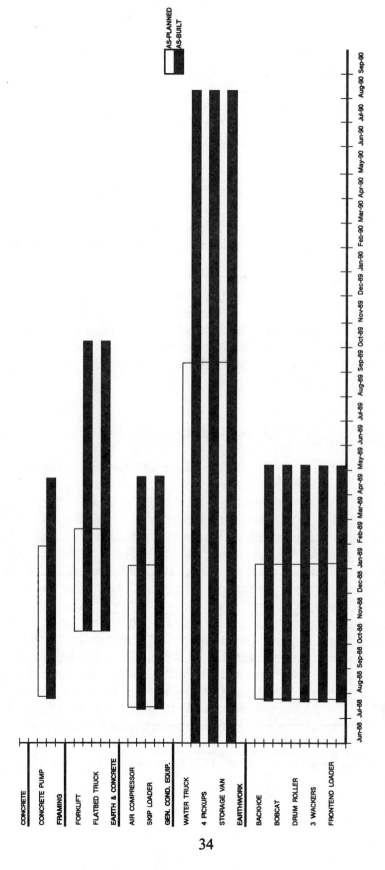

Figure 3–1. As-planned versus as-built durations for work items requiring equipment.

34

Table 3–1

As-Planned versus As-Built Equipment Use

Cost Code	Total Cost	Days Used	$/Day	Days Estm'd	Days Overrun	Add'l Cost Due to Ext'd Duration
1760 Compressors	$127,954	993	$ 19.54	304-10 mo.	689	$ 13,463.06
1780 Truck Crane	123,659	549	225.24	304-10 mo.	245	55,183.80
1790 Hydro Crane	78,017	639	122.09	213- 7 mo.	426	52,010.34
1830 Loader	88,061	959	68.91	274- 9 mo.	685	47,203.35
1840 Backhoe	28,647	670	42.76	92- 3 mo.	580	$ 24,800.80
	$346,338					$192,661.35

possible to re-create them by determining the cost for the appropriate equipment over the entire time the work was performed and then dividing it by the total number of work units to determine the equipment cost per work unit. This can then be multiplied by the number of additional work units to determine the additional equipment cost.

The additional equipment cost can also be determined by estimating the equipment to be used and the work units to be performed for each time period. An example would be as follows:

Backhoe	6 weeks at $1,100 per week—	$ 6,600
Wheel loader	6 weeks at $ 800 per week—	$ 4,800
Crawler tractor dozer	3 weeks at $1,400 per week—	$ 4,200
TOTAL		$15,600
Unit cost	$\dfrac{\$15,600}{8000 \text{ yards}} = \$1.95$ per yard	

One method used to calculate the number of additional equipment hours for a delay claim is to assume that each piece of equipment on the job was used for a full workday for each additional day of contract performance. This approach assumes that the equipment is chargeable to that project until it is reassigned to another project. Although the equipment may not be used a full workday every day, the full cost is charged to the project.[5]

Another method of calculating additional hours for a claim in which delays are asserted is to correlate equipment hours to the additional labor hours expended. This is a relatively simple task when one operator is assigned to one specific piece of equipment. The claim preparer should assume that whatever additional time the operator worked, the equipment also was used for that amount of time.

---

[5] R. Nash, Government Contract Changes 396 (1975).

If the equipment is used by more than one operator, calculating additional equipment hours is more difficult. However, it is usually possible to correlate a piece of equipment to a particular crew. For example, assume that a contractor had a crew of 25 assigned to various items of equipment, including one crane. It can be assumed that in one workday a crew of 25 would use the crane 8 hours, resulting in a ratio of 200 labor hours (25 workers times 8 hours per day) to 8 crane hours, which can be reduced to 25/1 or 0.04. Thus, 0.04 is the ratio of labor hours to equipment hours. Because an additional 34,300 labor hours were expended on excavation, the number of additional crane hours would be as follows:

$$34,300 \text{ labor hours} \times 0.04 = 1372 \text{ additional crane hours}$$

§ 3.4   —Standby versus Operating Costs

When additional equipment costs are required because of extended job duration, it is necessary to determine not only that the equipment was on-site longer but also whether it was less productive or whether it sat idle part of the time because of the extension of the schedule. When the equipment is idle, it is not appropriate to charge rates reflecting operating costs, that is, fuel, oil, gas, operators, and similar items that are incurred only when the equipment is operating. This distinction becomes more difficult to make when dealing with equipment related to job overhead or considered general conditions such as office trailers, storage vans, superintendents' trucks, or man lifts. When dealing with such general conditions items, it can generally be assumed that they are being operated or used all the time. To recover costs for idle equipment, the contractor must establish that, but for the delay, the equipment could have been otherwise productively employed.[6]

Another consideration is whether the contractor made reasonable efforts to reassign the equipment to avoid leaving it idle on the project in question. Of course, the uniqueness of the equipment, whether it was specifically designed and purchased for one project, and the location of the job are factors to consider in determining whether the equipment could be reassigned reasonably. Proving exactly when equipment was assigned to a contract and then reassigned can be difficult.[7]

---

[6] C.L. Fairley Constr. Co., ASBCA No. 32,581, 90-2 BCA (CCH) ¶ 22,665 (1990).

[7] *See* William Lagnion, ENGBCA No. 4287, 82-2 BCA (CCH) ¶ 15,939 (1982) (full equipment hours allowed from date an item of equipment first appeared on daily log to last date). *See also* United States Steel Corp. v. Missouri Pac. R.R., 668 F.2d 435 (8th Cir.), *cert. denied,* 459 U.S. 836, 103 S. Ct. 80 (1982) (equipment hours were allowed to accrue from date equipment was released from prior job).

§ 3.5   Cost of Equipment

The contractor's actual incurred equipment costs are the costs it is entitled to recover. The actual equipment costs are usually the contractor's booked or recorded costs, provided there is no contractual or regulatory obligation to the contrary. In *Meva Corp. v. United States,*[8] the court stated:

> In the absence of a regulation or directive such as in *Nolan Brothers, Inc. v. United States,* 437 F.2d 1371, 194 Ct. Cl. 1 (1971), the burden is on the party seeking to substitute AGC costs for the contractor's own actual booked costs to demonstrate that the contractor's own costs (as shown) are inadequate or incomplete or do not fairly represent the full costs rightly attributable to the particular contract. In this case, plaintiff did not succeed in bearing that burden; its effort to invoke AGC costs consisted mainly of general testimony as to the normal practice of building contractors, not criticism directed specifically to the $2,448,938 of costs associated from its own actual, booked equipment costs in this particular instance. The plaintiff has simply failed to prove that in this case actual, booked costs are inadequate or incomplete or do not represent the full costs rightly attributable to the contract.[9]

The best indicia of the cost of equipment are invoices from third-party vendors, assuming the equipment was rented and not owned by the claiming party. The contractor is reimbursed for the actual rent paid to the equipment supplier.[10] For certain federal government contracts, regulations provide for the payment of outside rentals.[11] If the contractor owns the equipment, the best source to determine equipment costs are the contractor's actual internal equipment rates.

Many contractors maintain separate equipment divisions or companies for the express purpose of standardizing equipment costs and maintaining adequate internal equipment rental charges. This allows the equipment to be leased to individual construction projects. Usually, these intracompany leases will be treated as any other lease. The lease or rent amounts incurred are costs that can be claimed. However, with respect to public contracts, the amount charged through intracompany lease can be limited to the actual ownership cost.[12] Thus, it should be assumed that the owners' representatives will closely scrutinize any intracompany leasing arrangements.[13]

---

[8] 511 F.2d 548, 559 (Ct. Cl. 1975).

[9] *Id.*

[10] A.S. Thomas, Inc., ASBCA No. 10,745, 66-1 BCA (CCH) ¶ 5438 (1966).

[11] FAR 31.105(2)(ii), 31.205–36(b).

[12] *Id.* 31.205–36(b)(3).

[13] *See, e.g.,* Isaac Degenaars Co., ASBCA Nos. 11,045, 11,083, 72-2 BCA (CCH) ¶ 9764 (1972). The board found that a husband controlled his wife's interest in an equipment rental company even though he owned no stock, even in the absence of any other

The intracompany equipment rates should include depreciation, interest, overhaul, repairs, property taxes, storage, insurance, in addition to actual equipment usage. These items are defined as follows:

Depreciation.   Depreciation is that internal charge that reflects the decline of equipment value due to age, usage, condition, and obsolescence. It is an amount that is charged each accounting period to reflect the diminution in value of the equipment over the economic life of the equipment. Even though a piece of equipment may be depreciated fully for tax purposes, it does not mean that depreciation as a component of equipment rates should not be charged. A piece of equipment that has been fully depreciated for tax purposes may well retain functional value.

Interest or cost of facilities capital.   Interest is the cost of the funds used to purchase the equipment. This is an appropriate charge even when the contractor paid for the funds out of capital rather than borrowing the money.

Overhaul.   Certain types of equipment, particularly heavy equipment, require periodic major overhauls or the replacement of significant parts. Such overhaul costs should be considered in the equipment rate.

Repairs.   Repairs are those normal, recurring maintenance procedures necessary to keep equipment in running order and maintain its value. These may be reflected in the operating costs of the equipment as opposed to the rental rate.

Property taxes.   Property taxes are those taxes paid on the equipment annually.

Storage.   The cost to store equipment during the portion of the year it is not in use.

Insurance.   Insurance is the cost of insuring the equipment.

---

financial interest in the company. On appeal, the United States Claims Court agreed with the Board's decision, stating:

> Plaintiff . . . argues that since Rae did not have legal ownership of the equipment, the family ties are irrelevant and AED rates should apply. The legal test to avoid AGC rates, however, in a case of delay and increased work is that the contractor must show that the equipment was actually rented. Cornell Wrecking Co. v. United States, 184 Ct. Cl. 289, 291 (1968). As noted by this Board, AGC rates include profit and depreciation factors, 75-1 BCA (CCH) ¶ 10,998 at 52,381, which in some circumstances involving fully depreciated equipment can lead to a windfall profit for the owners. L.L. Hall Construction Co. v. United States, 177 Ct. Cl. 870, 379 F.2d 559 (1966).

Degenaars Co. v. United States, 2 Cl. Ct. 482, 492 (1983).

Operating period. The operating period is the time period in which the equipment can actually be used. Even though a contractor owns a piece of equipment an entire year, it does not mean the appropriate monthly charge is one-twelfth of the annual cost. Many pieces of equipment are used far less than 12 months of the year. The rental rate must reflect this lowered usage. For example, a specialized piece of equipment that is used only four months of the year should have its entire annual cost divided by four rather than twelve for the appropriate monthly rate. On the other hand, if this piece of equipment is idle due to delay, this factor must be taken into account because the rate was calculated assuming specific idle months of the year.

All of these factors must be considered in analyzing a contractor's internal equipment rates. It is appropriate that these items be charged, but they must be charged in a reasonable manner to determine the contractor's internal equipment rates fairly and accurately.

§ 3.6 Industry Guides

A number of industry manuals exist for determining equipment rates. In addition to the commonly used manuals listed here, most contractor trade associations have a rental rate manual or rate survey available.

§ 3.7 —*Contractor's Equipment Cost Manual*

The Associated General Contractor's of America (AGC) *Contractor's Equipment Cost Manual,* published annually by Data Quest, Inc., has reached widespread acceptance. In fact, the use of the AGC *Manual* is required on certain federal government contracts,[14] after receiving approval by the United States Court of Claims.[15] Other government agencies have allowed it even though not required by regulation. The usefulness of the AGC *Manual* was recognized by the Department of Transportation Board of Contract Appeals. In *Foster Construction Co. & Williams Brothers Co.,*[16] the Board stated:

> The Government's auditor took the position that the contractor's equipment ownership expenses should consist of the actual rentals and the actual depreciation expense on the equipment. He, therefore, allowed only these

---

[14] DAR 15-402.1(c) (use of AGC *Manual* applies only to contracts let prior to April 1, 1984, for defense-related projects).

[15] Nolan Bros. v. United States, 437 F.2d 1371 (Ct. Cl. 1971).

[16] DOT CAB 71-16, 73-1 BCA (CCH) ¶ 9869 (1973) at p. 46,151.

items, and as noted before, lumped them into an overhead pool for distribution to the claims.

The appellant, on the other hand, contends that an appropriate amount of equipment ownership expense may be obtained by the use of generally recognized industrywide average experience rates. More specifically, appellant contends that it should be permitted to apply AGC rates to its equipment acquisition costs to determine the amount of ownership expense. We, thus, have a dispute very much like those presented in *Nolan Bros. v. U.S.,* [16 CCF ¶ 80,119], 194 Ct. Cl. 1 (1971); *L.L. Hall Construction Co. v. U.S.,* [11 CCF ¶ 80,791], 177 Ct. Cl. 870 (1966), and *Bennett v. U.S.,* [11 CCF 80,884], 178 Ct. Cl. 61 (1967), where the Government argues for the use of "actual costs" as opposed to the contractor's use of "average rates." Quite predictably, each party cites us to the prior decision favorable to its position.

In the present case, we think the better argument lies with the appellant, even though it is recognized that neither the agency's practice nor the instant contract was or is subject to the ASPR regulations, as was the case in *Nolan Bros., supra,* which mandated the use of AGC rates. This is because the auditor's use of "actual depreciation expense," standing alone, is far too narrow a base for a reasonable determination of the contractor's overall equipment ownership expense. Although the contractor's evidence on the point is not overly plentiful, there is enough of record to show all of the other manifold factors encompassed by the AGC rates (i.e., major repairs, overhaul, interest, taxes, insurance, storage, etc.) were in some measure applicable to the instant claims. The use of "average rates," therefore, is the more preferable means of determining a reasonable figure for claims allowance.

The Armed Services Board of Contract Appeals has held that the usual method of calculating equipment standby costs is to use the "AGC rates reduced by half to reflect the lack of fines and thus, less profit."[17] In another recent case, the contractor was limited to the AGC rates unless it could establish higher actual costs.[18]

In another case, the court stated that the use of AGC rates would have been preferable to the use of fair rental value for idle equipment, but refused to overrule a jury verdict based on the latter rate when the defendant failed to raise the issue until appeal.[19]

The AGC *Manual* provides guideline rental rates for equipment of specific models and years. The rates do not include expenses for equipment operators or general cost items such as overhead and profit. The AGC *Manual* is divided according to types of equipment and in order to use it, very specific information is needed about the particular equipment, including the specifications of both model year and capacity. If that information is

---

[17] C.L. Fairley Constr. Co., ASBCA No. 32,581, 90-2 BCA (CCH) ¶ 22,665 (1990) at p. 113,870.

[18] Holloway Constr. Co. v. United States, 18 Cl. Ct. 326 (1989).

[19] W.G. Cornell Co. v. Ceramic Coating Co., 626 F.2d 990 (D.C. Cir. 1980).

available, the AGC *Manual* will give an approximate base price for the equipment, the economic hours of use, and the annual use-hours upon which the rates are based. Additionally, the *Manual* will give the specific amounts for each component in the hourly ownership expenses, including depreciation, taxes, insurance, and the hourly repair and fuel expenses broken down by labor, parts, supplies, tires, fuel, and lubrication. Last, the *Manual* gives combined ownership and repair expenses with monthly, weekly, daily, and hourly figures. Given this level of information, it is possible to check the actual project equipment usage against the assumptions contained within the rates. When the actual factors differ from the assumption in the AGC *Manual,* the rates must be adjusted.

The AGC *Manual,* as indicated in its foreword, is intended to serve the entire construction industry by providing guideline figures for equipment costs.

§ 3.8   —*Rental Rates Compilation*

The Associated Equipment Dealers (AED) annually publishes a commonly used rental rate manual, which is referred to as the *Rental Rates Compilation.* This manual has been developed by surveying third-party equipment dealers for the actual rates used. The rates are averaged for age, condition, and operating efficiency of the equipment. As a result, its rates, which include overhead and profit, tend to be higher than the AGC rates. The AED rates are not comparable to the internal cost of owning equipment in most cases.

Although certain federal government contracts require the use of AGC rates for contractor-owned or contractor-controlled equipment,[20] the government may accept the AED rates if the contractor can show that these rates form the basis of the rates charged the contractor by a third-party vendor. The two types of rates are discussed in the appeal of *Blake Construction Co.*[21]:

A.G.C. and A.E.D.

To advert again to the appellant's method of estimating its costs, we do not believe that the A.E.D. rates are appropriate for use when, as here, the equipment used by the contractor was owned by him, not rented. We believe that the A.G.C. rates are more proper for application in such circumstances, with modifications as appropriate, but not necessarily modified as did the sub here. We agree, basically, with the following passage pertaining to the

---

[20] DAR 15-402.1(c) (use of AGC *Manual* applies only to contracts let prior to April 1, 1984, for defense-related projects).

[21] GSBCA No. 1176, 66-1 BCA (CCH) ¶ 5589 at pp. 26,126–27 (1966).

matter quoted from a recent excellent decision of the Armed Services Board of Contract Appeals:

"Equipment rates require a more extended discussion. [Appellant] believed that A.E.D. rates or their equivalent were a proper basis for computing the claim for equipment charges. Two pieces of equipment appellant rented from another contractor and for these has charged the actual rent paid. We have allowed those rates for those two pieces of equipment. The appellant-prime contractor owned all of the other equipment for which it makes claim. Use of A.E.D. rates is not proper when a contractor is charging for equipment which he owns. A.E.D. rates are compiled by an organization of, and published for use by, dealers engaged in the business of renting equipment. Such business has its own peculiar risks and intangible costs and the rates its practitioners charge must cover such, plus a profit —. The rates charged by such dealers are truly rental rates. The charges which a construction contractor may properly make for equipment performing construction work, or waiting to perform it, are charges designed to reimburse that contractor for the cost to him of owning and maintaining that equipment. These charges are properly designated equipment ownership expenses or rates; average ownership charges are set forth in The Associated General Contractors' manual. This distinction between rental rates and its rates is made clear in the A.G.C. manual, —. We have previously pointed out that the distinction between A.G.C. and A.E.D. rates and the impropriety of applying the latter to contractor-owned equipment. *David L. Brewer,* ASBCA No. 9781, 18 December 1964, 65-1 BCA ¶ 4591. *See also Continental Illinois National Bank and Trust Company of Chicago v. United States,* 126 Ct. Cl. 631, 678 (1953). We recognize that this careful distinction in terminology between rental and ownership 'expenses is often not made in everyday conversation within construction circles or even by the courts. The term "rental rates" is often used loosely to refer to any charges made for equipment whether owned or rented by the party operating the equipment, whether arrived at from A.E.D. or A.G.C. schedules, or whether determined by private agreement or private experience. Loose uses of words should not blur the clear and valid distinctions between true equipment rental rates and equipment ownership expenses . . . ."' *See, J.D. Shotwell Company,* ASBCA No. 8961, 65-2, ¶ 5243.[22]

§ 3.9 —*Rental Rate Bluebook for Construction Equipment*

Another commonly used industry standard is the *Rental Rate Bluebook for Construction Equipment,* commonly referred as the *Blue Book,* published by the machinery division of Data Quest, Inc. This manual is updated monthly and lists virtually all equipment that has been manufactured within the last five years. As with the AGC rates, the *Blue Book* rates are

[22] *Id.*

broken down in detail, which permits analysis of the basic assumptions of the rates. The costs included in the *Blue Book* are intended "as guidelines paralleling amounts an equipment owner should charge during rental or contractual periods to recover equipment-related costs." Thus, it can be used by a contractor for its owned equipment.

The use of the *Blue Book* was addressed in the case of *Arcon Construction Co. v. South Dakota Cement Plant,*[23] in which the owner had established that the contractor's bid equipment rates were approximately one-tenth of the *Blue Book* rates. The court held:

> A careful consideration of these authorities leads us to conclude that rental rates, such as those in the blue book, may be used as a guide to show damages resulting from idle equipment, providing they do not result in an unreasonable amount of damages. Of course, determining whether an amount is reasonable or unreasonable is the most difficult question. However, it is safe to say that when the blue book projects a cost for equipment which is ten times the amount of the figure the contractor used in his bid, as is the case here, the blue book amounts are unreasonable. Since the jury award in this case is far more than Arcon would have received for equipment costs under its bid, had it completed the project on time, we find the award to be unreasonable and we reverse on the issue of damages.

> . . . In order to give the trial court some guidance on retrial of the damage issue, we suggest the following:

> 1) Blue book figures may be admitted by the trial court in its discretion if the court determines that this evidence would aid the jury on the issue of damages under the facts of this case.

> 2) If the blue book is admitted, it should be with the following admonitions to the jury: a) Any sum allowed must be reasonable and should be premised in the first instance on an allocation of the cost of equipment for the period involved, based on the figure Arcon submitted for cost of equipment in its bid. b) This may be supplemented by evidence of other continuing costs of owning the equipment during the period it remained idle, as long as such costs can be proven with reasonable certainty. Examples of such costs include, but are not limited to, security, maintenance, taxes, interest on investment, etc. c) This may be further supplemented by a showing, if any, of lost profits during the period the equipment was idle, as long as the profits can be proven with reasonable certainty. d) All of the factors outlined above must be counter-balanced by any showing of decreased costs which flow naturally from non-use of the equipment.

> Keeping those guidelines in mind, the jury should be able to come up with a figure which is not unreasonable, and yet will fairly compensate Arcon for its equipment which remained idle due to the cement plant's breach of contract.[24]

---

[23] 349 N.W.2d 407 (S.D. 1984).

[24] *Id.*

Thus, the use of the *Blue Book* rates may be allowed in order to establish equipment damages even when the *Blue Book* rates are not specified. The *Blue Book* rates may be particularly helpful if the contractor could establish that its bid rates or internal charge rates were unrealistically low.

The *Blue Book* was also addressed in *Alaska v. Northwestern Construction, Inc.*[25] The court held it was appropriate to apply the *Blue Book* rates when they were allowed but not required by the contract even though "actual rates" were available.

§ 3.10   —*Tool and Equipment Rental Schedule*

The National Electrical Contractors Association (NECA) publishes a pamphlet, *Tool and Equipment Rental Schedule,* containing average rates for a variety of equipment and tools commonly used by the electrical contracting industry. These rates are all-inclusive rates and assume the equipment is used on the project on a continuous basis. The rates include all costs except maintenance operators, energy, and delivery to site.

§ 3.11   —Other Schedules

Government agencies such as the Corps of Engineers and state highway departments also provide standard equipment rental rates. These rate schedules are often specifically incorporated in the contracts and must be used when calculating changes under the contract.

§ 3.12   When Rates Are Inapplicable

Whenever equipment rates are used, it is important to verify that the assumptions behind the rates fit the actual conditions. One significant assumption is the average annual usage implied in the rate. If this annual usage varies significantly from that represented on the project, the rate may be significantly too high or too low to be applicable. Another example would be a case in which the equipment is being utilized on a shift basis so that the usage is far greater than the single-shift basis most rates are based upon. It would be appropriate, in this situation, to increase the daily or weekly equipment rates significantly because the equipment will wear out much more quickly than usual. If hourly rates are used, no such adjustment is necessary.

---

[25] 741 P.2d 235 (Alaska 1987).

Operating conditions that are more severe than expected also provide a reason to increase operating rates. If the equipment is working under severe conditions, such as extremely abrasive soils or adverse climatic conditions, it may be appropriate to increase equipment rates. By the same token, if the equipment is idle much more often than anticipated in the rate, it may be appropriate to reduce the equipment rate to reflect diminished wear and tear.

COST OF ADDITIONAL SMALL TOOLS

§ 3.13   Introduction

Small tools are an integral part of any construction project. Small tools do not necessarily represent small costs, however. The cost of small tools can often amount to 5 percent of a contractor's direct labor costs.[26] The cost of additional small tools is a recoverable element in construction claims and may be calculated through a variety of methods.

§ 3.14   Small Tools Defined

Small tools range from shovels, picks, and rakes to electric power tools.[27] Small tools are usually defined by their cost. For example, under Washington Metropolitan Area Transit Authority contracts, small tools are tools costing less than $200.[28] The life of small tools is limited because they frequently break, are lost, or are stolen. Therefore, small tools are expected to be consumed on a project, meaning that they will not be used on future projects.

In calculating damages in construction claims, it is important to distinguish between small tools and equipment.[29] It is assumed that equipment will later be used on some other project. Thus, although small tools are chargeable only to the project on which they were consumed, equipment is

---

[26] *See* Harrison W./Franki Denys, ENGBCA No. 5577, 90-3 BCA (CCH) ¶ 22,991 (1990); Fireman's Fund Ins. Co., ASBCA No. 39,666, 91-1 BCA (CCH) ¶ 23,372 (1990).

[27] Tools are defined as, "In construction, a saw, shovel, hammer, trowel, etc., called hand tools." Greater Phoenix Chapter, National Association of Women in Construction, Construction Dictionary (4th ed. 1980).

[28] *See* Washington Metro. Area Transit Auth. Contract, Special Provisions.

[29] See § 3.1. *Equipment* is defined as, "all machinery and equipment together with the necessary supplies for upkeep and maintenance." Greater Phoenix Chapter, National Association of Women in Construction, Construction Dictionary (4th ed. 1980).

chargeable to the project only for the time it was actually employed on the project. Contractors often fail to distinguish between small tools and equipment in calculating construction claims.

§ 3.15   Reasons for Increased Small Tool Costs

At the bidding stage, small tool costs are fairly easy to predict and are usually computed as a percentage of direct labor costs or other costs. Contractors may include the cost of small tools as a separate line item in the bid or the cost of small tools may be included as an element of other costs.

Additional small tool costs may arise from a variety of reasons. Owner-directed changes may result in the need for additional or substituted work. Additional or extra work requires increased labor hours that, increases the use and consumption of small tools. Additional small tool costs resulting from owner-directed changes are recoverable.[30]

Owner-caused delay may result in extended contract performance that also increases the need for and use of small tools. Additional small tool costs resulting from delay are also recoverable.[31] In sum, the cost of additional small tools resulting from an owner's actions or inactions is another recoverable cost in construction claims.[32]

§ 3.16   Calculation of Additional Small Tool Costs

Courts and boards of contract appeals have permitted contractors to calculate the cost of additional small tools through a variety of methods.[33] There is no uniformly accepted method for calculating additional small tool costs. Courts and boards of contract appeals appear to allow any method of calculation as long as the method chosen is reasonable in light of the situation at hand.

---

[30] Harrison W./Franki Denys, ENGBCA No. 5577, 90-3 BCA (CCH) ¶ 22,991 (1990).

[31] George Hyman Constr. Co., ENGBCA No. 4541, 85-1 BCA (CCH) ¶ 17,847 (1985).

[32] Harrison W./Franki Denys, ENGBCA No. 5577, 90-3 BCA (CCH) ¶ 22,991 (1990); George Hyman Constr. Co., ENGBCA No. 4541, 85-1 BCA (CCH) ¶ 17,847 (1985).

[33] Harrison W./Franki Denys, ENGBCA No. 5577, 90-3 BCA ¶ 22,991 (1990) (percentage of total labor markup); John Driggs Co., ENGBCA No. 4913, 88-2 BCA (CCH) ¶ 20,530 (1988) (percentage of direct labor markup); New York State Elec. & Gas Corp. v. Goettsche, 48 Misc. 2d 786, 265 N.Y.S.2d 809 (1965) (percentage of total labor markup); Kelly v. Grimshaw, 161 Kan. 253, 167 P.2d 627 (1946) (included as part of overhead).

§ 3.17   —Percentage of Total Labor Markup Calculation

The cost of additional small tools may be calculated by marking up the total labor costs by a certain percentage. This method of calculation divides the total cost of small tools by the total labor costs.[34] The quotient is the percentage which the cost of small tools bears to the total cost of labor. The percentage, or markup, is then multiplied by the increased labor costs. The resulting figure is the amount of additional small tool costs incurred on the project. An example of the total labor markup calculation is as follows:

Total small tool costs = $352,610
Total labor costs = $7,052,800

$$\text{Small tools as a percentage of labor} = \frac{352,610}{7,052,800} = 5\%$$

Additional labor costs = $500,000
Additional small tool costs = 5% × 500,000 = $25,000

When the majority of the claim is for additional work, the total labor markup method is a reasonable and accepted manner in which to calculate the costs of additional small tools.[35] When additional labor is expended because of a loss of productivity resulting in extension of the project's duration, however, the percentage of labor method provides a claimed cost that often is significantly less than the costs actually incurred on the project. In such cases, contractors should consider alternative methods to calculate additional small tool costs.

§ 3.18   —Percentage of Direct Labor Markup Calculation

In some cases, the total labor cost may be an inappropriate basis for calculating the cost of additional small tools.[36] When the labor costs attributable to field support and field office are high relative to the direct field labor, direct labor costs may be the appropriate basis for calculating the cost of additional small tools.[37] The direct labor calculation is similar to the total labor calculation with the exception that the direct labor base is usually smaller than the base used in the total labor method. The direct labor

---

[34] *See* Lew F. Stilwell, Inc., ASBCA No. 9423, 1964 BCA (CCH) ¶ 4128 (1964).

[35] *Id.*

[36] *See* John Driggs Co., ENGBCA No. 4913, 88-2 BCA (CCH) ¶ 20,530 (1988).

[37] *Id.*

method does not necessarily result in decreased recovery for additional small tool costs, however.

§ 3.19   —Combined Percentage of Labor Markup Calculation

In some cases, contractors mark up labor costs to account for the combined cost of additional small tools, supplies, taxes, and insurance.[38] Under the combined percentage method, the ratio of small tools to labor is irrelevant and a lump sum percentage is applied to the labor costs.

In *Dodge Street Building Corp. v. United States,*[39] the contractor was allowed a 12-percent markup on the cost of labor for the increased costs of small tools, taxes, and insurance.[40] Other contractors have recovered the cost of additional small tools in large percentage adjustments for the combined cost of supervision and supplies.[41] Combined cost calculations are not usually used to calculate additional small tool costs, however.

§ 3.20   —Recovery of Additional Small Tool Costs in Overhead

Many federal government contracts prohibit separate recovery for small tools in subsequent claims under the contract.[42] In such cases, contractors must recover the cost of additional small tools as an overhead item. An illustrative example is found in *Shumate Constructors, Inc.*[43]

In *Shumate Constructors,* the contractor claimed increased costs incurred as a result of performing additional work.[44] As part of its claim, the contractor calculated its small tools expense as a 3 percent markup on labor.[45] The changes clause in the contract provided that additional small tool costs could be recovered only in claims for overhead and profit.[46]

---

[38] Dodge St. Bldg. Corp. v. United States, 341 F.2d 64 (Ct. Cl. 1965).

[39] *Id.*

[40] *Id.*

[41] *See* Steve P. Rados, Inc., AGBCA No. 77-130-4, 82-1 BCA (CCH) ¶ 15,624 (1982).

[42] *See* Shumate Constr., Inc., VABCA No. 2772, 90-3 BCA (CCH) ¶ 22,946 (1990); Freeman-Darling, Inc., GSBCA No. 7112, 89-2 BCA (CCH) ¶ 21,882 (1989); Smith-Cothran, Inc., DOT CAB Nos. 1931, 2022, 89-1 BCA (CCH) ¶ 21,554 (1989).

[43] VABCA No. 2772, 90-3 BCA (CCH) ¶ 22,946 (1990).

[44] *Id.*

[45] *Id.*

[46] The contract clause stated, "[O]verhead and contractor's fee percentages shall be considered to include insurance other than mentioned herein, field and office supervisors and assistants, security police, use of small tools, incremental job burdens, and no separate allowance will be made therefor." *Id.* at p. 115,190.

In various other cases, the boards of contract appeals have not permitted contractors to recover the cost of additional small tools as a separate allowance.[47]

§ 3.21   —Extended Daily Overhead
Rate Calculation

The cost of additional small tools may be included in the contractor's claim for extended daily overhead.[48] This type of calculation considers the cost of additional small tools as a component of the contractor's daily direct overhead cost along with wages, salaries, and other costs traditionally associated with overhead. This method of calculating the cost of additional small tools has been accepted by the boards of contract appeals.[49]

In *Gracon Corp.*,[50] the contractor included the cost of small tools in its average daily overhead rate.[51] The small tool cost component was based on the contractor's actual expenses incurred during the fiscal quarter immediately preceding the delay.[52] The average daily overhead rate was then multiplied by the number of days of delay, which resulted in the contractor's extended, unabsorbed overhead costs for the delay period.[53] This manner of calculating and recovering the cost of additional small tools was accepted without question by the Department of Interior Board of Contract Appeals.[54]

§ 3.22   —Cost Modeling

Small tool costs are affected by both time and labor. If additional labor is required, then additional small tools will be required because the performance of construction work virtually always requires the use of tools. The relationship between labor and small tool costs is frequently linear. That is, a 10-percent increase in labor will result in 10-percent higher small tool costs. The relationship between time and small tool costs is also roughly

---

[47] Freeman-Darling, Inc., GSBCA No. 7112, 89-2 BCA (CCH) ¶ 21,882 (1989); Smith-Cothran, Inc., DOT CAB Nos. 1931, 2022, 89-1 BCA (CCH) ¶ 21,554 (1989); Regan/Nager Constr., PSBCA No. 1070, 85-1 BCA (CCH) ¶ 17,778 (1984).

[48] Atlas Constr. Co., GSBCA Nos. 7903, 8143, 8593, 8653, 90-2 BCA (CCH) ¶ 22,812 (1990); Gracon Corp., IBCA No. 2271, 89-1 BCA (CCH) ¶ 21,232 (1988).

[49] Atlas Constr. Co., GSBCA Nos. 7903, 8143, 8593, 8653, 90-2 BCA (CCH) ¶ 22,812 (1990); Gracon Corp., IBCA No. 2271, 89-1 BCA (CCH) ¶ 21,232 (1988).

[50] IBCA No. 2271, 89-1 BCA (CCH) ¶ 21,232.

[51] *Id.*

[52] *Id.* at p. 107,103.

[53] *Id.*

[54] *Id.*

linear. If a project takes longer than originally estimated, it is axiomatic that there will be additional small tool costs because small tools break, wear out, or are lost over time. When a project is both extended in duration and labor is increased, that small tool costs increase is a function of both the increase in time and the increase in labor. For example, if both the required time period and labor double, small tool costs can be expected to increase by a factor of four. This relationship is expressed below:

Predicted small tool costs =

$$\frac{\text{actual labor costs}}{\text{estimated labor costs}} \times \frac{\text{actual duration}}{\text{estimated duration}} \times \frac{\text{estimated small}}{\text{tool costs}}$$

This type of cost modeling frequently will predict actual small tool costs. When a portion of the schedule duration increases due to both parties and a portion of the labor increases due to both parties, it is necessary to modify the equation variables properly to allocate the added small tool costs between the parties.

An actual example of calculating predicted small tool costs compared to actual costs is shown below:

Estimated small tools cost	$ 24,240
Estimated labor cost	$ 821,297
Estimated duration	16 months
Actual labor cost	$1,685,992
Actual duration	33 months

$$\frac{1,685,992}{821,297} \times \frac{33}{16} \times 24,240 = \$102,632 \text{ (Predicted expense)}$$

The predicted expense must be compared to the actual expense.

This method has been found to be reasonably accurate in predicting small tool costs on a troubled project. Cost modeling is a means to validate actual costs. It is important that the estimate be correct, that the actual costs of small tools be determined in a reasonable manner, and that it be consistent with the estimate.

§ 3.23   —Agreement of Parties

The easiest and least costly way to calculate and recover the cost of additional small tools is through a fixed agreement of the parties.[55] In this situation, the parties stipulate in advance as to the additional fixed cost of small

---

[55] See Columbus & S. Ohio Elec. Co. v. J.P. Sand & Gravel Co., 22 Ohio App. 3d 98, 489 N.E.2d 830 (1985).

tools or the fixed percentage of labor attributable to additional small tool costs. Mutual agreement as to the cost of additional small tools, however, may not be possible given the circumstances of the particular case.

§ 3.24   Secondary Considerations

Contractors should consider all factors before calculating the cost of additional small tools. Various site conditions may contribute to higher-than-normal small tool costs. Traditionally, projects based in and around bodies of water consume small tools at a rate higher than normal due to increased chances of loss and breakage. The same is true for bridge or highrise construction. Contractors, therefore, should thoroughly consider the nature of the project and its effect on small tools consumption.

The location of the project may also affect the degree of small tools consumption. Projects in high crime areas usually have higher small tool costs due to theft and pilferage.[56] The effect of theft should be factored into all calculations of additional small tool costs.

---

[56] Harrison W./Franki Denys, ENGBCA No. 5577, 90-3 BCA (CCH) ¶ 22,991 (1990).

CHAPTER 4

MATERIAL COSTS

§ 4.1   Introduction

This chapter addresses recovering the cost of materials in construction claims. Material cost claims can be divided into two categories: claims for additional material and claims for the escalated cost of material. For a variety of reasons attributable to the owner, contractors may be forced to purchase materials which were unanticipated at the time of bidding. Also, contractors may be required to purchase materials at prices higher than anticipated. It is well recognized that contractors can recover the costs of additional and escalated materials.[1]

---

[1] Luria Bros. & Co. v. United States, 177 Ct. Cl. 676 (1966); Levering & Garrigues Co. v. United States, 73 Ct. Cl. 566 (1932); Kelly & Kelly v. United States, 31 Ct. Cl. 361

Claims for additional or escalated material, however, are relatively uncommon because contractors can usually predict such costs well in advance of performance of the project. Additional or escalated material costs are more easily calculable than home office overhead costs. Contractors, however, should be aware of the potential costs associated with additional or escalated material claims.

Claims for additional material may serve as a useful first test of the validity of a claim. If a project has substantial labor, equipment, and material overruns, there is a strong possibility that the contractor underestimated the scope of the work. Contractors, therefore, should not take lightly the calculation and assertion of claims for costs associated with additional or escalated material.

§ 4.2 Materials Defined

Material is "any substance specified for use in the construction of the project and its appurtenances."[2] Thus, materials are the bricks, mortar, steel, paint, and fixtures brought to the site; assembled, they constitute the final structure.[3] Materials can also include a subcategory of items known as components.[4] *Components* are items which are physically incorporated in construction materials.[5] For example, concrete is a material and sand is a component of concrete.[6] The distinction between materials and components is significant only for purposes of compliance with Buy American Act provisions in federal procurement contracts and for recovering the cost of taxes incurred in purchasing additional materials.[7]

A further distinction exists between materials and supplies. Supplies are items needed to perform the work but not incorporated into the final physical structure. *Supplies* are "[T]hings other than labor, which are consumed in, but do not become a physical part of the structure and are distinguished from the used materials which are things becoming a physical part of the structure."[8] The cost of supplies incurred as a result of additional material requirements is also recoverable as an element of construction claims.

(1896); Annotation, *Right of Building or Construction Contractor to Recover Damages Resulting From Delay Caused by Default of Contractee,* 115 A.L.R. 65 (1958).

[2] National Association of Women in Construction, Construction Dictionary (4th ed. 1980).

[3] 9 J. McBride & T. Touhey, Government Contracts § 50.110(2)(1991).

[4] *Id.*

[5] *Id.; see* Dick Hollan, Inc., ASBCA No. 21,304, 77-1 BCA (CCH) ¶ 12,540 (1977).

[6] 9 J. McBride & T. Touhey, Government Contracts § 50.110(2)(1991).

[7] *See* Dick Hollan, Inc., ASBCA No. 21,304, 77-1 BCA (CCH) ¶ 12,540 (1977).

[8] National Association of Women in Construction, Construction Dictionary (4th ed. 1980).

§ 4.3   Reasons for Material Claims

The three most common reasons for material claims are owner-caused delay,[9] defective specifications,[10] and owner-directed changes.[11]

§ 4.4   —Costs Attributable to Owner-caused Delay

In cases of owner-caused delay, contractors seek primarily to recover the escalated cost of the material.[12] In times of inflation, delay in the progress of a job often results in an increase in the cost of material. The effect of inflation is particularly acute in the construction industry, where the cost of labor and materials escalate rapidly,[13] and is particularly pronounced when the material is based on a petroleum product.[14] Claims for escalated material costs are not restricted to inflationary economic periods, however. This fact is aptly illustrated by *Levering & Garrigues Co. v. United States.*[15]

In *Levering,* the contractor entered into a contract with the Navy in 1919 to construct an addition to an existing power house located in Annapolis, Maryland.[16] The contractor could not obtain the exact brick that was used in the original building and sought to substitute a similar brick with the Navy's approval. The Navy took over four months to approve the substitution, during which time the price of the brick escalated.[17]

In determining that the contractor could recover the increased cost of the brick, the United States Court of Claims stated:

> The plaintiff during this period of delay repeatedly called the defendant's attention to the fact that the market price of bricks was advancing. The delay

---

[9] Mead Corp. v. McNally-Pittsburg Mfg. Corp., 654 F.2d 1197 (6th Cir. 1981); Abbett Elec. Corp. v. United States, 162 F. Supp. 772 (Ct. Cl. 1958); Levering & Garrigues Co. v. United States, 73 Ct. Cl. 566 (1932); Foley Eng'g & Constr., Inc., ASBCA No. 32,958, 87-2 BCA (CCH) ¶ 19,747 (1987); C. Walker Constr. Co., VABCA No. 1527, 82-2 BCA (CCH) ¶ 15,799 (1982).

[10] C.F.I. Constr. Co., DOT CAB Nos. 1782, 1801, 87-1 BCA (CCH) ¶ 19,547 (1987); Berkeley Constr. Co., VABCA No. 1962, 88-1 BCA (CCH) ¶ 20,259 (1987); Thurmont Constr. Co., ASBCA No. 13417, 69-1 BCA (CCH) ¶ 7602 (1969).

[11] ADCO Constr., Inc., PSBCA Nos. 2355, 2455, 2465, 2480, 90-3 BCA (CCH) ¶ 22,944 (1990); J. Tieder & J. Hoffar, Proving Construction Contract Damages 180 (1990).

[12] *See* Mead Corp. v. McNally-Pittsburg Mfg. Corp., 654 F.2d 1197 (6th Cir. 1981); Abbett Elec. Corp. v. United States, 162 F. Supp. 772 (Ct. Cl. 1958); Levering & Garrigues Co. v. United States, 73 Cl. Ct. 566 (1932).

[13] Sherman R. Smoot Co. v. United States, 516 F. Supp. 260 (D.D.C. 1981).

[14] Heron, *Impact of Material and Fuel Shortages on Contracting,* 11 Forum 1005 (1976).

[15] 73 Ct. Cl. 566 (1932).

[16] *Id.* at 572.

[17] *Id.* at 576.

of four months in making approval of the brick submitted by plaintiff was unreasonable and arbitrary and plaintiff is entitled to recover the amount of increase which it was required to pay.[18]

The thrust of *Levering* remains unchanged in that contractors may recover the escalated cost of materials due to owner-caused delay.[19]

Although most claims for escalated material costs resulting from owner-caused delay seek the increased cost of the material, contractors should not limit their claims to the increase in the cost of the material. As discussed in §§ **4.7** through **4.11**, other costs associated with the cost of additional or escalated material may also be recoverable.

§ 4.5   —Costs Attributable to Defective Specifications

Defective specifications obviously require correction, and compliance with corrected specifications may result in the contractor substituting another material at no additional cost to the owner.[20] Often, however, it is impossible for contractors to substitute materials at no additional cost. Contractors may be able to recover the increased cost of material substitutions in the following situations.

In the absence of a contractual provision to the contrary, an owner impliedly warrants the sufficiency of its specifications.[21] Accordingly, contractors may recover the increased cost of performing in accordance with an owner's defective plans and specifications. A common example involves specifications that require the use of inadequate structural components. The substituted component will most likely be larger, stronger, and more costly than the deficient component called for by the specifications. The increased cost of the substituted component is a recoverable material cost in construction claims.[22]

Another type of defective specification claim that causes particular difficulties arises when the specifications require an item which is not available. Increased material costs attributable to the unavailability of an item are also recoverable. In considering such a situation, the Armed Services Board of Contract Appeals in *Thurmont Construction Co.*[23] stated:

---

[18] *Id.*

[19] *See* C. Walker Constr. Co., VABCA No. 1527, 82-2 BCA (CCH) ¶ 15,799 (1982).

[20] Berkeley Constr. Co., VABCA No. 1962, 88-1 BCA (CCH) ¶ 20,259 (1987).

[21] United States v. Spearin, 248 U.S. 132 (1918); Berkeley Constr. Co., VABCA No. 1962, 88-1 BCA (CCH) ¶ 20,259 (1988).

[22] *See, e.g.,* United States v. Spearin, 248 U.S. 132 (1918); Berkeley Constr. Co., VABCA No. 1962, 88-1 BCA (CCH) ¶ 20,259 (1988).

[23] ASBCA No. 13,417, 69-1 BCA (CCH) ¶ 7602 (1969).

The evidence shows that no door meeting all contract requirements was available on the market. No such door was even manufactured at the time.

* * *

However, the evidence indicates that, at that time, no such product was being or had ever been manufactured, much less as a "standard product." Accordingly the specifications were defective in specifying an unattainable requirement. When the Government changed the specifications to provide for an attainable requirement it was required to make an equitable adjustment in the contract price if the change caused an increase in the contractor's cost of performance.[24]

Contractors should be aware that along with the additional costs of the substituted item, contractors may also recover for delay associated with complying with the defective specifications. Once again, contractors should not limit claims solely to the increased cost of the material.[25]

§ 4.6 —Costs Attributable to Owner-directed Changes

Practically all construction contracts permit an owner to direct changes to the work while the work is in progress.[26] Owner-directed changes may require the addition or deletion of a section to the structure.

An owner-directed change may require the contractor to substitute more costly materials or require the contractor to provide additional materials.[27] Moreover, a change order may render previously purchased material unsuitable or unusable. Such material costs are recoverable elements of construction claims.

§ 4.7 Other Costs Associated with Material Claims

Contractors should be aware of costs other than the direct cost of the additional or escalated material. Although these expenses may be tangentially related to the actual cost of the material, such costs are recoverable and should be included in all construction claims.

---

[24] *Id.* at p. 35,308.

[25] See §§ **4.7–4.11 & 4.17.**

[26] *See* AIA Doc. A201 § 7.2 (1987); Federation Internationale des Ingenieurs–Conseils, Conditions of Contract for Electrical and Mechanical Works § 31.1.

[27] *See generally* O&M Constr., Inc. v. State, 576 So. 2d 1030 (La. Ct. App. 1991).

§ 4.8 —Additional Material Handling and Storage Costs

Contractors may recover costs associated with additional handling and processing of material that results from acts of the owner. Such costs were allowed by the United States Claims Court in *Luria Bros. & Co. v. United States.*[28] In *Luria Bros.,* the court stated:

> Many materials which had been ordered and delivered to the job prior to December 1, 1953, could not be used in the normal course of construction because of the interruptions to job progress previously described. As a result it was necessary for plaintiff to incur additional cost in sheltering and storing such materials. It was maintained in storage for almost one year and during that time a certain amount of deterioration occurred which required reinforcing repair prior to erection for the pouring of the arch. The total cost to plaintiff for the protection and handling of this material amounted to $5,935.81.[29]

The additional expenses allowed in *Luria Bros.* represented the additional labor costs involved in handling and refinishing the materials.

Contractors may also be able to recover material storage costs that would not have been incurred but for acts of the owner.[30] In addition to *Luria Bros.,* an illustrative example is found in *American Bridge Co. v. State.*[31] In *American Bridge,* the prime contractor entered into a contract with the State of New York for work to be done on the Mid-Hudson Bridge in Poughkeepsie, New York. A prior contractor, however, delayed the prime contractor's progress. Although the state knew that the prime contractor could not start on the date anticipated, the state directed the contractor to fabricate the steel necessary for construction.

The prime contractor incurred unanticipated expenses in storing the fabricated steel.[32] Although the state conceded that its directive to fabricate the steel resulted in damage to the contractor, the state asserted that any such damages were barred by a no damages for delay clause.[33] The court determined, however, that the state was liable for the cost of storing the material.[34]

---

[28] 177 Ct. Cl. 676 (1966).

[29] *Id.* at 741–42.

[30] American Bridge Co. v. State, 245 A.D. 535, 283 N.Y.S. 577 (1935).

[31] *Id.*

[32] 283 N.Y.S. at 579.

[33] *Id.* at 581.

[34] *Id.*

Contractors should consider whether they have incurred storage costs and material handling costs that they would not have incurred but for acts of the owner. On large projects, storage and handling costs may be excessive, and such costs should not be overlooked in calculating damage claims.[35]

§ 4.9 —Additional Transportation Costs

A contractor may also be entitled to the cost of transporting additional or substituted material to a job site.[36] In most cases, however, contractors will be able to recover only the cost for the usual method of moving that type of material. Therefore, extraordinary transportation expenses are not recoverable unless required by the owner.

§ 4.10 —Additional Overrun Costs

Contractors should not limit claims to the exact amount of the additional or substituted materials incorporated into the project. Invariably, material purchases are for a quantity greater than actually needed in order to account for spoilage and minor overruns. The Federal Acquisition Regulation (FAR) permits recovery of additional material costs for items not actually used on the project. Specifically, it states: In computing material costs, consideration will be given to reasonable overruns, spoilage or defective work (unless otherwise provided in any contract provision of the contract relating to inspecting and correcting of defective work).[37]

§ 4.11 —Taxes

A final cost related to material expenses is sales or use tax paid by contractors for the material used on a project. In private projects, contractors may recover excess sales and use taxes incurred as a part of an owner's delay or change. Many public projects, however, are exempt from sales tax, and contractors may not recover this extra expense.[38] In *John McShain,*

---

[35] *Id.; see also* Hartford Accident & Indem. v. District of Columbia, 441 A.2d 969 (D.C. 1982); Cushman et al., Delays and Disruptions in Construction Litigation (1981).

[36] *See generally* C.F.I. Constr. Co., DOT CAB Nos. 1782, 1801, 87-1 BCA (CCH) ¶ 19,547 (1987); J. Tieder & J. Hoffar, Proving Construction Contract Damages 183 (1990).

[37] FAR 31.205.26(a) (19___).

[38] John McShain, Inc. v. District of Columbia, 205 F.2d 882, 884–85 (D.C. Cir. 1953).

Inc. v. District of Columbia, the United States Court of Appeals for the District of Columbia denied a contractor's claim for sales tax based on § 1101(d) of the Internal Revenue Code. Specifically, the court stated:

> In respect of contracts with the Federal Government and the District, the Tax Court gave petitioner the benefit of this regulation to certain items (e.g., cinders and rubble) which it held to be physically incorporated in, and part of, the real property. Other items which were consumed in the course of construction, such as lumber for making forms, paper towels and cups, office supplies, oil, and gasoline, were held by the Tax Court to be outside the scope of Section 1101(d). The Tax Court said that the regulation "means that the material . . . must be physically present or incorporated in the structure. It is the antithesis of consumption." We agree with this statement, and find no indication that the Tax Court incorrectly applied it. (citations omitted)[39]

Although the court denied the contractor's claim for taxes paid for the material, the court permitted the contractor to recover the taxes paid for supplies used on the project.[40]

§ 4.12   Calculating Additional Material Quantities

Calculating additional material quantities is a fairly simple process because material quantities are easily identifiable. Maintaining accurate records facilitates establishing the quantity of additional material used on a project.

In the absence of records or other supporting data, contractors may establish and calculate the quantity of additional material by reference to the project's drawings. The difference between the quantity of material required by the original drawings and the quantities actually used on the project is the amount of additional material required on the project.

If no drawings are available, the quantity of additional material may be determined by comparing the contractor's original estimate for material with the actual quantity of material used. The quantity of material used, however, must be verified by purchase orders, delivery tickets, or other procurement documents. As discussed in § **4.16**, this method of calculating additional material quantities is subject to certain limitations. Also, any calculation of additional material quantities should consider overrun, spoilage, and defective items.

---

[39] *Id.* at 884.

[40] The distinction between supplies and materials is discussed in § **4.2**.

§ 4.13   Calculating Additional Costs

Contractors must consider whether they are seeking the cost of additional material, the cost of material escalation, or both. Although calculating the cost of additional material is relatively simple, calculating the cost of material escalation can be problematic.[41]

§ 4.14   —Calculating and Proving the Cost of Additional Material

To calculate the cost of additional material, the quantity of additional material is multiplied by the cost or unit price of the material.[42] For example, if a contractor is required to purchase ten additional I beams at $1000 apiece, the calculation would be as follows:

$$10 \text{ I beams} \times \$1000 \text{ per beam} = \$10,000$$

An invoice from the supplier and proof that it was paid is usually sufficient to establish the cost of the additional material.[43]

In many instances, however, it is not possible to segregate the cost of additional materials from basic contract materials. This is especially true of fungible items such as concrete or backfill. In these situations, a supplier's invoice establishing the unit price for the material at the time the added work was performed will usually be sufficient to establish the increased costs. In the absence of invoices, it may be necessary to have the supplier testify or provide a price list for the applicable time period in order to establish the contractor's additional material costs.

§ 4.15   —Calculating and Proving the Cost of Material Escalation

Material escalation costs may be calculated through the use of direct and indirect methods.[44] The direct method compares the estimated cost of the material and the actual, escalated cost of the material as purchased.[45]

---

[41] *See* George Hyman Constr. Co., ENGBCA No. 4541, 85-1 BCA (CCH) ¶ 17,847 (1985).

[42] *See* Tieder, Hoffar & Cox, *Calculating and Proving Construction Damages,* 82-3 Construction Briefings (1982).

[43] *Id. See, e.g.,* ADCO Constr. Co., PSBCA Nos. 2353, 2453, 2480, 90-3 BCA (CCH) ¶ 22,944 (1990).

[44] George Hyman Constr. Co., ENGBCA No. 4541, 85-1 BCA (CCH) ¶ 17,847 (1985).

[45] *See* Levering & Garrigues Co. v. United States, 73 Ct. Cl. 566 (1932).

The difference between the cost of the material as originally estimated and the actual cost of the material is the amount of recoverable material escalation. Once again, invoices are the best proof of the escalated cost of material.

The indirect method is used when the contractor does not have invoices or other supporting data to establish the cost of the material.[46] A good example of an indirect method of calculation is found in *George Hyman Construction Co.*[47] In this case, instead of offering the material costs estimated at the time of bidding, the contractor used indices published by the *Engineering News Record* to establish the material costs "and worked backwards to determine a 'deflated' cost of material or purported 'what the material would have cost had the work been performed at the time originally planned.'"[48] Under the indirect method, the escalated material cost is the difference between the deflated cost and the actual cost of materials.[49] Trade journals other than the *Engineering News Record* may be used to determine escalated material costs.[50]

Certain mistakes are common in calculating and proving escalated material costs, regardless of which method is used. Often, contractors assume that delay automatically results in the escalation of material costs for which the owner is liable.[51] Contractors may only recover material escalation costs that result from owner-caused delay. In *Thorn Construction Co.*,[52] the contractor's claim for material escalation during a period of delay was denied because the owner was not responsible for the delay.[53]

Also, contractors often duplicate costs and seek to recover the total cost of the material, that is, both the original cost of the material and the escalated cost of the material. Claims for material escalation should seek only the difference between the original estimated cost and the actual cost because the original cost was factored in the bid price. Finally, contractors often fail to consider the additional costs associated with material escalation as discussed in §§ 4.7–4.11.

---

[46] George Hyman Const. Co., ENGBCA No. 4541, 85-1 BCA (CCH) ¶ 17,847 (1985).

[47] *Id.*

[48] *Id.* at p. 89,342.

[49] *Id.*

[50] In *George Hyman Constr. Co.*, the Corps of Engineers Board of Contract Appeals permitted a subcontractor to use escalation figures from Iron Age Magazine. *Id.* at p. 89,351.

[51] See Thorn Constr. Co., IBCA No. 1254-3-79, 83-1 BCA (CCH) ¶ 16,230 (1983); C. Walker Constr. Co., VABCA No. 1327, 82-2 BCA (CCH) ¶ 15,799 (1982).

[52] 83-1 BCA (CCH) ¶ 16,230 (1983).

[53] *Id.* at p. 80,638.

§ 4.16   Mitigating Factors in Recovering Additional Costs

Contractors should be aware of their responsibilities and obligations in bidding on and performing work on a project. In certain cases, the contractor may be responsible for the need for additional material or the escalated cost of material. Conversely, although the contractor may not be at fault for the additional or escalated material, recovery of such costs may be barred by provisions of the contract.

Contractors who knowingly bid on specifications which are defective may not recover the cost of additional, substituted, or escalated materials.[54] Thus, a contractor's claim for additional material costs may be denied if an owner can establish that a contractor knew or should have known of a deficiency in the specifications. This is especially true in federal government contracts.[55]

Also, contractors must determine the availability of materials at the time of bid.[56] In the absence of impossibility, contractors will not be able to recover the escalated cost of material or the cost of additional material resulting from the inability to obtain material specified in the contract. This fact is clearly illustrated in *C.E. Lowther & Son.*[57] In this case, the contract called for the application of a coal tar enamel coating.[58] The contractor submitted, and the government approved, a substitute coating material to be used on one section of the project.[59] Thereafter, the government required the contractor to use the coating as called for by the contract. The contractor, however, was unable to locate the material specified by the contract.[60] In considering the contractor's claim for such costs, the Armed Services Board of Contract Appeals stated: "The availability of the specified coal tar enamel should have been determined by the appellant at the time it bid. It has not shown that the government forced it to use a more costly product."[61]

Moreover, if material costs have escalated because the contractor was remiss in writing purchase orders, the contractor will not be able to recover the escalated amounts. Similarly, contractors will not be able to recover for

---

[54] *See generally* Berkley Constr. Co., VABCA No. 1962, 88-1 BCA (CCH) ¶ 20,259 (1987).

[55] Delphi Indus., Inc., AGBCA No. 76-160-4, 84-1 BCA (CCH) ¶ 17,053 (1983).

[56] Granite Constr. Co., ENGBCA No. 4172, 89-2 BCA (CCH) ¶ 21,683 (1989); C.E. Lowther & Son, ASBCA No. 26760, 85-2 BCA (CCH) ¶ 18,144 (1985).

[57] C.E. Lowther & Son, ASBCA No. 26760, 85-2 BCA (CCH) ¶ 18,149 (1985).

[58] *Id.* at p. 91,107.

[59] *Id.*

[60] *Id.*

[61] *Id.*

additional or escalated material costs due to expiration of quotations from suppliers.

§ 4.17   Credit for Deleted Materials

In many cases, certain quantities of material may be deleted from the original contract requirements, or specified materials may be replaced by others. In both situations, it may be necessary for the contractor to credit the owner for the deleted items. These deductive changes cause frequent disagreements on construction projects.

The measure of downward adjustment in contract price usually equals the cost the contractor would have incurred had the work not been deleted.[62] Naturally, when certain work is deleted from the contract, actual costs are not in issue. Instead, because the deleted work has not been performed, the parties will be dealing with estimates of the amount that would have been incurred had the contractor not deleted or changed certain work.

The owner bears the burden of proving a decrease in the contractor's cost due to a deductive change.[63] This principle is clearly stated in *Nager Electric Co. v. United States.*[64] In *Nager Electric,* the United States Court of Claims stated:

> Another principle which is integrally involved in this case is that the Government (the owner) has the burden of proving how much of a downward equitable adjustment in price should be made on account of the deletion of the original values. Just as the contractor has that task when an upward adjustment is sought under the Changes Clause, so the defendant (the owner) has the laboring oar, and bears the risk of failure of proof, when a decrease is at issue.[65]

§ 4.18   Price Escalation or Revision Clauses

Public and international construction contracts may contain a material escalation provision. For example, in New York public contracts, a contractor may receive a price adjustment when the increased cost of materials exceeds 15 percent of the contract price.[66] However, price escalation or price

---

[62] G&M Elec. Contractors Co., ASBCA No. 4771, 78-2 BCA (CCH) ¶ 13,452 (1978).

[63] Nager Elec. Co. v. United States, 442 F.2d 936 (Ct. Cl. 1971).

[64] *Id.*

[65] *Id.* at 946.

[66] *See* John Grace & Co., Inc. v. State Univ. Constr. Fund, 44 N.Y.2d 84, 375 N.E.2d 377, 404 N.Y.S.2d 316 (1978). For further discussion on increased contract cost due to the escalated price of petroleum products, see Heron, *Impact of Material and Fuel Shortages on Contracting,* 11 Forum 1005 (1976).

revision clauses are not common practice in construction contracts in the United States.

It is standard practice in international construction contracts, however, for the contract to include a price revision clause.[67] Price revision clauses protect contractors from increases in material costs which cannot be predicted at the time of bidding.[68] Contractors should be aware of the importance of price revision clauses in international construction contracts, especially if the contract will be performed in a country with historically high inflation.[69]

---

[67] *See* Norris, *Price Adjustment: Contract Currencies and Rates of Exchange,* 6 Int'l Construction L. Rev. 317 (1989); Gauch, *Price Increase or Contract Termination in the Event of Extraordinary Circumstances,* 4 Int'l Construction L. Rev. 264 (1987).

[68] *See* Blount Bros. Corp. v. Government of Islamic Republic of Iran, Iran Hous. Co., Case No. 52 (215-52-1), XII Y.B. Int'l Comm. Arb. 299 (Iran-U.S. Cl. Trib. 1985).

[69] *See* French Contractor v. Minister of Irrigation of African Country X; Case No. 65 (221-65-1) XII Y.B. Int'l Comm. Arb. 90 (1986).

CHAPTER 5

BOND AND INSURANCE COSTS

§ 5.1 Introduction

The expense for bonds and insurance can be considerable on construction projects. Contractors may incur additional bond and insurance costs due to the actions or inactions of the owner. Owner-directed changes often result in an increase in the amount of the contract, which requires the contractor to pay increased bond premiums. Owner-caused delay may also require the contractor to pay increased bond premiums. Owner-directed changes or owner-caused delay may also cause the contractor to incur additional insurance costs. Additional bond and insurance costs are recoverable elements of construction claims.[1]

---

[1] Luria Bros. v. United States, 369 F.2d 701 (Ct. Cl. 1966); Fidelity Constr. Co., DOT CAB No. 1113, 81-2 BCA (CCH) ¶ 15,345 (1981); Owen L. Schwam Constr. Co., ASBCA No. 22,407, 79-2 BCA (CCH) ¶ 13,919 (1979).

§ 5.2   Construction Contract Bonds

Virtually all public and many private contracts require that a contractor provide bonds to the owner guaranteeing performance of the contract and payment to subcontractors. In addition, many contractors require their subcontractors to provide comparable bonds guaranteeing performance of the subcontract and payment of second-tier subcontractors.[2] Essentially, bonds shift and spread the risks of nonperformance and nonpayment faced by owners, contractors, and suppliers.[3]

Three types of bonds are used in the construction industry: bid bonds, payment bonds, and performance bonds. *Bid bonds* protect the owner when the lowest bidder on a contract refuses or fails to execute the contract in accordance with its bid.[4] Bid bonds are not of concern in calculating damages in construction claims.

Payment bonds protect owners when contractors default on payments to subcontractors and suppliers. Payment bonds protect owners from liability for subcontractor and supplier claims when the owner has previously paid the prime contractor. In cases of contractor default, the surety becomes liable for payment and the surety must seek recourse against the prime contractor if it wishes to recover.

Performance bonds protect the owner against nonperformance of the prime contractor. Increasingly, prime contractors are requiring subcontractors to post performance bonds as protection against subcontractor nonperformance. In the event of default by the prime contractor, sureties may choose to complete the project, hire a completion contractor, or finance the defaulting contractor to complete the project.

§ 5.3   Bonds on Public Projects

The Miller Act requires contractors to post performance and payment bonds on all federal construction contracts.[5] In accordance with the Miller Act, the Federal Acquisition Regulation (FAR) provides:

(a) The Miller Act (40 U.S.C. 270A-270(F)) requires performance and payment bonds for any construction contract exceeding $25,000.00 except that

---

[2] *See* FAR 28.102; Mayor of Baltimore v. Fidelity & Deposit Co., 282 Md. 431, 386 A.2d 749 (1978); Cal. Bus. & Prof. Code §§ 7071.5-7071.12 (West).

[3] 3 Stein, Construction Law § 17.01 (1991).

[4] *Id.*

[5] *See* 40 U.S.C. § 270a-270(f) (1986); FAR 28.102-1.

this requirement may be waived (1) by the contracting officer for as much of the work as is to be performed in a foreign country upon finding that it is impracticable for the contractor to furnish such bond, or (2) as otherwise authorized by the Miller Act or other law.[6]

On federal contracts, contractors must post performance bonds equaling 100 percent of the original contract price.[7] Contractors may be able to post performance bonds in an amount less than the contract price if the contracting officer determines that the lesser sum would adequately protect the government.[8] On federal contracts, contractors must also post payment bonds in amounts between 40 and 50 percent of the contract price, depending on the amount of the contract.[9]

Most states have enacted "Little Miller Acts."[10] Although the federal Miller Act may be instructive in determining the operation of Little Miller Acts, differences between the federal act and the various state acts exist. In Virginia, for example, contractors are required to furnish performance and payment bonds in the amount of any contract exceeding $100,000.[11] Also, the surety chosen by the contractor must be authorized to do business in Virginia.[12] Contractors should be aware of the particular provisions of the applicable state's Little Miller Act.

§ 5.4 Bonds on Private Projects

On private projects the contractor is increasingly required to provide the owner with performance and payment bonds. In most cases, however, no bonding is required on private projects, and statutorily enacted mechanics' liens protect contractors, material suppliers, and subcontractors from the risks of nonpayment and nonperformance. On many private projects, therefore, bonding costs are not considerations in the calculation of damages.

---

[6] *See* FAR 28.102-1.

[7] *Id.* 28.102-2.

[8] *Id.*

[9] FAR 28.102-2(2)(b) provides that on contracts less than $1 million, contractors must post payment bonds in the amount of 50% of the contract price. On contracts more than $1 million but less than $5 million, contractors must post bonds in the amount of 40% of the contract price. On contracts more than $5 million, contractors must post payment bonds in the amount of 50% of the contract price.

[10] *See, e.g.,* Conn. Gen. Stat. Ann. § 49-41 (West); Mass. Ann. Laws. ch. 149, § 29 (Law. Co-op.); Va. Code Ann. § 11-58 (Michie).

[11] Va. Code Ann. § 11-58(1) & (2) (Michie).

[12] *Id.*

§ 5.5 Reasons for Increased Bond Costs

Contractors incur additional bond costs primarily in two situations: owner-directed changes[13] and owner-caused delay.[14] The costs of additional bond premiums in either situation are recoverable and should be included in all claims.

As discussed more fully in **Chapter 4**, owner-directed changes more often than not result in increased costs to the contractor and an increase in the value of the contract. Bond premiums are computed on a percentage of the contract value, and any increase in the value of the contract accordingly increases the amount of the bond premium.[15] Owner-caused delay may also require contractors to obtain additional bonding and incur increased bonding costs. Courts and boards of contract appeals recognize that increased bonding costs due to delay are recoverable.[16]

§ 5.6 Calculating Costs of Increased Bond Premiums

The cost of additional bond premiums may be calculated by two basic methods. Additional bond premiums may be calculated indirectly based on a percentage of the equitable adjustment,[17] or they may be calculated directly by multiplying the bond rate by the amount of additional contract value.[18]

---

[13] Mann Constr. Co., EBCA No. 361-6-86, 89-3 BCA (CCH) ¶ 22,176 (1988); Algernon Blair, Inc., VACAB No. 952, 70-2 BCA (CCH) ¶ 8367 (1970).

[14] J.D. Hedin Constr. Co. v. United States, 456 F.2d 1315 (Ct. Cl. 1972); *see* Loughman Cabinet Co. v. C. Iber & Sons, Inc., 361 N.E.2d 379 (Ill. 1977)(contract contained a no damages for delay clause with an exception which allowed recovery for extra bond premiums in cases of jury-caused delay).

[15] *See* Tieder, Hoffar & Cox, *Calculating and Proving Construction Damages,* 83-3 Construction Briefings (1982).

[16] Fidelity Constr. Co., DOT CAB No. 1113, 81-2 BCA (CCH) ¶ 15,345 (1981); J.D. Hedin Constr. Co. v. United States, 456 F.2d 1315 (Ct. Cl. 1972).

[17] Fidelity Constr. Co., DOT CAB No. 1113, 81-2 BCA (CCH) ¶ 15,345 (1981).

[18] Owen L. Schwam Constr. Co., ASBCA No. 22,407, 79-2 BCA (CCH) ¶ 13,919 (1979).

§ 5.7   —Calculating Bond Premiums as a Percentage of the Equitable Adjustment

The most common method of calculating and recovering increased bond premiums is to mark up the equitable adjustment by a certain percentage.[19] In *Fidelity Construction Co.,*[20] the Department of Transportation Contract Appeals Board marked up the contractor's equitable adjustment by 1.2 percent as compensation for increased bond premiums.[21] The amount of adjustment to the equitable adjustment for increased bond costs may, however, depend on the provisions of the contract and the available proof. The average markup for increased bonding costs ranges between 0.5 percent and 1.2 percent of the equitable adjustment.[22]

§ 5.8   —Calculating Bond Premiums Based on Contract Value

Because bond premiums are based on the value of the work being performed, they are usually calculated per increment of contract value. Bond premiums normally decrease as the contract amount increases. The decrease is based on only the incremental increase. Additionally, bond premiums are normally quoted for jobs of 24 months or less in duration. Frequently, there is an adder to the bond premium for each month in excess of 24 months. An example of a bond rate table follows:

THE BOND PREMIUM IS CALCULATED AS FOLLOWS:

$14.40/Thousand Dollars for first	$ 500,000
$ 8.70/Thousand Dollars for next	$2,000,000
$ 6.90/Thousand Dollars for next	$2,500,000
$ 6.30/Thousand Dollars for next	$2,500,000
$ 5.76/Thousand Dollars over	$7,500,000

Premium increased by 1% for every month over 24 months

---

[19] Excavation Constr., Inc., ENGBCA No. 3858, 82-1 BCA (CCH) ¶ 15,770 (1982); Olsberg Excavating Corp., DOT CAB No. 1288, 84-1 BCA (CCH) ¶ 16,931 (1983); Fidelity Constr. Co., DOT CAB No. 1113, 81-2 BCA (CCH) ¶ 15,345 (1981); A. Campo, Inc., ASBCA No. 14,830, 72-1 BCA (CCH) ¶ 9377 (1972).

[20] DOT CAB No. 1113, 81-2 BCA (CCH) ¶ 15,345 (1981).

[21] *Id.* at p. 76,017.

[22] See Excavation Constr., Inc., ENGBCA No. 3858, 82-1 BCA (CCH) ¶ 15,770 (1982) (equitable adjustment marked up by 0.47% to accommodate increased bond costs); Fidelity Constr. Co., DOT CAB No. 1113, 81-2 BCA (CCH) ¶ 15,345 (1981)(equitable adjustment marked up by 1.2% to accommodate the increased bond costs).

When calculating increased bond costs, it is important not only to calculate the additional bond premium on the contract value increase but also to calculate the additional bond premium if the project overall is extended. The following calculation of additional bond cost utilizes both an increase in contract amount and period for performance in excess of 24 months.

CONTRACT AMOUNT	$5,500,000
INCREASE	$1,000,000
ORIGINAL DURATION	20 Months
DURATIONS AS EXTENDED	32 Months

ADDITIONAL PREMIUM ON ADDITIONAL CONTRACT
    AMOUNT IS:

    $1,000,000 × 0.0063 = $ 6,300

THE ADDITIONAL PREMIUM FOR CONTRACT DURATION IN EXCESS OF 24 MONTHS IS 1% OF THE TOTAL PREMIUM PER MONTH FOR THE 8-MONTH EXTENSION IN DURATION. THE ADDITIONAL COST IS:

    32 Months − 24 Months = 8 Months

    Bond premium on total contract amount of $6,500,000 is calculated as follows:

    0.0144 × $ 500,000 = $ 7,200
    0.0087 × $2,000,000 = $17,400
    0.0069 × $2,500,000 = $17,250
    0.0063 × $1,500,000 = $ 9,450
                          $51,300

ADDITIONAL PREMIUM FROM ADDITIONAL TIME IS:

    8 Months × 1%/Month × $51,300 = $ 4,104

    TOTAL ADDITIONAL PREMIUM: $10,404

The direct method of calculating additional bond premium costs multiplies the base cost of the bond by the amount of increased contract value. The Armed Services Board of Contract Appeals has permitted excess bond costs to be calculated by use of the direct method.[23]

In *Owen L. Schwam Construction Co.,* the Board permitted the contractor to recover the additional bond premium incurred according to the increase in contract value.[24] Specifically, the Board stated: "The terms of the General Contractor's bond provides for a premium of $6.50 per $1000 of

---

[23] Owen L. Schwam Constr. Co., ASBCA No. 22,407, 79-2 BCA (CCH) ¶ 13,919 (1979).

[24] *Id.* at p. 68,332.

work performed in addition to that originally required by the contract."[25]
The board, in determining that the contract had been increased by
$56,398, calculated the contractor's increased bond costs as follows:

$56,398.00 (increased cost of contract)
    $6.50 (bond cost per $1000 of contract value)
$6.50 × 56.3 = $365.95 (total of recovery for insurance bond costs)

The direct method is simply an alternative to the percentage markup
method and does not usually result in a greater figure than arrived at
through the use of the percentage markup method.

§ 5.9   —Secondary Considerations in Calculating Bond Costs

Owner-directed changes or owner-caused delay may also increase the bonding costs incurred by subcontractors on a project. In most cases, subcontractors will pass on these increased costs to the prime contractor. Prime
contractors may recover the additional bonding costs incurred by subcontractors.[26] This cost, although recoverable, is often overlooked by contractors in the calculation of construction claims. On large projects such costs
can be considerable.

Contractors should also be aware that increased bonding costs are determined by the total adjustment or the total increase in contract price without regard to the penal sum of the bond.[27] In *Fidelity Construction Co.,*[28]
the Department of Transportation Contract Appeals Board stated: "The
total premium charged by a corporate surety is based upon the final price
of a construction contract, with a postcompletion adjustment of premiums
to reflect the final contract price, and not upon the penal sum of the
bond."[29] Thus, additional bond costs are computed based on the final contract price.[30]

Contractors may be liable for an owner's increased bonding costs if the
contractor is found to have breached the contract.[31] In *McDevitt & Street v.*

---

[25] *Id.*

[26] Algernon Blair, Inc., VACAB No. 952, 70-2 BCA (CCH) ¶ 8367 (1970).

[27] Olsberg Excavating Corp., DOT CAB No. 1288, 84-1 BCA (CCH) ¶ 16,931 (1983).

[28] DOT CAB No. 1113, 81-2 BCA (CCH) ¶ 15,345 (1981).

[29] *Id.* at p. 76,017.

[30] *Id.;* Olsberg Excavating Corp., DOT CAB No. 1288, 84-1 BCA (CCH) ¶ 16,931 (1983).

[31] McDevitt & Street Co. v. Marriott Corp., 713 F. Supp. 906 (E.D. Va. 1989).

Marriott Corp.,[32] the United States District Court for the Eastern District of Virginia determined that the owner could recover increased bond and insurance costs resulting from the contractor's breach of the contract.[33] The court allowed the owner to recover the increased costs of bonding as administrative costs which were foreseeable damages in the event of a breach.[34]

§ 5.10   Loss of Bonding Capacity

If an owner's acts result in extended contract performance, contractors may recover for loss of bonding capacity. Claims for loss of bonding capacity are based on the theory that extended performance at significant losses will result in an inability to obtain future bonding and the inability to obtain future work.[35] These claims often fail because of the highly speculative nature of future profits and the difficulty in proving future profits. To successfully recover for loss of bonding capacity, the contractor must establish that (1) projects were available during the extended period of performance, (2) the extended project's negative cash flow prevented the contractor from obtaining future bonds, and (3) it is reasonably certain that the contractor would have profited on the anticipated work.[36] To recover, contractors must prove their historical rate of gross over a period of years and establish a causal connection between the extended performance period and the inability to obtain bonding.

§ 5.11   Increased Insurance Costs

Insurance is a significant and growing cost element of construction contracts. On some contracts, insurance costs may be 1 percent of the total price of the contract. An owner's action or inaction may cause the contractor to incur increased insurance costs that are recoverable elements of construction claims.[37]

General liability and builder's risk insurance represent the majority of insurance costs of construction contracts. General liability insurance is intended to replace numerous specific policies and provide contractors with umbrella coverage against liability to third parties. General liability

---

[32] *Id.*

[33] *Id.* at 935.

[34] *Id.*

[35] Tieder, Hoffar & Cox, *Calculating and Proving Construction Damages,* 82-3 Construction Briefings (1982).

[36] *See* Raymond Int'l, Inc. v. Baltimore Constr., 412 A.2d 1246 (Md. 1980).

[37] Luria Bros. & Co. v. United States, 369 F.2d 701 (Ct. Cl. 1966).

insurance is intended to cover liabilities arising out of the construction process that are not directly related to the work itself.

Conversely, builder's risk insurance protects against loss or damage to the structure during construction.[38] Builder's risk insurance is either carried by the owner or the general contractor. In projects involving multiple prime contractors, builder's risk insurance may be carried by all prime contractors on the project as it relates to their own work. Therefore, the recovery of the excess cost of this type of insurance depends on the nature and extent of the insurance coverage carried by the contractor.

§ 5.12   —Reasons for Increased Insurance Costs

There are two reasons for increased insurance costs: owner-directed changes and owner-caused delay. In some cases, insurance premiums are based on the dollar amount of the contract. Owner-directed change orders increasing the amount of the contract will necessarily result in increased insurance premiums. Also, owner-caused delay may require that existing insurance policies be renewed for the extended period of performance. The excess cost of insurance in both cases is recoverable.[39]

§ 5.13   —Calculating Increased Insurance Costs

When owner-directed changes increase the amount of the premium, the contractor is entitled to recover the difference between the original premium price and the increased premium price. No further calculation is required to establish the increased cost of the insurance premiums.

When the contractor incurs increased insurance costs due to delay, the entire cost of the extended or new policy is often recoverable.[40] In *Luria Brothers & Co. v. United States,*[41] the United States Court of Claims permitted the contractor to recover the entire amount of the increased insurance premium. Specifically, the court stated: "[t]he trial commissioner has determined that the plaintiff suffered delay damages and additional expenditures directly attributable to the defendant's breaches . . . [including] wage and material price increases plus 100 percent of an insurance premium plaintiff was required to pay."[42]

---

[38] For a further discussion of builder's risk insurance, see Annotation, *Coverage under Builders Risk Insurance Policy,* 97 A.L.R.3d 1270 (1980).

[39] Contractors should consider whether actions or inactions of the owner have resulted in increased insurance premiums.

[40] Luria Bros. & Co. v. United States, 369 F.2d 701 (Ct. Cl. 1966).

[41] *Id.* at 709.

[42] *Id.*

In federal government contracts, contractors may also be able to recover self-insurance costs in addition to the costs of purchased insurance.[43] Self-insurance costs must be approved and required by the FAR to be recoverable.[44]

---

[43] *See* FAR 31.205(19).

[44] *See id.* 28.308(9).

CHAPTER 6

HOME OFFICE OVERHEAD

§ 6.1   Introduction

Contractors are entitled to recover increased costs due to delays in performance caused by the owner.[1] A contractor may claim delay damages for various actions or inactions of the owner,[2] and the ability to recover such

---

[1] Guy James Constr. Co. v. Trinity Indus., Inc., 644 F.2d 525 (5th Cir.), *modified,* 650 F.2d 93 (5th Cir. 1981); ACS Constr. Co., ASBCA No. 35,872, 89-1 BCA (CCH) ¶ 21,314 (1988).

[2] J.R. Pope, Inc., DOT CAB No. 78-55, 80-2 BCA (CCH) ¶ 14,562 (1980); Bates & Rogers Constr. Corp. v. North Shore Sanitary Dist., 92 Ill. App. 3d 90, 414 N.E.2d 1274 (1980).

delay damages may stem from an express contractual provision providing for such recovery or from an implied covenant of noninterference.[3] Home office overhead costs are well-recognized items of delay damages.[4] Claims for extended home office overhead resulting from delay have been sharply criticized and, hence, are the most litigated of all delay claims.[5] The majority of disputed claims involve the manner in which home office overhead is calculated.[6] The *Eichleay* formula has been accepted by some courts and federal boards of contract appeals as one method to calculate home office overhead costs.[7] However, the *Eichleay* formula has been the subject of great debate regarding federal government contracts, and it has not been unanimously accepted at the state level. In addition to the *Eichleay* formula, home office overhead may be calculated by other methods depending on the project and the nature of the contractor's business.

This chapter deals with the calculation and recovery of home office overhead costs as an element of damages in construction contracts.

§ 6.2   Home Office Overhead Costs Defined

Home office overhead is often characterized as an indirect cost in construction contracts.[8] Home office overhead costs, unlike the direct costs of

---

[3] Kenworth v. State, 236 Cal. App. 2d 378, 46 Cal. Rptr. 396 (1965).

[4] Southern New England Contracting Co. v. State, 165 Conn. 644, 345 A.2d 550 (1974); Guy James Constr. Co., 644 F.2d 525 (5th Cir.), *modified,* 650 F.2d 93 (5th Cir. 1981); W.G. Cornell Co. v. Ceramic Coating Co., 626 F.2d 990 (D.C. Cir. 1980); J.D. Hedin Constr. Co. v. United States, 347 F.2d 235 (Ct. Cl. 1965); Edlin Elec., Inc., ASBCA No. 30,766, 85-3 BCA (CCH) ¶ 18,410 (1985).

[5] George Hyman Constr. Co. v. Washington Metro. Area Transit Auth., 816 F.2d 753 (D.C. Cir. 1987); Capital Elec. Co. v. United States, 729 F.2d 743 (Fed. Cir. 1984); *In re* Stein, 57 B.R. 1016 (Bankr. E.D. Pa. 1986); Tectonics Inc. v. United States, 10 Cl. Ct. 296 (1986); C-Ran Corp., ASBCA No. 37,643, 90-3 BCA (CCH) ¶ 23,201 (1990); Bromley Contracting Co., VABCA No. 2822, 90-3 BCA (CCH) ¶ 23,110 (1990); IPS Group, Inc., ASBCA No. 33,182, 83-3 BCA (CCH) ¶ 21,142 (1988); Eichleay Corp., ASBCA No. 5183, 60-2 BCA (CCH) ¶ 2688 (1960); Southern New England Contracting Co., 165 Conn. 644, 345 A.2d 550 (1974); Berley Indus., Inc. v. City of N.Y., 45 N.Y.2d 683, 385 N.E.2d 281, 412 N.Y.S.2d 589 (1978); Nebraska Pub. Power Dist. v. Austin Power, Inc., 773 F.2d 960 (8th Cir. 1985).

[6] Capital Elec. Co. v. United States 729 F.2d 743 (Fed. Cir. 1984); Eichleay Corp., ASBCA No. 5183, 60-2 BCA (CCH) ¶ 2688 (1960); Berley Indus. 45 N.Y.2d 683, 385 N.E.2d 281, 412 N.Y.S.2d 589 (1978).

[7] The *Eichleay* formula derives its name from the Armed Services Board of Contract Appeals' decision in Eichleay Corp., ASBCA No. 5183, 60-2 BCA (CCH) ¶ 2688 (1960).

[8] Capital Elec. Co., GSBCA Nos. 5316, 5317, 83-2 BCA (CCH) ¶ 16,458 (1983), *rev'd,* 729 F.2d 743 (Fed. Cir. 1984).

labor, materials, or equipment, are not incurred solely for a particular project. Therefore, from an accounting viewpoint, these costs cannot be directly allocated to one project.[9] Home office overhead typically includes the cost of accounting and payroll services, general insurance, the salaries of upper-level management, and marketing costs.[10] In federal construction contracts, which are governed by the Federal Acquisition Regulation (FAR), certain costs may not be recovered as home office overhead.[11] Such unrecoverable costs include interest, advertising costs unrelated to recruitment of personnel, entertainment costs, bid preparation costs, and the cost of bad debts.[12] In any event, *home office overhead* is the actual dollar amount which is an essential part of a contractor's cost of doing business.[13]

Home office overhead costs are often relatively fixed expenses in that such costs remain constant even though a company's revenues may fluctuate.[14] Moreover, home office overhead costs may continue even when no direct project costs are being incurred.[15] Because of the fixed nature of these costs, when a project is extended, the contractor's home office is required to service the project longer than originally anticipated. Thus, delay may result in extended overhead costs, or it may result in unabsorbed overhead because the contractor is unable to obtain another project to absorb the home office overhead during the delay period.[16]

---

[9] Eichleay Corp., ASBCA No. 5183, 60-2 BCA (CCH) ¶ 2688 (1960).

[10] Coath & Gross, Inc. v. United States, 101 Ct. Cl. 702, 709–10 (1944). Among other costs associated with home office overhead are heat, electricity, taxes, and depreciation. *See generally* Reynolds, *Is* Eichleay *the Answer?: An In-depth Look at Home Office Overhead Claims,* 7 Construction L., No. 2 (1987) [hereinafter Reynolds]; Note, *Home Office Overhead as Damages for Construction Delays,* 17 Ga. L. Rev. 761 (1983) [hereinafter Note, *Home Office Overhead*].

[11] *See* FAR pt. 31, 48 C.F.R. §§ 31.000–31.703 (1990).

[12] *See* 48 C.F.R. §§ 31.205-1–31.205-23 (1990); *see also* Reynolds, *Recovering Delay Damages for Home Office Overhead,* 89-13 Construction Briefings (1989).

[13] G.S.&L. Mechanical & Constr., Inc., DOT CAB No. 1640, 86-3 BCA (CCH) ¶ 19,026 (1986); Wickham Contracting Co., IBCA No. 1301-8-79, 86-2 BCA (CCH) ¶ 18,887 (1986).

[14] See § **6.4**. The cost of heat, electricity, and general management, may of course fluctuate with seasonal conditions. However, in the short run, such costs remain constant regardless of construction activity or recovery obtained during a particular, limited duration. *See also* Reynolds.

[15] *See* Reynolds.

[16] The distinction between extended and unabsorbed overhead is discussed in § **6.3**.

§ 6.3   Extended and Unabsorbed
Overhead Costs Distinguished

The terms "extended home office overhead" and "unabsorbed home office overhead"[17] are often used interchangeably by courts and boards of contract appeals.[18] The terms are not synonymous; extended and unabsorbed overhead are actually two distinct concepts.[19] The term "extended home office overhead" is used in construction contracting; the term "unabsorbed overhead" is used in the manufacturing field.[20] However, construction contractors commonly incur unabsorbed home office overhead costs when performance of a contract is delayed.[21]

Extended home office overhead is a "concept unique to construction contracting."[22] The concept of extended home office overhead is based upon a premise that extension of the performance period increases overhead costs.[23] Usually, extended home office overhead costs are incurred only after the original date of completion specified by the contract.[24]

Although unabsorbed home office overhead is more commonly associated with the manufacturing field,[25] a construction contractor incurs unabsorbed home office overhead when the owner's delay prevents the contractor from obtaining other projects which would absorb the cost of overhead.[26]

---

[17] For purposes of clarity and accuracy, this chapter distinguishes between extended home office overhead and unabsorbed home office overhead. Some commentators, however, state that the decision in Capital Elec. Co. v. United States, 729 F.2d 743 (Fed. Cir. 1984), laid to rest the distinction between unabsorbed and extended home office overhead. *See* Reynolds.

[18] Golf Landscaping, Inc. v. Century Constr. Co., 39 Wash. App. 895, 696 P.2d 590 (1984); K.L. Conwell Corp., ASBCA No. 35,489, 90-1 BCA (CCH) ¶ 22,487 (1990); Manshul Constr. Corp. v. Dormitory Auth., 79 A.D.2d 383, 436 N.Y.S.2d 724 (1981) (extended home office overhead at issue); Kent & Waters, *Recovering Indirect Costs,* 80-6 Construction Briefings 245 (1980).

[19] *See* Golf Landscaping, Inc. v. Century Constr. Co., 39 Wash. App. 895, 696 P.2d 590 (1984); Manshul Constr. Corp. v. Dormitory Auth., 79 A.D.2d 383, 436 N.Y.S.2d 724 (1981).

[20] *See* Note, *Home Office Overhead;* Reynolds.

[21] Golf Landscaping, Inc. v. Century Constr. Co., 39 Wash. App. 895, 696 P.2d 590 (1984); Capital Elec. Co., GSBCA No. 5317, 83-2 BCA (CCH) ¶ 16,548 (1983), *rev'd on other grounds,* 729 F.2d 743 (Fed. Cir. 1984).

[22] Capital Elec. Co., GSBCA Nos. 5316, 5317, 83-2 BCA (CCH) ¶ 16,548 (1983), *rev'd on other grounds,* 729 F.2d 743 (Fed. Cir. 1984).

[23] *Id.* at p. 82,311.

[24] Lane, *Recovering Damages for Home Office Overhead,* 89-13 Construction Briefings (1989) [hereinafter Lane].

[25] Capital Elec. Co., GSBCA Nos. 5316, 5317, 83-2 BCA (CCH) ¶ 16,548 (1983), *rev'd on other grounds,* 729 F.2d 743 (Fed. Cir. 1984).

[26] Golf Landscaping, Inc. v. Century Constr. Co., 39 Wash. App. 895, 696 P.2d 590 (1984).

The General Services Board of Contract Appeals has defined *unabsorbed overhead* as, "The consequence of the increase in the rate of allocation of indirect costs to work other than that which was delayed or disrupted. . . . [T]he contract's share of overhead is diminished; the overhead share of all other contract work is increased."[27] Thus, owner-caused delay which reduces the number of contracts to which a contractor's overhead expenses are charged may give rise to a claim for unabsorbed overhead.[28]

It is well-established that home office overhead costs are a recoverable element of delay damages.[29] The distinction between extended and unabsorbed home office overhead, however, will not affect the ultimate resolution of the claim for such costs.[30]

§ 6.4   Fixed Costs versus Variable Costs

Claims for home office overhead can include both fixed and variable costs.[31] *Fixed overhead costs,* as the name implies, are those costs which do not vary with activity on the project.[32] Rather, these costs are incurred merely because of the passage of time. *Variable costs,* however, are those costs that vary according to the level of activity on the project.[33] Typically, these costs increase when direct costs on the project increase.[34]

Home office overhead costs can be a mixture of fixed and variable costs.[35] It is difficult to distinguish precisely fixed home office overhead costs from variable home office overhead costs,[36] and courts and boards often gloss over whether the cost in question is fixed or variable.[37] In light of the difficulty in distinguishing between fixed and variable costs, one state

---

[27] Capital Elec. Co., GSBCA Nos. 5316, 5317, 83-2 BCA (CCH) ¶ 16,548 (1983), *rev'd on other grounds,* 729 F.2d 743 (Fed. Cir. 1984).

[28] Golf Landscaping, Inc. v. Century Constr. Co., 39 Wash. App. 895, 696 P.2d 590 (1984).

[29] Southern New England Contracting Co. v. State, 165 Conn. 643, 345 A.2d 550 (1974); Edlin Elec. Inc., ASBCA No. 30,766, 85-3 BCA (CCH) ¶ 18,410 (1985).

[30] *See* Lane.

[31] Autotrol Corp. v. Continental Water Sys. Corp., 918 F.2d 689 (7th Cir. 1990).

[32] *Id. See* Note, *Home Office Overhead.*

[33] Autotrol Corp. v. Continental Water Sys. Corp., 918 F.2d 689 (7th Cir. 1990).

[34] *Id.*

[35] The fixed costs of heat and electricity may increase or decrease depending on the seasonal conditions present. *See* Southern New England Contracting Co. v. State, 165 Conn. 644, 345 A.2d 550 (1974); *see also* Note, *Home Office Overhead.*

[36] Salt City Contractors, VACAB No. 1362, 80-2 BCA (CCH) ¶ 14,713 (1980); Golf Landscaping, Inc. v. Century Constr. Co., 39 Wash. App. 895, 696 P.2d 590 (1984).

[37] *See* Autotrol Corp. v. Continental Water Sys. Corp., 918 F.2d 689 (7th Cir. 1990) (engineers' salary determined to be fixed); Kemmons-Wilson, Inc., ASBCA No. 16,167, 72-2 BCA (CCH) ¶ 9689 (1972) (home office overhead considered to be almost a 100% fixed expense).

court has stated that it is unrealistic to require a plaintiff to completely segregate fixed and variable costs before recovery for unabsorbed overhead is permitted.[38] The use of a formula approach may not be permissible to calculate home office overhead costs which are variable.[39] Contractors, therefore, should examine closely their home office overhead expenses to ascertain fully whether they are fixed or variable before selecting a method of calculation.[40]

§ 6.5 *Eichleay Corp.:* A Simple Approach to Calculating Home Office Overhead

In *Eichleay Corp.,*[41] the Armed Services Board of Contract Appeals approved the method of calculating home office overhead expenses suggested by the appellant, Eichleay Corporation.[42] Although *Eichleay* is generally cited as the genesis of the *Eichleay* formula, the method of calculation used in *Eichleay* was not new to government contracts. By the Board's own admission, the formula proposed by the appellant had been used previously by the United States Court of Claims.[43]

In *Eichleay,* the appellant entered into a contract with the government for construction of a Nike missile site in Pennsylvania.[44] Three individual contracts were actually involved in construction of the facility, and none of the contracts was completed within the specified time.[45] The home office overhead costs sought by the appellant resulted from government delay in issuing change orders.[46] The contracting officer determined the amount of home office overhead owed to the appellant, and the appellant appealed that determination to the Armed Services Board of Contract Appeals.[47] Solely at issue in *Eichleay* was the proper allocation of home office

---

[38] Golf Landscaping, Inc. v. Century Constr. Co., 39 Wash. App. 895, 696 P.2d 590, 593 (1984).

[39] *Cf.* Salt City Contractors, VACAB No. 1362, 80-2 BCA (CCH) ¶ 14,713 (1980).

[40] *Id.;* Golf Landscaping, Inc. v. Century Constr. Co., 39 Wash. App. 895, 696 P.2d 590 (1984).

[41] ASBCA No. 5183, 60-2 BCA (CCH) ¶ 2688 (1960).

[42] *Id.* at p. 13,576.

[43] *Id.* at 13,574. Specifically, the *Eichleay* formula had been used by the Court of Claims in Fred R. Comb Co. v. United States, 103 Ct. Cl. 174 (1945); Houston Ready-Cut House Co. v. United States, 96 F. Supp. 629 (Ct. Cl. 1951).

[44] Eichleay Corp., ASBCA No. 5183, 60-2 BCA (CCH) ¶ 2688 (1960).

[45] *Id.* at p. 13,567.

[46] *Id.*

[47] *Id.* at 13,568.

expenses incurred during the period of suspension.[48] The Board approved the appellant's method of calculating home office overhead. The appellant's method allocated the contractor's main office expenses by finding a ratio of contract billings to total billings for the performance period and multiplying that ratio by the main office overhead for the performance period. That figure is then divided by the number of days of performance to determine a daily rate of overhead. The daily rate is then multiplied by the number of days of delay.[49] The appellant's method of calculating home office overhead resulted in a figure $97,000 greater than the figure arrived at under the formula proposed by the government.[50]

§ 6.6   *Eichleay* Formula Accepted, Criticized, and Modified

The *Eichleay* formula has been accepted by several courts and boards as an appropriate method of calculating unabsorbed and extended home office overhead.[51] However, its use has been severely criticized. The *Eichleay* formula was viewed with disdain as soon as the Armed Services Board of Contract Appeals (ASBCA) approved of its use in 1960.[52] As discussed in § **6.10**, state courts have not enthusiastically adopted the *Eichleay* formula as an appropriate method for calculating home office overhead. Accordingly, contractors must realize that the mere application of the *Eichleay* formula does not guarantee a successful claim. It is only one of the many methods that may be used to calculate home office overhead costs.[53]

---

[48] *Id.* at 13,573.

[49] *Id.* at 13,574. See § **6.7**.

[50] Eichleay Corp., ASBCA No. 5183, 60-2 BCA (CCH) ¶ 2688 (1960) at p. 13,578.

[51] Capital Elec. Co. v. United States, 729 F.2d 743 (Fed. Cir. 1984); Boublis Elec., Inc., ASBCA No. 34,056, 89-3 BCA (CCH) ¶ 22,094 (1989); Gregory Constructors, Inc., ASBCA No. 35,960, 88-3 BCA (CCH) ¶ 20,934 (1988); IPS Group, ASBCA No. 33,182, 88-3 BCA (CCH) ¶ 21,142 (1988); Golf Landscaping, Inc. v. Century Constr. Co., 39 Wash. App. 895, 696 P.2d 590 (1984); PDM Plumbing & Heating v. Findlen, 13 Mass. App. 950, 431 N.E.2d 594 (1982).

[52] In *Eichleay Corp.,* the government strongly opposed the appellant's calculation of home office overhead expenses and the arguments asserted by the government therein have been repeated numerous times. More recently, commentators have heralded the death of *Eichleay* as a result of the General Services Board of Contract Appeals decision in Capital Elec. Co. v. United States, 729 F.2d 743 (Fed. Cir. 1984).

[53] Boublis Elec., Inc., ASBCA No. 34,056, 89-3 BCA (CCH) ¶ 22,094 (1989); Gregory Constructors, Inc., ASBCA No. 35,960, 88-3 BCA (CCH) ¶ 22,934 (1989); Nebraska Pub. Power Dist. v. Austin Power, Inc., 773 F.2d 960 (8th Cir. 1985). Other methods of calculating home office overhead are the direct markup method, the labor allocation method, and the *Hudson* formula.

In *Capital Electric Co.,*[54] the contracting officer denied the appellant's claim for costs allegedly incurred as a result of government-caused delay.[55] Appeal was taken to the General Services Board of Contract Appeals, which rejected the *Eichleay* formula as a method of calculating extended home office overhead.[56] Specifically, the Board stated:

> The daily rate concept of recovery of extended overhead that *Eichleay* represents comports with neither the pervasive principles nor the broad operating principles that encompass generally accepted accounting principles. It neither associates cause with effect nor allocates costs that cannot be so associated to a specific accounting period or periods. It does not assign indirect costs to an appropriate cost objective during the period in which those indirect costs were incurred. [57]

The *Eichleay* formula was resurrected on appeal, however,[58] and the United States Court of Appeals for the Federal Circuit held that the Board wrongly ignored the 40-year use and acceptance of the *Eichleay* formula.[59] Thus, the court reaffirmed that the *Eichleay* formula was an appropriate method of calculating home office overhead in federal government contracts.[60]

Although *Eichleay* is generally recognized as one of the appropriate methods to calculate home office overhead,[61] criticisms of the formula still exist. The *Eichleay* formula is criticized for its assumption that a contractor has, in fact, incurred home office overhead that it would have otherwise avoided if the project was not extended.[62] The *Eichleay* formula has also been criticized as producing amounts that have a tenuous relationship to the damages actually incurred by the contractor.[63] Courts and boards, however, have recognized that home office overhead cannot be proven with mathe-

---

[54] GSBCA Nos. 5316, 5317, 83-2 BCA (CCH) ¶ 16,458 (1983), *rev'd,* 729 F.2d 743 (Fed. Cir. 1984).

[55] *Id.* at p. 82,300.

[56] *Id.*

[57] *Id.* at 82,313.

[58] Capital Elec. Co. v. United States, 729 F.2d 743 (Fed. Cir. 1984).

[59] *Id.* at 746.

[60] *Id.* at 747.

[61] *See* J.V. Bailey, ENGBCA No. 5348, 90-3 BCA (CCH) ¶ 23,179 (1990) (*Eichleay* formula applied without question); Pittsburgh-Des Moines Corp., EBCA No. 314-3-84, 89-2 BCA (CCH) ¶ 21,739 (1989) ("*Eichleay* formula is commonly accepted by the courts and boards").

[62] *See* Reynolds.

[63] Berley Indus., Inc. v. City of N.Y. 385 N.E.2d 281, 412 N.Y.S.2d 589 (1978) (citing dissenting opinion of Justice Murphy in *id.,* 59 A.D.2d 644, 398 N.Y.S.2d 353 (1977)).

matical certainty and that the *Eichleay* formula is an appropriate method to estimate the amount of home office overhead damages in question.[64]

Throughout the years, contractors have successfully and unsuccessfully attempted to modify the original calculation used in *Eichleay*.[65] Illustrations of the original *Eichleay* calculation and the subsequent modifications thereto appear in § 6.7.

§ 6.7   Standard *Eichleay* Calculation

As approved by the ASBCA in *Eichleay Corp.*,[66] the standard *Eichleay* calculation is as follows:

$$\frac{\text{Total Contract Billings}}{\text{Total Company Billings for Contract Period}} \times \frac{\text{Home Office Overhead for Actual Contract Period}}{} = \frac{\text{Home Office Overhead Allocable to Contract}}{}$$

$$\frac{\text{Home Office Overhead Allocable to Contract}}{\text{Actual Days of Contract Performance}} = \text{Daily Home Office Overhead Allocable to Contract}$$

$$\text{Daily Home Office Overhead Allocable to Contract} \times \text{Number of Days of Delay} = \text{Extended Home Office Overhead}$$

This calculation contains several potential flaws, however. The standard *Eichleay* formula assumes a proportional relationship between the price of a contract and the home office overhead associated with the contract.[67] Furthermore, if a contractor has reasonably constant overhead percentages, the total overhead allocable to the contract does not fluctuate due to the delay. As a result, no matter how long the delay, the allocable overhead remains roughly constant. In other words, critics of the formula often assert that the contractor would have incurred these costs in any event. Commentators have also suggested that the *Eichleay* formula is limited by the

---

[64] George Hyman Constr. Co. v. Washington Area Metro. Transit Auth., 816 F.2d 753 (D.C. Cir. 1987); Nebraska Pub. Power Dist. v. Austin Power, Inc., 773 F.2d 960 (8th Cir. 1986).

[65] *See* Ricway, Inc., ASBCA No. 30,056, 86-3 BCA (CCH) ¶ 19,138 (1986) (contractor's calculation of contract billings and overhead for period of suspension by using a percentage of annual billings and overhead was impermissible). *See also* Gregory Constructors, Inc., ASBCA No. 35,960, 88-3 BCA (CCH) ¶ 20,934 (1988) (formula using data which did not reflect actual time was rejected).

[66] ASBCA No. 5183, 60-2 BCA (CCH) ¶ 2688 (1960).

[67] *See* Note, *Home Office Overhead.*

assumption that home office overhead costs are wholly fixed costs.[68] Thus, because the *Eichleay* formula does not consider the variable nature of fixed costs, the formula does not accurately measure the actual costs incurred by the contractor as a result of delay in performance of the contract.[69]

§ 6.8 *Eichleay* Modified: Variation 1

To address the problems inherent in the original *Eichleay* formula, a number of variations on the calculation have been used. One of these variations is the following:

$$\frac{\text{Original Contract Price}}{\substack{\text{Total Company Billings} \\ \text{for Original Contract Period} \\ \text{(adjusted to include contract as} \\ \text{though it had been performed)}}} \times \substack{\text{Total Home Office} \\ \text{Overhead for Actual} \\ \text{Contract Period}} = \substack{\text{Home Office Overhead} \\ \text{Allocable to Contract}}$$

$$\frac{\text{Allocable Home Office Overhead}}{\text{Original Days of Contract Performance}} = \substack{\text{Daily Home Office} \\ \text{Overhead Allocable} \\ \text{to Contract}}$$

$$\substack{\text{Daily Home Office Overhead} \\ \text{Allocable to Contract}} \times \substack{\text{Number of Days} \\ \text{of Delay}} = \substack{\text{Extended Home Office} \\ \text{Overhead Damages}}$$

This modified version of the *Eichleay* formula results in a greater daily home office overhead figure than arrived at through the standard *Eichleay* calculation.[70] The modified formula utilizes the original days of contract performance as the denominator in the second step rather than the actual days of contract performance as used in the standard *Eichleay* calculation. Thus, the overhead allocation is multiplied by the extended number of days. This variation assumes, however, that the increased home office overhead is directly proportional to time: if a project takes twice as long to complete, there will be twice as much overhead allocated to it. Courts and boards, however, have rejected this modified version of the *Eichleay* formula.[71]

---

[68] *Id.* Although the standard *Eichleay* calculation does not explicitly exclude computation of variable costs, an assumption by a court or tribunal that home office overhead costs are fixed essentially excludes computation of variable costs.

[69] Kemmons-Wilson, Inc., ASBCA No. 16,167, 72-2 BCA (CCH) ¶ 9689 (1972); Note, *Home Office Overhead.*

[70] *See* Lane.

[71] Capital Elec. Co. v. United States, 729 F.2d 743 (Fed. Cir. 1984) (record did not support use of modified *Eichleay* formula); Gregory Constr., Inc., ASBCA No. 35,960, 88-3 BCA (CCH) ¶ 20,934 (1988).

§ 6.9   *Eichleay* Modified: Variation 2

Another variation of the standard *Eichleay* formula includes contract billings for the period in which the contract was extended. This modification considers only fixed overhead costs.[72] Moreover, this calculation attempts to compensate for the fact that the overhead is spread over a longer period of time. In doing so, the overhead is allocated over a larger base and the calculated amount of home office overhead is lower than that arrived at through the original *Eichleay* formula or Variation 1. This variation of the *Eichleay* formula is as follows:

$$\frac{\text{Original Contract Price}}{\substack{\text{Total Contracts Billings for} \\ \text{Original Contract Period} + \\ \text{Contract Billings for} \\ \text{Extended Period}}} \times \substack{\text{Total Fixed Home} \\ \text{Office Overhead} \\ \text{for Original} \\ \text{Contract Period}} = \substack{\text{Fixed Home Office} \\ \text{Overhead Allocable} \\ \text{to Contract}}$$

$$\frac{\substack{\text{Fixed Home Office Overhead} \\ \text{Allocable to Contract}}}{\substack{\text{Original Days of} \\ \text{Contract Performance}}} = \substack{\text{Daily Fixed Home} \\ \text{Office Overhead} \\ \text{Allocable to Contract}}$$

$$\substack{\text{Daily Fixed Home} \\ \text{Office Overhead} \\ \text{Allocable to Contract}} \times \substack{\text{Number of Days} \\ \text{of Delay}} = \substack{\text{Extended Home Office} \\ \text{Overhead Damages}}$$

The genesis of this variation is not known,[73] and it has not been accepted by the Boards of Contract Appeals to which it has been proffered.[74]

§ 6.10   Calculating Home Office Overhead in State and Private Contracts

State courts have not unanimously approved of the *Eichleay* formula as a means of calculating home office overhead expenses.[75] In asserting a claim

---

[72] The standard *Eichleay* formula theoretically excludes variable home office overhead costs from the calculation, but this modified formula explicitly excludes variable overhead costs. See §§ **6.7–6.8.**

[73] *See* G.S.&L. Mechanical & Constr., Inc., DOT CAB No. 1640, 86-3 BCA (CCH) ¶ 19,026 (1986) ("[modified *Eichleay* formula] arose from a source which we have been unable to locate and which has not been cited to us").

[74] *Id.* Schindler Haughton Elevator Corp., GSBCA No. 5390, 80-2 BCA (CCH) ¶ 14,871 (1980).

[75] Berley Indus., Inc. v. City of N.Y., 45 N.Y.2d 683, 385 N.E.2d 281, 412 N.Y.S.2d 589 (1978) (*Eichleay* formula calculation criticized as having tenuous relation with actual damages incurred); Manshul Constr. Corp. v. Dormitory Auth., 79 A.D.2d 383, 436

for home office overhead costs in state or private contracts, contractors should be familiar with the method accepted by their jurisdiction. To date, Massachusetts, Washington, and Nebraska are the only states that have accepted the *Eichleay* formula by name.[76]

In *PDM Heating & Plumbing v. Findlen,*[77] the Massachusetts Appeals Court addressed the issue of whether the *Eichleay* formula was a permissible method to calculate the home office overhead component of damages incurred by a subcontractor. The delay was caused in part by the owner and in part by the general contractor.[78] The Massachusetts court found that the *Eichleay* formula was a fair method to calculate the home office overhead expenses incurred by the subcontractor.[79] Specifically, the court stated:

> In circumstances such as those presented here, the master was not compelled to use any one particular method of computing office overhead expenses attributable to the delay; it was only necessary for him to use a fair method. . . . (W)e conclude that the calculations made by the master were reasonably calculated to achieve a fair estimate of the plaintiff's actual damages attributable to overhead expenses.[80]

Similarly, in *Golf Landscaping, Inc. v. Century Construction Co.,*[81] the Washington Court of Appeals determined that the *Eichleay* formula is "a reasonable basis for estimating the amount of unabsorbed home office overhead occasioned by construction delays."[82] In *Nebraska Public Power District v. Austin Power, Inc.,*[83] the United States Court of Appeals for the Eighth Circuit denied the claim that the Nebraska Supreme Court would not follow the *Eichleay* formula.[84] Thus, the court held that, in absence of contrary authority, the *Eichleay* method is a permissible method to compute home office overhead in Nebraska.[85]

N.Y.S.2d 724 (1981) ("current state of the law in this area is uncertain and fluid"); Fehlhaber Corp. v. State, 65 A.D.2d 119, 410 N.Y.S.2d 920 (1978); *see also* Novak & Co. v. Facilities Dev. Corp., 116 A.D.2d 891, 498 N.Y.S.2d 492 (1986); Golf Landscaping, Inc. v. Century Constr. Co., 39 Wash. App. 395, 696 P.2d 590 (1984); PDM Plumbing & Heating, Inc. v. Findlen, 13 Mass. App. 590, 431 N.E.2d 594 (1982).

[76] PDM Plumbing & Heating, Inc. v. Findlen, 13 Mass. App. 950, 431 N.E.2d 594 (1982); Golf Landscaping, Inc. v. Century Constr. Co., 39 Wash. App. 395, 646 P.2d 590 (1984).

[77] 13 Mass. App. 590, 431 N.E.2d 594 (1980).

[78] *Id.* at 595.

[79] *Id.*

[80] *Id.*

[81] 39 Wash. App. 895, 696 P.2d 590 (1984).

[82] 696 P.2d at 593.

[83] 773 F.2d 960 (8th Cir. 1985).

[84] *Id.* at 972.

[85] *Id.*

New York courts, however, have criticized the *Eichleay* formula.[86] In *Berley Industries, Inc. v. City of New York,*[87] the New York Court of Appeals stated that the *Eichleay* formula traditionally has been applied without analysis and for reasons of administrative convenience.[88] Moreover, the court stated that application of the *Eichleay* formula in the case would result in a home office overhead figure unrelated to the damages actually incurred by the plaintiff.[89] However, in a concurring opinion, Judge Jones stated that the *Eichleay* formula may be an acceptable means of calculating home office overhead expenses incurred as a result of delay.[90] Subsequently, in *Novak & Co. v. Facilities Development Corp.,*[91] the New York Supreme Court, Appellate Division, rejected application of an *Eichleay*-type formula to calculate home office overhead costs.[92]

State courts are not bound by the precedent set in *Capital Electric v. United States,*[93] which recognized the *Eichleay* formula as an acceptable method of calculating home office overhead. State courts, however, appear to be concerned more with proof of damage than the manner in which home office overhead is calculated.[94] Rather than concentrating on the precise method to be used, state courts appear to calculate home office overhead by any manner which is fair in light of the facts.[95] In claiming damages for extended or unabsorbed home office overhead at the state

---

[86] Manshul Constr. Corp. v. State, 79 A.D.2d 383, 436 N.Y.S.2d 724 (1981); Berley Indus., Inc. v. City of N.Y., 385 N.E.2d 281, 412 N.Y.S.2d 589 (1978).

[87] 385 N.E.2d 281, 412 N.Y.S.2d 589 (1978).

[88] 412 N.Y.S.2d at 592.

[89] *Id.* (citing Justice Murphy's dissenting opinion in Berley Indus., Inc. v. City of N.Y., 59 A.D.2d 664, 398 N.Y.S.2d 353 (1977)).

[90] 385 N.E.2d at 593 (Jones, J., concurring).

[91] 116 A.D.2d 891, 498 N.Y.S.2d 492 (1986).

[92] 498 N.Y.S.2d at 494.

[93] 729 F.2d 743 (Fed. Cir. 1984).

[94] *See* General Fed. Constr. v. D.R. Thomas, 52 Md. App. 700, 451 A.2d 1250 (1982) (*Eichleay* method mentioned by the court without analysis or objection); Guy James Constr. Co. v. Trinity, 644 F.2d 523 (5th Cir. 1981), *modifying* 630 F.2d 43 (5th Cir. 1980) (emphasis on lack of causal connection); Berley Indus. v. City of N.Y. 385 N.E.2d 281, 412 N.Y.S.2d 589 (1978) ("depending on the proof, the *Eichleay* method might be an acceptable means of measuring this [home office overhead] component") (Jones, J., concurring).

[95] *See* PDM Plumbing & Heating v. Findlen, 13 Mass. App. 950, 431 N.E.2d 594 (1982) ("The test is whether the method adopted is reasonably calculated to measure loss resulting from the breach"); Golf Landscaping, Inc. v. Century Constr. Co., 39 Wash. App. 895, 696 P.2d 590 (1984) ("*Eichleay* formula affords reasonable basis for estimating amount of unabsorbed overhead"); Kansas City Bridge Co. v. Kansas City Structural Steel Co., 317 S.W.2d 370 (Mo. 1958) ("In the view we take, we are not particularly concerned with the method used to compute the daily overhead allocable to the job").

level therefore, contractors should thoroughly examine the law in their jurisdiction. In many states, home office overhead costs may be calculated by any method, including the *Eichleay* method, if the court deems the method to be fair in light of the particular circumstances.[96]

§ 6.11   Establishing a Prima Facie Case for Recovery of Home Office Overhead

Before bringing a claim, contractors should consider whether they can establish a prima facie case for recovery of home office overhead costs. The lack of a prima facie case will render moot the method chosen to calculate home office overhead expenses.

In certain cases, contractors have assumed that owner-caused delay automatically entitled them to recover overhead costs.[97] This erroneous assumption apparently dates back to *Eichleay Corp.*[98] In *Eichleay Corp.*, the Armed Services Board of Contract Appeals stated:

> It has, however, been sufficiently demonstrated by the mere fact of prolongation of the time of performance, and the continuation of main office expenses, that more of such expenses were incurred during the period of performance than would have been except for the suspension, Fred R. Combs Co. v. United States, 103 C. Cls. 174 (1945); Henry Ericson v. United States, 62 F. Supp. 312 (1945).[99]

Based upon *Eichleay Corp.,* contractors equated delay with recovery of home office overhead costs.[100]

---

[96] See § **6.6**.

[97] Boublis Elec., Inc., ASBCA No. 34,056, 89-3 BCA (CCH) ¶ 22,934 (1989); Bromley Contracting Co., VABCA No. 2822, 90-3 BCA (CCH) ¶ 23,110 (1990).

[98] ASBCA No. 5183, 60-2 BCA (CCH) ¶ 2688 (1960). On reconsideration, however, the Army Appeals Panel stated:

> The partial suspensions were lifted at innumerable, varying intervals over a prolonged period of time with the issuance of the numerous modifications providing for changes in the contracts. Under these circumstances it would not have been prudent or practical for appellant either to risk the layoff of Home Office Personnel and facilities or, on the other hand, to absorb personnel and facilities so made idle by taking on new commitments. The mere showing of these facts is sufficient to transfer to the government the burden of going forward with proof that appellant suffered no loss or should have suffered no loss.

Eichleay Corp., ASBCA No. 5183, 61-1 BCA (CCH) ¶ 2894 (1961).

[99] ASBCA No. 5183, 60-2 BCA (CCH) ¶ 2688 at p. 13,574 (1960).

[100] *See* PDM Plumbing & Heating v. Findlen, 13 Mass. App. 950, 431 N.E.2d 594 (1982) ("The test is whether the method adopted is reasonably calculated to measure loss resulting from the breach"); Golf Landscaping, Inc. v. Century Constr. Co., 39 Wash.

Courts and boards have determined that a contractor is not automatically entitled to recover home office overhead costs when performance of the contract has been delayed.[101] In order to establish a prima facie case of entitlement to home office overhead, a contractor must show that (1) performance of the contract was delayed due to inexcusable actions or inactions of the owner, and (2) the contractor suffered actual damages as a result of the delay,[102] and either (3) the nature of the delay made it impractical for the contractor to undertake the performance of other work,[103] or (4) the nature of the delay made it impractical to reduce home office overhead costs.[104] In calculating potential home office overhead damages in federal contracts, contractors should consider whether they satisfy these elements of a prima facie case. In state and private contracts, contractors should be equally, if not more, concerned about meeting the standards of proof necessary to recover home office overhead costs.[105]

§ 6.12   Reserving the Right to Claim for Home Office Overhead

Although it is not an immediate consideration in calculating home office overhead expenses, contractors must properly reserve their rights to bring the claim. In federal, state, and private contracts, it is imperative that the right to bring a claim for home office overhead be preserved. Moreover, contractors should be cognizant of any notice provisions contained in their

---

App. 895, 696 P.2d 590 (1984) ("Eichleay formula affords reasonable basis for estimating amount of unabsorbed overhead"); Kansas City Bridge Co. v. Kansas City Structural Steel Co., 317 S.W.2d 370 (Mo. 1958) ("In the view we take, we are not particularly concerned with the method used to compute the daily overhead allocable to the job"). *See also* Montoya Constr. Co., ASBCA No. 21,575, 89-1 BCA (CCH) ¶ 21,575 (1989).

[101] George Hyman Constr. Co. v. Washington Metro. Area Transit Auth., 816 F.2d 753 (D.C. Cir. 1987); Capital Elec. Co. v. United States, 729 F.2d 743 (Fed. Cir. 1984); W.G. Cornell Co. v. Ceramic Coating Co., 626 F.2d 990 (D.C. Cir. 1980); Bromley Contracting Co., VABCA No. 2822, 90-3 BCA (CCH) ¶ 23,110 (1990); J.V. Bailey, ENGBCA No. 5348, 90-3 BCA (CCH) ¶ 23,179 (1990).

[102] George Hyman Constr. Co. v. Washington Metro. Area Transit Auth., 816 F.2d 753, 757 (D.C. Cir. 1987).

[103] W.G. Cornell Co. v. Ceramic Coating Co., 626 F.2d 990 (D.C. Cir. 1980). This is a prime example of the home office overhead not being absorbed by other contracts, i.e., unabsorbed overhead.

[104] Eichleay Corp., ASBCA No. 5183, 61-1 BCA (CCH) ¶ 2894 (1961). This is a prime example of extended overhead. *See generally* George Hyman Constr. Co. v. Washington Metro. Area Transit Auth., 816 F.2d 753, 757 (D.C. Cir. 1987).

[105] See § **6.10**.

contract.[106] A contractor may be precluded from recovery if the owner has not been provided with proper notice or the claim has not been preserved as required by the terms of the contract.[107]

In *Pan Alaska*, [108] the appellant executed a release after submitting a final progress payment request.[109] In signing the release, the appellant's project manager added the following sentence: "Release is complete for all contract activities except extended overhead claim pending."[110] The contracting officer subsequently denied the appellant's claim for extended overhead costs.[111] On appeal, the Armed Services Board of Contract Appeals granted the respondent's motion for summary judgment.[112] The Board determined that the appellant's claim for extended home office overhead was barred by the payments clause of the contract, which required that all claims be preserved in stated amounts excepted from the operation of the release.[113] Moreover, the suspension of work clause required that claims be asserted in a stated amount not later than the date of final payment.[114] In any event, contractors should be fully aware of provisions of the contract that may inhibit their ability to recover home office overhead costs in cases of delay.

§ 6.13   Secondary Considerations in Calculating Home Office Overhead

Once the amount of home office overhead is calculated by the *Eichleay* formula or the methods discussed in § **6.16**, contractors should carefully examine the costs they have attributed to home office overhead. As discussed in § **6.2**, various costs may not be recovered as overhead in federal contracts.[115] In addition to the unallowable costs enumerated in the FAR, courts and boards have been hesitant to allow recovery of various other costs in claims for home office overhead.

---

[106] *See* Quin Blair Enters., Inc. v. Julien Constr. Co., 597 P.2d 945 (Wyo. 1979) (failure to provide owner with timely notice precluded recovery).

[107] *Id. See also* Southern Rd. Builders, Inc. v. Lee County, 493 So. 2d 189 (Fla. Dist. Ct. App. 1986).

[108] ASBCA No. 38,525, 90-3 BCA (CCH) ¶ 23,050 (1990).

[109] *Id.* at p. 115,715.

[110] *Id.*

[111] *Id.*

[112] *Id.*

[113] *Id.*

[114] ASBCA No. 38,525, 90-3 BCA (CCH) ¶ 23,050 at p. 115,715 (1990).

[115] See § **6.2**.

Contractors must be careful that their calculation of home office over-head does not duplicate costs.[116] In *R.G. Beer Corp.,*[117] the Corps of Engineers Board of Contract Appeals reduced the appellant's overhead figure arrived at through the *Eichleay* formula. The appellant's claim was reduced by the amount of the fixed expense portion of home office overhead markup with respect to direct costs paid to the appellant during the period on which the *Eichleay* calculation was based.[118] Otherwise, the Board determined that the appellant would twice recover the same fixed expenses, once through normal overhead allocable to the project and once through the *Eichleay* award.[119] Boards and courts have similarly reduced *Eichleay* awards in order to prevent double recovery.[120]

Courts and boards have also questioned the validity of certain home office overhead expenses. In *Irby Steel v. W.R. Fairchild Construction Co.,*[121] the Louisiana Court of Appeal denied the defendant's counterclaim for home office overhead costs.[122] Although the court denied the claim on grounds of insufficient proof, the court determined that it would be improper for one of the owners of the defendant company to charge his salary as part of home office overhead.[123] In any event, contractors should be aware that all home office overhead calculations and cost items contained therein will be thoroughly scrutinized by the reviewing tribunal.

§ 6.14   Other Methods of Calculating Home Office Overhead

Although the *Eichleay* formula represents the most accepted method of calculating home office overhead in federal contracts,[124] contractors may use a number of other methods to calculate their home office overhead. Contractors, therefore, should choose the method which is most advantageous in light of the facts of the particular situation.

---

[116] R.G. Beer Corp., ENGBCA No. 4885, 86-3 BCA (CCH) ¶ 19,012 (1986).

[117] *Id.*

[118] *Id.* at p. 96,031.

[119] *Id.* at 96,032.

[120] *Id. See also* Sovereign Constr. Co., ASBCA No. 17,792, 75-1 BCA (CCH) ¶ 11,251 (1975) (home office award reduced by amount of overhead payments for change order work).

[121] 270 So. 2d 233 (La. Ct. App. 1972).

[122] *Id.* at 242.

[123] *Id. See also* Singleton Contracting Corp., GSBCA Nos. 9614, 9615, 9616, 9617, 9637, 9702, 90-3 BCA (CCH) ¶ 23,125 (1990).

[124] See §§ **6.6–6.8.**

§ 6.15   —Direct Cost Formulas

The direct cost formulas are alternatives to the *Eichleay* formula for calculating home office overhead. The two most commonly used direct cost methods are the *Allegheny* method[125] and the *Carteret* method.[126] The *Allegheny* method permits recovery of underabsorbed overhead by utilizing an allocation rate differential between anticipated and actual allocation rates for either the delay period alone or during the actual period of contract performance. That figure is then multiplied by an acceptable allocation base, such as contract manufacturing costs, contract billings, or direct labor costs. The *Allegheny,* or burden fluctuation method,[127] is calculated as follows:

$$\text{Overhead Rate During Delay} - \text{Projected Overhead Rate} = \text{Excess Overhead Rate}$$

$$\text{Excess Overhead Rate} \times \text{Contract Base For Delay} = \text{Claimable Overhead Rate}[128]$$

The *Allegheny* method is advantageous in that it simulates the effect of delay, suspension, or extension on allocable overhead during the accounting period of the delay.[129] This method, however, does not account for the balancing of costs deferred into subsequent accounting periods.[130]

The *Carteret* method, however, deducts the normal overhead rate from the overhead rate experienced during delay to arrive at the excess overhead rate.[131] The *Carteret* calculation is as follows:

$$\text{Overhead Rate Experienced During Delay Period} - \text{Normal Overhead Rate for Project} = \text{Excess Rate}$$

$$\text{Excess Rate} \times \text{Contract Base for Delay} = \text{Recoverable}[132] \text{ Overhead}$$

---

[125] Allegheny Sportswear Co., ASBCA No. 4163, 58-1 BCA (CCH) ¶ 1684 (1958); *see also* Allied Materials & Equip., ASBCA No. 17,318, 75-1 BCA (CCH) ¶ 11,150 (1975).

[126] Carteret Work Uniforms, Inc., ASBCA No. 1647, 6 CCF § 61,651-1951 (1954).

[127] *See* Allied Materials, ASBCA No. 17,318, 75-1 BCA (CCH) ¶ 11,150 (1975).

[128] For further discussion of the *Allegheny* method, see R. Cushman et al., *Delay Claims,* in Proving and Pricing Construction Claims (R. Cushman & D. Carpenter eds., John Wiley & Sons 1990).

[129] Capital Elec. Co., GSBCA Nos. 5316, 5317, 83-2 BCA (CCH) ¶ 16,458 (1983), *rev'd on other grounds,* 729 F.2d 743 (Fed. Cir. 1984).

[130] *Id.*

[131] *See* Carteret Work Uniforms, Inc., ASBCA No. 1647, 6 CCF ¶ 21,501 (1954).

[132] *Id.*

This method, however, fails to account for the length of the delay involved and has been rejected in favor of the *Eichleay* formula.[133] Although the boards of contract appeals have not recently used the *Carteret* method, it may still be a viable method to calculate home office overhead.

Labor costs are frequently used as the allocation base in these direct cost methods. The labor expended on the project is compared to the total labor used by the entire company. Accordingly, the overhead is increased on projects which are labor-intensive.

Another method of overhead calculation is the direct markup percentage formula.[134] In this formula, a contractually agreed overhead percentage is applied to the additional direct costs incurred during the delay period.[135] This method is frequently used in small change orders and small claims when it would not be feasible to attempt to allocate home office overhead to the contract. Moreover, use of the direct percentage markup approach is appropriate only when extra work is involved.[136]

§ 6.16   *—Hudson* Formula

The *Hudson* formula, which is commonly used in Great Britain,[137] is an alternative formula for calculating home office overhead. The formula, which also includes a profit allocation, represents an extension of the established contract home office and attributes a profit percentage to the delay period. The formula is as follows:

$$\frac{\text{Home Office Overhead/Profit Percentage}}{100} \times \frac{\text{Contract Sum}}{\text{Contract Period}} \times \frac{\text{Period of Delay}}{\text{(in weeks)}}$$
$$(\text{e.g., in weeks})$$

As with any other allocation method, the contractor must prove that the underlying cost assumptions are reasonable and realistic before recovery will be allowed.

---

[133] *See* Dawson Constr. Co., GSBCA No. 4956, 79-2 BCA (CCH) ¶ 13,989 (1979); *see also* Kent & Waters, *Recovering Indirect Costs,* 80-6 Construction Briefings (1980).

[134] *See* ACS Constr. Co., ASBCA No. 35,872, 89-1 BCA (CCH) ¶ 21,314 (1988) (payment to appellant for changes resulting from delay included on allowance for home office overhead as a percentage of direct costs).

[135] *Id.*

[136] *See* Note, *Home Office Overhead.*

[137] J.F. Finnegan Ltd. v. Sheffield City Council, 43 Build. L.R. 124 (Q.B. 1989).

§ 6.17 Comparative Calculation of Home Office Overhead

Appendix B contains an example of an extended/unabsorbed home office overhead calculation using both a labor-based allocation and the *Eichleay* formula. This example is based on a calculation of one branch of a multi-branch company. As a result, overhead exists in both the branch and the home office.

CHAPTER 7

JOBSITE OVERHEAD

§ 7.1   Introduction

Most construction contractors have two distinct types of overhead. The first type is home office overhead, which was discussed in **Chapter 6**. The second kind is that which occurs directly on the jobsite. If contract performance is extended, a contractor often continues to incur expense at the jobsite. Like home office overhead, jobsite overhead consists of those items which are required specifically for the project but cannot be reasonably allocated to any specific work item within the project.

§ 7.2   Jobsite Overhead Defined

Normal jobsite overhead, also referred to as general conditions items, includes costs that increase as a result of the passage of time on a project, such as:

1. Project managers
2. Superintendents
3. Secretarial and clerical workers
4. Timekeepers
5. Office trailers
6. Storage trailers
7. Office equipment
8. Office supplies
9. Temporary electricity
10. Temporary water

11. Temporary sewer
12. Telephone costs
13. Sanitary facilities
14. Trucks and automobiles.

All of these costs are time-related and may be recoverable.[1] If an item usually included in jobsite overhead can be clearly segregated, a court or board may list it as a distinct item of damages.[2] Jobsite costs may be recovered only as direct damages on certain federal government projects, although on other federal projects the items allowable are often specified (and hence limited) by the contract documents.[3]

It should be noted that courts and boards sometimes do not separate jobsite overhead from general overhead but apply an accepted percentage markup for all overhead costs to the direct costs established in the claim.[4]

Overhead costs are frequently segregated within the job costing system under headings such as general conditions or field overhead costs. When pricing change orders or added work that does not change contract duration, a reasonable way to calculate the costs of these items is as a percentage of direct cost. The proportion of general conditions costs to all other direct costs in the project can be calculated and the resulting percentage calculation can be applied to the change order. It may be appropriate to calculate the general conditions cost as a percentage of direct project labor costs rather than to allocate. This is because many general conditions costs are affected more by labor than subcontract or material costs. However, this method is unreasonable when significant extensions of time are involved. It is also unreasonable when the nature of a change increases the overhead required.

§ 7.3   Calculation Methods

A change in work method, such as going to shifts or weekend work, could require additional supervision, tools, and equipment. Such a change may well increase general conditions costs far more than the application of the jobsite percentage to the additional cost would indicate. If this is the case, the additional cost should be calculated and included as part of the change even though it is a jobsite overhead or general conditions cost. Other more subtle examples of extra jobsite overhead include the imposition of

---

[1] Lee Elec. Co., FAA CAP No. 67-26, 67-1 BCA (CCH) ¶ 6263 (1967); Hardeman-Monier-Hutcherson, ASBCA No. 11,785, 67-1 BCA (CCH) ¶ 6210 (1967).

[2] *See, e.g.,* Fehlhaber Corp. v. State, 419 N.Y.S.2d 773 (App. Div. 1979).

[3] *See, e.g.,* FAR 31.105.

[4] *See* Blake Constr. Co., GSBCA No. 1176, 66-1 BCA (CCH) ¶ 5589 (1966) (applying the "usual and customary" 10% markup).

additional reporting requirements, additional timekeeping requirements, additional quality control, more complex scheduling methods, and the control and maintenance of revised drawings. Any of these could require additional office supplies and clerical staff at the jobsite. It is common for the general contractor to be required to furnish the owner or its agent with a fully equipped trailer and telephone. These costs can increase with both time and changes in the work.

When additional time is required but there are no significant work method changes, one method frequently used to calculate the additional general conditions costs is to take the actual costs of these items for the project to date and divide the total by the number of days to date. This method has been adopted in many cases.[5] It produces a daily cost for general conditions, which can be multiplied by the additional number of days. An example of this calculation is shown in **Table 7–1**.

The type of calculations shown in **Table 7–1** are appropriate for cases in which the contractor is forced to staff and support the project beyond its anticipated completion date due to owner actions and inactions. The total cost of field overhead in this example is $850,794, which was spent over the course of 1,011 days. This results in a cost per day of $841, compared to the $701 per day originally budgeted.

Because the project continued 509 days past the reasonably anticipated completion date, the contractor is entitled to 509 days times $841 per day or $428,069 for extended field overhead.

During the original contract period, the contractor increased its overhead as a result of actions by the owner, especially in the areas of concrete, inspection, and available work areas. For example, concrete operations lasted eight months longer than originally planned. Needless to say, supervision and support costs for the concrete work increased. The contractor suffered the damages as a result of additional owner-caused overhead costs during the original contract period. In the example in **Table 7–1**, this was $140 per day ($841–701) for 502 days, or $70,280.

Thus, the total additional field overhead to which the contractor is entitled is:

Extended field overhead	$428,069
Additional field overhead during construction period	70,280
Total	$498,349

This method of calculation has the advantage of being based on actual historic costs. However, when field overhead costs vary widely with time, this method of calculation may be inappropriate. If the majority of the job

---

[5] *See* Shirley Contracting Corp., ASBCA No. 29,848, 85-1 BCA (CCH) ¶ 17,858 (1985); Kemmons-Wilson, Inc., ASBCA No. 16,167, 72-2 BCA (CCH) ¶ 9689 (1972).

Table 7-1

Calculating Additional General Conditions Costs

Code	Cost Type	Description	Original Estimate	Cost to Date	Adjustment for Approved Change Orders	Adjusted Total Cost
001040	M	Subsistence	0	4,342		4,342
001150	M	Job Office	3,215	3,550		3,550
001160	M	Engineer Office	2,285	5,181		5,181
001170	M	Tool Shed	3,800	3,750		3,750
001180	M	Chemical Toilets	8,720	8,124		8,124
001190	M	Signs	410	668		668
001204	M	Repairs		106		106
001260	M	Storage of Materials	16,760	16,014		16,014
001290	M	Job Communications	1,920	5,822		5,822
001300	M	Drinking Water	580	612		612
001310	M	Unload & Haul	2,745	19,824		19,824
001315	M	Unload & Haul Equip.	2,410	1,312		1,312
001330	M	Temp Power-Install		8,552		8,552
001350	M	Temp Power-Cords	12,860	7,157		7,157
001360	M	Temp Water-Install	4,900	6,095		6,095
001390	M	Telephone	9,320	12,635		12,635
001410	M	Printing-Supplies	825	624		624
001420	M	Blueprinting	770	896		896
001440	M	Photographs	825	223		223
001450	M	Office Equipment	590	9,324	(1,360)	7,964
001460	M	Arch Office Equip	1,535	2,403		2,403
001470	M	First Aid	825	1,547		1,547
001480	M	Hard Hats	1,030	1,921		1,921
001500	M	Fire Extinguisher	620	1,481		1,481
001520	M	Cleanup-Final	20	2,822		2,822
001590	M	Travel & Entertain		5,087		5,087
001610	M	Move on-off		4,018		4,018
001620	M	Layout	2,100	379		379
001630	M	Layout-Reg. Engineer	200	263		263
001680	M	Portable Generators	830	9,564	(1,600)	7,964
001720	M	Survey Equipment	3,000	6,101		6,101
001740	M	Pickup Trucks	3,730	17,532		17,532
001750	M	Flatbed Trucks	8,580	8,990		8,990
001850	M	Scaffold	3,600	808		808
001860	M	Fuel, Oil & Grease	1,000	71,060		71,060
001870	M	Superintendent	49,525	14,776	(400)	14,376
017800	M	Fringe Benefits		2,022		2,022
01790	X	Liability Insurance		1,045		1,045
		Total Non-Labor Cost	151,810	266,630	(3,360)	263,270
		Total Number Days	502			1,011
		Cost per Day	302			260

Code	Cost Type	Description	Original Budget	Total Actual Cost
001150	L	Job Office	470	316
001160	L	Engineer Office	470	782
001170	L	Tool Shed	160	11
001190	L	Signs	160	189
001260	L	Storage of Materials	6,300	10,054
001300	L	Drinking Water	1,480	91
001310	L	Unload & Haul	6,060	17,678
001490	L	Guard Rails	390	1,202
001510	L	Cleanup-Periodic	2,370	38,292
001520	L	Cleanup-Final	720	36,255
001610	L	Move on-off	1,050	133
001630	L	Layout	3,000	22,851
001860	L	Maintenance	2,000	11,477
001870	L	Superintendent	32,420	163,176
001880	L	Asst. Superintendent	66,016	88,989
001890	L	Field Engineer	14,984	49,690
001910	L	Timekeeper		13,424
		Subtotal	138,050	454,620
010400		Subsistence	51,520	56,018
017600		Payroll Taxes	3,054	38,006
01770		Workers' Comp Ins	3,054	27,532
17800		Fringe Benefits	4,614	11,348
		Total Labor Cost	$200,292	$587,524
		Total Number Days	502	1,011
		Cost per Day	399	581
Total All Cost			$352,102	$850,794
Total Number Days			502	1,011
Total Cost per Day			701	841

March 17, 1982 to July 31, 1983 = 502 days in the original schedule
July 31, 1983 to December 21, 1984 = 509 days overrun due to owner-caused delays.

Total project days				1,011

is completed and additional field overhead costs are significantly less than the historical costs, the calculations may be overstated. Additionally, if field overhead costs include such things as layout, surveying, surety bond, or other items, the daily rate will be distorted upward over the delay period because these expenses were incurred early in the project. Thus, it is important when using this method to analyze each line item of cost and include only those line items applicable to the delay.

Some jobsite general conditions costs that are not readily apparent are also affected by delay. One example is warranty costs. Virtually all projects, no matter how well constructed, have some warranty costs. Extending the duration of the project when part of the project is already complete will, in all likelihood, increase warranty costs because a greater period will pass before the warranty starts. Although calculating such costs can be difficult, and often can be only approximated, it is appropriate to include warranty costs as an additional cost of delay and of change orders.

If a project is delayed to the extent that it is demobilized and then later remobilized, it is appropriate to include both demobilization and remobilization costs as part of the extended general conditions cost. When there is an extended delay, a decision to cease work is both reasonable and prudent. When the job is clearly going to be delayed for an extended period, the contractor may have a duty to demobilize in order to mitigate damages. The best method of calculating demobilization and remobilization costs is to use the actual costs incurred; such costs change depending upon how the demobilization and remobilization occurred.

When part of the contractor's responsibilities include maintenance of temporary roads at the site or the maintenance of open excavation or trenches, these costs can be significantly affected by delay. Although the dirt roads on a site may not seem to require much maintenance, in fact maintenance costs can be significant. In drier climates, maintenance may include watering the roads daily, which quickly becomes expensive for the contractor.

If the delay extends into seasons with different weather conditions than those during which the work was originally intended to be performed, work that is weather-dependent can be significantly affected. Extensive increases in general conditions costs may be related to such a shift in season. A common example is the moving of concrete work from late summer or fall into winter. Such a move may result in significant added costs to temporarily enclose, cover, and heat the work area. These costs are significant although frequently less than the project owner's cost to shut the project down and restart when weather conditions improve. Such costs are properly included as part of the cost of the delay.

For example, due to the actions and inactions of the owner, a project was delayed and continued through an unexpected period of winter conditions. The extreme conditions forced the contractor to provide material and labor

Table 7–2

Additional Winter Conditions Costs

Code	Cost Type	Description	Original Budget	Cost to Date	Change Order Adjustment	Add. Cost
001320	L	Winter Conditions	6,380	38,676	(11,000)	21,296
001380	L	Temp Heat	1,090	5,212		4,122
			7,470	43,888		28,418
		Subsistence	0	0		
017600	L	Payroll Taxes	165	3,913		3,748
017700	L	Workers' Comp.	165	2,754		2,588
017800	L	Union Fringe Benefits	250	812		563
		Total Labor	8,050	51,367		35,317
001320	M	Winter Conditions	2,615	11,245		8,630
001380	M	Temp Heat	9,410	19,833	(10,423)	
		Total	12,025	31,078	(11,000)	19,053
		Total Cost	$20,075	$82,445	($11,000)	$51,370

Total added cost for winter conditions and temporary heat is $51,370.

Source: Work in Process Reports, Owner Change Order #2.

for temporary heat, snow and ice removal, and temporary enclosures. Sample calculations for the cost of such a delay are shown in **Table 7–2**.

To avoid claiming the same amount twice, the claim preparer should be careful not to include jobsite cost items in the home office overhead claim amount.[6]

Overhead calculations are often scrutinized by courts and auditors to insure that the charges are not duplicated in other items in the claim and that these items have not been compensated through change orders.[7] In addition, most courts require factual proof that jobsite overhead costs in fact increased due to the circumstances claimed.[8]

---

[6] Two State Constr. Co., DOT CAB Nos. 78-31, 1006, 1070, 1081, 81-1 BCA (CCH) ¶ 15,149 (1981); Kenyon Magnetics, Inc., GSBCA No. 5263, 80-2 BCA (CCH) ¶ 14,624 (1980).

[7] *See* J.D. Hedin Constr. Co. v. United States, 347 F.2d 235 (Ct. Cl. 1965).

[8] *See* Paccon, Inc., ASBCA No. 7890, 65-2 BCA (CCH) ¶ 4996 (1965); A.A. Baxter Corp. v. Colt Indus., Inc., 10 Cal. App. 2d 144 (1970).

CHAPTER 8

PROFIT

§ 8.1 Introduction

Profit is a contractor's incentive to perform work, the lifeblood that sustains a contractor's business. Except in unusual circumstances, owners cannot expect contractors to perform additional work without additional profit. Accordingly, profit is a well-recognized although often disputed element of construction claims.[1]

Claims for profit are usually divided into three categories: profit on work performed, profit on work not performed, and lost profits or lost business revenue. Profit on additional work performed is fairly easy to establish and calculate. Profit for unperformed work and lost business revenues is often difficult to prove, calculate, and recover, however.

Profit on federal government contracts is governed by the Federal Acquisition Regulations (FAR). The FAR provides criteria to determine what amount of profit would compensate a contractor fairly for work performed. The FAR also governs the recoverability of profit when contracts are terminated for the convenience of the government. Regardless of whether the contract is public or private, profit should not be overlooked in calculating damages in construction claims.

---

[1] Bennett v. United States, 371 F.2d 859 (Ct. Cl. 1967); J&T Constr. Co., DOT CAB No. 73-4, 75-2 BCA (CCH) ¶ 11,398 (1975); Lester N. Johnson Co. v. City of Spokane, 588 P.2d 1214 (Wash. Ct. App. 1978); Metropolitan Sewage Comm'n v. R.W. Constr., Inc., 255 N.W.2d 293, 301 (Wis. 1977).

§ 8.2 Profit Defined

A contractor's profit is usually a percentage of the cost of material, direct labor, equipment, and subcontracts. Profit may be divided into two categories: gross profit and net profit. Generally speaking, gross profit is the difference between the cost of performing the work and the total contract revenues received. Gross profit margins can vary widely between contractors and projects because contractors may include different cost items in their overhead. Gross profit margins are often inaccurate reflections of a contractor's rate of return, and in most cases contractors are entitled to recover net profits rather than gross profits.

Net profit is profit earned after the application of overhead costs but before the application of state and federal taxes. In most cases, the net profit margin more accurately reflects the recoverable profit percentage in construction claims. For example, gross profits should not be claimed concurrently with extended overhead costs if some costs are charged against the contractor's gross profit as well as in the contractor's overhead. Therefore, the net profit margin is more appropriate when extended overhead is claimed because use of net profits prevents double recovery for overhead expenses.

§ 8.3 Profit on Work Performed

It is well-recognized that contractors may recover profit on additional or extra work performed.[2] To deny a contractor profit on the performance of additional work would confer a benefit on the owner to the detriment of the contractor.[3] Without the recovery of profit on additional work, the contractor would not be made whole.[4]

Various situations may give rise to claims for additional profit. Profit may be recovered on additional work resulting from owner-directed changes.[5] An example is found in *Bennett v. United States*.[6] In that case, the contractor was awarded a contract for construction of a levee on the Missouri

---

[2] United States v. Callahan Walker Constr. Co., 317 U.S. 56 (1942); General Builders Supply Co. v. United States, 409 F.2d 246 (Ct. Cl. 1969); New York Shipbuilding Co., ASBCA No. 16,164, 76-2 BCA (CCH) ¶ 11,979 (1976); Melvin Grossmann v. Sea Air Towers, Ltd., 513 So. 2d 686 (Fla. Dist. Ct. App. 1987); Lester N. Johnson Co. v. City of Spokane, 588 P.2d 1214 (Wash. Ct. App. 1978); Metropolitan Sewage Comm'n v. R.W. Constr., 255 N.W.2d 293, 301 (Wis. 1977).

[3] New York Shipbuilding Co., ASBCA No. 16,164, 76-2 BCA (CCH) ¶ 11,979 (1976).

[4] *Id.* at p. 57,427.

[5] Bennett v. United States, 371 F.2d 859 (Ct. Cl. 1967).

[6] *Id.*

River.[7] The contractor sought additional compensation for removal of 105,870 cubic yards of earth that the contractor asserted was not required by the plans and specifications.[8] The Engineering Board of Contract Appeals initially denied the contractor's claim for additional compensation.[9]

In a de novo proceeding, the United States Claims Court permitted the contractor to recover its costs and a 6 percent profit for the additional excavation work.[10] Specifically, the court stated:

> The key is always to put the contractor in as good a position as he would have been but for the defendant's wrongful action. In this case, that point cannot be achieved if the profit to be allowed is to be limited to the contract price alone. Accordingly, it is our judgement that the allowance of a 6 percent profit on the additional work will provide plaintiff with a reasonably just return.[11]

Courts and boards permit the recovery of additional profit when differing site conditions require the performance of work that was not originally anticipated.[12] For example, in *J&T Construction Co.,*[13] the contractor entered into a contract with the Federal Highway Administration Bureau of Public Roads for the improvement of a section of the Oregon Forest Highway.[14] The contractor sought an equitable adjustment of $169,738.93 for increased costs incurred as a result of differing site conditions, namely halloysite clay and boulders.[15] On appeal, the Department of Transportation Contract Appeals Board permitted the contractor to recover its costs and a 10 percent profit thereon.[16] The Board stated that "courts and boards have held consistently that the inclusion of a percentage for profit is an appropriate element for consideration where the government exacts a measure of performance for which the contract did not call for."[17]

In addition to profit on additional work, courts and boards have permitted contractors to recover profit on the cost of additional materials supplied. For example, in *Carvel Walker,*[18] the Corps of Engineers Board of

---

[7] *Id.* at 860.

[8] *Id.*

[9] Bennett v. United States, 371 F.2d 859, 861 (Ct. Cl. 1967).

[10] *Id.* at 864.

[11] *Id.*

[12] J&T Constr. Co., DOT CAB No. 73-4, 75-2 BCA (CCH) ¶ 11,398 (1975).

[13] *Id.*

[14] *Id.* at p. 54,249.

[15] *Id.* at 54,248.

[16] *Id.* at 54,271.

[17] *Id.*

[18] ENGBCA No. 3744, 78-1 BCA (CCH) ¶ 13,005 (1977).

Contract Appeals permitted an asphalt contractor to recover a 12 percent profit on additional asphalt seal coating which was not required by the contract.[19]

Generally, profit may not be recovered when a contractor is simply delayed in the performance of its work.[20] The rationale for denying profit in cases of delay is that the contractor has not performed additional or extra work for which it should profit. An example of this reasoning is aptly illustrated by the United States Court of Claims in *Laburnum Construction Corp. v. United States,*[21] wherein the court denied a contractor's claim for profit on costs incurred during a period of government-caused delay.[22] The court stated that the profit sought simply represented profit on the delay damages incurred by the contractor and that the contractor was not deprived of anticipated profits as a result of the delay. As discussed in §§ **8.6** and **8.7**, recovery of profit is often difficult if the contractor has not actually performed additional or extra work.

§ 8.4   Determining Profit Percentages on Work Performed

Profit on additional work is an easy item to calculate in construction claims because the additional costs incurred are simply marked up or multiplied by a figure which represents the profit percentage. The difficulty lies in determining the appropriate profit percentage by which to mark up the costs of performing the additional work. Numerous methods or factors may be used to arrive at the appropriate profit percentage on the cost of performing additional work. On all contracts and claims, however, the profit percentage should be fair and reasonable under the circumstances of the project.[23]

Often, the contract may specify the profit percentage. For example, on United States Postal Service contracts, 10 percent is the maximum profit percentage allowed on claims for equitable adjustments.[24] The Federal Highway Administration limits profit to 15 percent of the cost of labor and materials on all contracts it administers.[25] Although these profit ceilings

---

[19] *Id.* at p. 63,442.

[20] Chaney & James Constr. Co. v. United States, 421 F.2d 728 (Ct. Cl. 1970); Laburnum Constr. Corp. v. United States, 325 F.2d 451 (Ct. Cl. 1963).

[21] 325 F.2d 451 (Ct. Cl. 1963).

[22] *Id.* at 459.

[23] Keco Indus., Inc., ASBCA No. 18,730, 74-2 BCA (CCH) ¶ 10,711 (1974); New York Shipbuilding Co., ASBCA No. 16,164, 76-2 BCA (CCH) ¶ 11,979 (1976).

[24] Ginsburg, Wilkinson & English, *Profit on U.S. Construction Contracts,* 86-11 Construction Briefings (1986).

[25] *Id.*

have been challenged as being in conflict with the FAR's changes clause, such challenges on the whole have not been successful.[26] Generally speaking, a 10 percent profit percentage has been accepted by courts and boards.[27]

Contractually specified profit percentages are often applied to minor changes as well as to major claims. Such application is frequently inappropriate because contractually specified profit percentages are usually intended to be applied only to small changes rather than to major claims. There is no direct bar to the use of predetermined profit percentage levels on major claims, however.

In absence of a contractually specified profit percentage, courts and boards may consider various factors in determining the applicable profit margin. The profit margin may be adjusted to reflect any increase in risk or difficulty incurred in performing additional work.[28] Other factors may also be considered in arriving at the appropriate profit percentage to be applied to changed or additional work.

Industry studies on profit margins provide a useful reference for determining appropriate profit margins.[29] For example, the National Electrical Contractors Association (NECA) publishes an annual survey of its members listing profit margins by region and volume of the contractor. Similar studies are published by the Construction Financial Management Association (CFMA). The CFMA Reports may be less useful to specialty contractors because all specialties are lumped together in one category. CFMA Reports are most useful to general or heavy contractors and are recognized as the most comprehensive survey on construction profitability.

Profit percentage rates may also be determined by reference to the contractor's historical profit margin. Historical profit margins should be readily ascertainable from the contractor's financial records and other financial data. A contractor's historical profit margin may not be useful if the claimed project constituted a major portion of the contractor's revenues for the previous several years, however. If this is the case, the contractor's historical profit margin must exclude the claimed project in order to arrive at a true historical average. As discussed in § 8.7, historical averages may also be inaccurate if the contractor performed several lines of work in addition to construction.

---

[26] *See* E.E. Steinlicht, IBCA No. 834-4-70, 71-1 BCA (CCH) ¶ 8767 (1971); Gulf-Tex Constr., Inc., VACAB Nos. 1341, 1342, 83-1 BCA (CCH) ¶ 16,355 (1983). *Cf.* Lecher Constr. Co., B-224357, 86-2 CPD ¶ 369 (1986) (except for statutory ceilings on profits, agencies may not create administrative ceilings); Ginsburg, Wilkinson & English, *Profit on U.S. Construction Contracts,* 86-11 Construction Briefings (1986).

[27] Walber Constr. Co., HUDBCA No. 79-385-C17, 81-1 BCA (CCH) ¶ 14,953 (1981); Carvel Walker, ENGBCA No. 3744, 78-1 BCA (CCH) ¶ 13,005 (1977).

[28] American Pipe & Steel Corp., ASBCA No. 7899, 1964 BCA (CCH) ¶ 4058 (1964).

[29] For example, Robert Morris Associates publishes extensive data on profit. Such information can usually be obtained through banks, sureties, or other financial institutions.

The profit margin used by the contractor in its original bid is also useful to determine the profit margin to be applied to changed work. In doing so, however, the bid must be thoroughly examined for errors, mistakes, or inaccuracies. Discrepancies due to mistakes in the bid may detract from the validity of the claim.

In negotiated federal defense contracts, however, the FAR provides guidelines to determine a contractor's profit margin.[30] In arriving at the profit percentage under the FAR, the contracting officer must consider the contractor's effort, the loss risk, the contractor's participation in federal socioeconomic programs, the contractor's capital investment, and any independent development initiative shown by the contractor.[31]

Basically, contractors are entitled to recover a fair and reasonable profit on the cost of additional work performed. Even if the contractor bid the job at no profit, a reasonable profit may be recovered for additional work performed under the contract.[32]

§ 8.5   Profit on Work Performed Prior to Termination

On private contracts, recovery of profit on work completed as of the date of contract termination is an open question. Under Article 14 of AIA Document A201, a contractor is entitled to recover loss with respect to materials, equipment, tools, construction equipment, and machinery, including reasonable profit and damages, if the contractor terminates the contract for one of the grounds provided for in that section.[33] This clause appears to allow for the recovery of profit for work completed as of the date of termination without defining profit or how it is to be proven. The contractor may recover additional profit on any increased costs of performance under AIA Document A201 if the owner suspends the contractor's work.[34] The AIA contract does not explicitly provide for the recovery of profit on work completed as of the date of termination when the owner terminates the contract, however. Other private contracts often expressly deny profit on work performed to date in the event of a termination.

On federal government contracts, the FAR governs the recoverability of profit when the contract is terminated for the convenience of the government. If terminated for convenience, a contractor may recover profit on

---

[30] 48 C.F.R. § 15.905.1 (1990).

[31] *Id.*

[32] Keco Indus., Inc., ASBCA Nos. 15,184, 15,547, 72-2 BCA (CCH) ¶ 9576 (1972).

[33] American Institute of Architects Document A201, General Conditions of the Contract for Construction (1987).

[34] *Id.*

work completed as of the date of termination.[35] Although any reasonable method may be used to arrive at the amount of profit recoverable, the FAR lists various factors to be considered in arriving at the appropriate profit percentage rate. Specifically, the criteria enumerated in the FAR are as follows:

1) Extent and difficulty of the work done by the contractor as compared with the total work required by the contract (engineering estimates of the percentage of completion ordinarily should not be required, but if available should be considered);

2) Engineering work, production scheduling, planning, technical study and supervision, and other necessary services;

3) Efficiency of the contractor, with particular regard to-

    i)   Attainment of quantity and quality production;

    ii) Reduction of costs;

    iii) Economic use of materials, facilities, and manpower; and

    iv) Disposition of termination inventory;

4) Amount and source of capital and extent of risk assumed;

5) Inventive and developmental contributions, and cooperation with the Government and other contractors in supplying technical assistance;

6) Character of the business, including the source and nature of materials and the complexity of manufacturing techniques;

7) The rate of profit that the contractor would have earned had the contract been completed;

8) The rate of profit both parties contemplated at the time the contract was negotiated; and

9) Character and difficulty of subcontracting, including selection, placement, and management of subcontracts, and effort in negotiating settlements of terminated subcontracts.[36]

If it can be established that the contractor would have lost money on the entire contract, the contractor will not be able to recover profit on the work completed.[37] Recovery of profit is denied in these situations because it is believed that the contractor would not have profited had it completed the work and it should not profit simply because it did not complete the work. This is often the subject of dispute because contractors often operate at a loss during the early phases of a contract due to learning curves and various cost allocations.

---

[35] 48 C.F.R. § 49.202 (1990).

[36] 49 C.F.R. § 202 (1990).

[37] 48 C.F.R. § 52.249-2 (1990).

§ 8.6   Profit on Unperformed Work

Claims for lost profit for work that was not performed usually arise when the contract has been breached. In cases of breach, the contractor has been deprived of the benefit of its bargain because it has been prevented from performing the work and obtaining the profit which it had anticipated. Profit in these cases is regarded as an element of damages, and the common law principles of contract law apply.[38] Often, contractors are denied profit on work not performed because such profits are considered too remote and speculative.[39] To date, profit has not been awarded as an element of damage on federal government contracts.[40]

Profit on unperformed work may be recovered when the contractor can establish that 1) it is reasonably certain that it would have profited but for the breach of contract, 2) the lost profit can be measured with reasonable certainty, and 3) the profits sought were reasonably within the contemplation of the parties when the contract was made.[41] The above elements were aptly summarized over 100 years ago by the United States Supreme Court in *United States v. Behan,*[42] wherein the Court denied a contractor lost profits on a contract that was wrongfully terminated by the government. The Court stated:

> Profits cannot always be recovered. They may be too remote and speculative in their character, and, therefore incapable of that clear and direct proof which the law requires. But when . . . they are 'direct and immediate fruits of the contract', they are free from this objection; they are then part and parcel of the contract [and are therefore recoverable]. (citations omitted)[43]

§ 8.7   Measuring Profit on Unperformed Work

Traditionally, the amount of profit recoverable for work that has not been performed is the difference between the actual cost of doing the work and the amount that the contractor would have been paid for the work.[44] Initial estimates for performing the work and the anticipated rate of return on the

---

[38] McGrath & Co., ASBCA No. 1949, 58-1 BCA (CCH) ¶ 1599 (1958); Ginsburg, Wilkinson & English, *Profit on U.S. Construction Contracts,* 86-11 Construction Briefings (1986).

[39] United States v. Behan, 110 U.S. 338 (1884).

[40] Savoy Constr. Co. v. United States, 2 Cl. Ct. 338 (1983); Ginsburg, Wilkinson & English, *Profit on U.S. Construction Contracts,* 86-11 Construction Briefings (1986).

[41] Burnett & Dody Dev. Co. v. Phillips, 84 Cal. App. 3d 384, 148 Cal. Rptr. 569 (Ct. App. 1978); Gouger & Veno, Inc. v. Diamondhead Corp., 224 S.E.2d 278 (N.C. Ct. App. 1976).

[42] 110 U.S. 338 (1884).

[43] *Id.* at 344.

[44] United States v. Behan, 110 U.S. 338 (1884).

work must be verified to further support the validity of the profit the contractor would have received but for the breach. As discussed in § **8.4**, historical return averages may be used to attest to the validity of a contractor's rate of return.

Historical rates of return should be carefully examined to ascertain if the claimed project is similar to the projects upon which the historical rate of return is based. If the claimed project has a much higher percentage of labor than previous projects performed by the contractor, the historical profit margin may be low compared to the profit margin on the claimed project. Also, if the contractor works in varied fields such as construction management or material supply, its historical profit margin may be distorted because of the traditionally low profit margins in those fields.

Some courts have permitted contractors to recover lost profits based on the contractor's expected gross profits rather than the contractor's expected net profits.[45] Lost profits have also been measured as the difference between contract price and the total labor and material costs which would have been incurred, regardless of the profit percentage.[46]

§ 8.8 Lost Business Revenues

In certain cases, recovery of actual costs plus profit may not be sufficient to fully reimburse the contractor for the breach of contract and make the contractor whole. For example, a contractor who works primarily in the public sector may have its bonding capacity diminished as a result of a pending or threatened claim.[47] Diminished bonding capacity could result in an immediate cessation of business and the recovery of the claimed costs and profit thereon years later would not adequately compensate the contractor for the losses actually incurred. These claims are often referred to as claims for lost revenue or claims for "lost market."

To recover for lost business revenue resulting from lost bonding capacity, a contractor must establish that 1) the contractor's ability to bid for public jobs was restricted as a result of lost bonding capacity, 2) the contractor had work upon which to bid, and 3) it was likely that the contractor would have been awarded one or more of the contracts for which it could have bid. Below is an example calculation of lost business revenues due to lost bonding capacity of a hypothetical contractor.

For purposes of illustration, assume that a contractor performs only fixed-price, bonded work for municipalities. Some municipalities require

---

[45] Covington Bros. v. Valley Plastering, Inc., 566 P.2d 814 (Nev. 1977).

[46] Magnolia Constr. Co. v. Causey, 421 So. 2d 990 (La. Ct. App. 1982), *writ denied*, 426 So. 2d 177 (La. 1983).

[47] **Ch. 5** discusses more fully the recovery of bond and insurance costs in construction claims.

surety bonds from bonding companies on the United States Treasury list while other municipalities require bonds from sureties licensed within that state. As a result of a large claim on a major project, the contractor lost its bonding capacity in mid-August. After a two-month delay the contractor was able to obtain bonding from a surety not listed with the Treasury. Six months later the claim was settled and the contractor again obtained bonding from a Treasury-listed surety. Approximately two-thirds of the contractor's historic business came from municipalities requiring Treasury-listed surety bonds, however. The contractor's adjusted revenue for the previous year was $5,960,336 and adjusted net profit was $587,986, the profit margin was 9.86 percent and average monthly revenue was $496,694. Because the contractor lost all business for two months and 68 percent of its business for six months, lost profit due to lost bonding capacity would be calculated as follows:

Lost profit for mid-August to mid-October:
$496,694 × 2months × 9.86% = $ 97,948

Lost profit mid-October to mid-April:
$496,694 × 6 months × 68% × 9.86% =   199,814

Total lost market profit $297,762

State courts have permitted contractors to recover damages for lost bonding capacity.[48] Recovery of damages for lost bonding capacity has been denied on federal government contracts, however.[49]

---

[48] *See* Tempo Inc. v. Rapid Elec. Sales & Serv., Inc., 347 N.W.2d 728 (Mich. Ct. App. 1984); Laas v. Montana State Highway Comm'n, 187 Mont. 121, 483 P.2d 699 (1971).

[49] C.F.I. Constr. Co., DOT CAB Nos. 1782, 1801, 87-1 BCA (CCH) ¶ 19,547 (1987); Clark v. Hirt, IBCA No. 1508-8-81, 84-1 BCA (CCH) ¶ 17,134 (1984).

CHAPTER 9

INTEREST

§ 9.1   Introduction

In protracted claim disputes, interest or financing costs to the contractor can be substantial. Most changes and disputes clauses in major construction contracts require the contractor to proceed with additional work even though a final price for the change has not been resolved. The result is that the contractor must commit its cash to perform the disputed work. Increased costs result when a contractor either directly finances additional work with debt or equity capital or keeps current with general operating expenses during the performance of the extra work by additional borrowing. The rules concerning recovery of interest as a cost of performance are circumscribed even though it is a real and significant expense.

§ 9.2   Borrowed Funds as a Cost of Performance

Interest on borrowed funds as a cost of performance is not an allowable cost under present federal contracts.[1] The Federal Cost Principles do not allow interest on the following: interest on borrowing (however presented), bond discounts, costs of financing and refinancing capital (net worth plus long-term liabilities), legal and professional fees paid in connection with the preparation of prospectuses, costs of preparation and issuance of stock rights, and costs related thereto.[2] As a result, interest on borrowed funds cannot be recovered on federal construction projects.[3]

In federal contracts not subject to the Federal Cost Principles,[4] some contractors were allowed to recover interest on actual borrowings.[5] However, the contractors had to prove that the interest costs were attributable to the performance of the changed work.[6] In a recent case, the Postal Service Board of Contract Appeals determined that the Federal Cost Principles were merely a guideline and awarded interest costs incurred solely to finance delays and changes.[7]

The boards of contract appeals have allowed the recovery of "imputed" interest by the contractor for the use of their own equity capital, rather than debt capital, in financing changed work. However, the court of claims has since ruled that the allowance of "imputed" interest would violate 28 U.S.C. § 2516(a). These decisions are discussed in § 9.3.

Recovery of the cost of money prior to judgment is considered to be generally covered by prejudgment interest statutes. However, one court

---

[1] FAR 31.205-20. FAR 31.000–31.703 contains the Federal Cost Principles, formerly the Contract Cost Principles and Procedures. They describe the procedures for (1) the pricing of contracts, subcontracts, and modifications to contracts and subcontracts whenever a cost analysis is performed; and (2) the negotiation, allowance, or determination when required by a contract.

[2] *Id.;* FAR 31.105(a) (expressly applicable to all construction contract modifications; applicable to military contracts, effective 1970, and applicable to civilian contracts, effective 1972).

[3] Erickson Air Crane Co., EBCA Nos. 50-6-79, 52-7-79, 85-7-79, 83-1 BCA (CCH) ¶ 16,145 (1982); Mecon Co., ASBCA No. 22,813, 78-2 BCA (CCH) ¶ 13,542 (1978); J.W. Bateson Co., ASBCA No. 22,337, 78-2 BCA (CCH) ¶ 13,523, *aff'd,* 79-1 BCA (CCH) ¶ 13,658 (1978).

[4] FAR 31.105(a) (expressly applicable to all construction contract modifications; applicable to military contracts effective in 1970 and applicable to civilian contracts effective in 1972).

[5] Bell v. United States, 404 F.2d 975 (Ct. Cl. 1978).

[6] *Id. See also* Keco Indus., Inc., ASBCA No. 15,131, 72-1 BCA (CCH) ¶ 9262 (1971); Sun Elec. Corp., ASBCA No. 13,031, 70-2 BCA (CCH) ¶ 8371 (1970).

[7] Automation Fabricators & Eng'g Co., PSBCA No. 2701, 90-3 BCA (CCH) ¶ 22,943 (1990).

determined that the cost of borrowed capital may be recovered in lieu of statutory interest if it can be proven that the borrowed funds were "primarily" used to finance the extra work.[8]

In another case, the court found that if the contractor prevails on the issue of entitlement in any of its multiple claims, the contractor is entitled to recover interest from the date of the change until the date of payment by the owner.[9] The court reasoned that the interest rates on borrowing represented a fair and reasonable approximation of the cost of money to the contractor attributable to the project.[10] In this case, the federal pricing of adjustments clause was "conspicuously" absent from the contract, thereby rendering the cost principles of the federal procurement regulations (FPRs) inapplicable. Furthermore, the court recognized that the contractor may be entitled to compounding of its interest costs as just compensation for the change. In its decision, the Board stated:

> The Armed Services Board of Contract Appeals in New York Shipbuilding Co., ASBCA No. 16164, 76-2 BCA ¶ 11,979 page 57,449, analyzed a somewhat similar problem and in that opinion decided that annual compounding was reasonable and just. One factor it considered was the conservative (low) rates used by the parties. It is possible that Rohr really paid the banks fees that equate with interest that is compounded more frequently than annually, and the parties could justifiably negotiate a settlement based on the actual compounding paid by Rohr. In this appeal Rohr chose to present its amended claim by compounding interest only annually. We conclude based on this record, that, if an equitable adjustment is due, compounding annually would result in a fair and reasonable approximation of the added cost to Rohr caused by the HVAC change.[11]

Another court, however, rejected a plaintiff's claim for interest because the plaintiff failed to show it would have not taken out the loans but for defendant's actions.[12]

§ 9.3   Imputed Interest

As discussed above, interest on borrowings as a cost of performance have been allowed by the courts and the boards of contract appeals. In addition,

---

[8] Havens Steel Co. v. Randolph Eng'g Co., 613 F. Supp. 514 (W.D. Mo. 1985).

[9] Rohr Indus., ENGBCA No. 4306, 83-1 BCA (CCH) ¶ 16,299 (1983).

[10] Id.

[11] Id. at p. 81,000.

[12] Seattle W. Indus., Inc. v. David A. Mowat Co., 750 P.2d 245 (Wash. 1988).

contractors have been allowed to recover "imputed" interest.[13] *Imputed interest* is equitable compensation for the financing of changed or delayed work using the contractor's own equity capital. The Armed Services Board of Contract Appeals recognized that the concept of "equitable adjustment" under the changes clause demanded that a contractor be fairly compensated for the use of private capital for changed work, regardless of whether the private capital was borrowed funds or equity capital. Accordingly, the contractor was allowed to recover imputed interest to compensate it for the use of its equity capital.[14]

Interest for the use of equity capital in this case was allowed as an element of profit rather than a cost of performance; nevertheless, the amount of recovery was determined according to the usual interest factors such as principal, type and rate of interest, and the period during which interest is calculated.[15] Subsequent decisions have also allowed imputed interest as an element of profit.[16] For example, when a contractor attempted but failed to prove that it specifically borrowed funds to finance changed work and thus should be entitled to recover interest as a cost of performance, it was still entitled to recover interest as an element of profit because the facts of the case were plain that the contractor had invested its equity or borrowed capital to finance the changed work.[17]

Although the federal boards have allowed contractors to recover imputed interest for the use of equity capital, the court of claims has refused to follow suit.[18] However, the court has considered the cost to contractors of using their own capital. In *Dravo Corp. v. United States,*[19] the court stated:

> Admittedly, plaintiff's contention has certain appeal. With a high rate of inflation, it is unrealistic to think that a delay in payment by the Government does not adversely affect plaintiff's financial situation, even in the absence of specific borrowings. The mere use of plaintiff's money for the changed work, without immediate reimbursement, clearly costs the plaintiff something. Moreover, to deny recovery is perhaps to draw an artificial distinction between smaller companies, with simple internal financing arrangements and which are entirely debt capitalized, and larger companies, with more complex financial organization which may employ equity as

---

[13] New York Shipbuilding Co., ASBCA No. 16,164, 76-2 BCA (CCH) ¶ 11,979 (1976).

[14] *Id.*

[15] *Id.*

[16] Fischbach & Moore Int'l Corp., ASBCA No. 18,146, 77-1 BCA (CCH) ¶ 12,300 (1976); *see also* Ingalls Shipbuilding Div., ASBCA No. 17,579, 78-1 BCA (CCH) ¶ 13,038, *motion for reconsideration denied,* 78-1 BCA (CCH) ¶ 13,216 (1978).

[17] *Id.*

[18] Framlau Corp. v. United States, 568 F.2d 687 (Ct. Cl. 1977).

[19] 594 F.2d 842 (Ct. Cl. 1979).

well as debt capital. The latter would be hard put to establish the stringent requirements for an interest claim on a debt capital theory, as plaintiff has failed to do here.[20]

Nevertheless, the court followed an earlier decision[21] and refused to adopt the equity capital theory because "the cost to the contractor of borrowing capital is clearly determinable while the value to him of the use of equity capital is not so readily ascertainable."[22]

It should be noted that these federal cases concerning borrowed funds and equity capital involved contracts which predate the mandatory application of the Federal Cost Principles contained in current regulations.[23] As stated previously, the allowance of interest on borrowed funds is now precluded by these regulations, and the allowance of interest on equity capital is now precluded by federal statute[24] as a result of *Dravo Corp. v. United States.*[25] Departing from its earlier decisions, the Armed Services Board of Contract Appeals has followed the court of claims' ruling in *Dravo Corp.* and has refused to allow interest on the use of equity capital.[26]

Notwithstanding the present bar against the recovery of imputed interest as profit, the Federal Cost Principles allow an imputed cost for interest on "facilities capital employed in contract performance . . . without regard to whether its source is equity or borrowed."[27]

§ 9.4   Interest on the Claim

On nonfederal projects, interest may be allowed to compensate a contractor for borrowing funds or using its own equity capital. In these circumstances interest is actually a part of the contractor's direct cost claim. Interest accrues from the time the contractor borrowed funds or invested its own capital. Therefore, the contractor should request interest as a cost or profit when it presents its claim. If interest accrues on a claim presented by a contractor, the contractor would seek to recover interest from the time payment is due.

---

[20] *Id.*

[21] Framlau Corp. v. United States, 568 F.2d 687 (Ct. Cl. 1977).

[22] *Id.; see also* Gevyn Constr. Corp. v. United States, 827 F.2d 752 (Fed. Cir. 1987).

[23] DAR 15-205.17 and FPR 1-15.205-17.

[24] 28 U.S.C. § 2516(a) (1965).

[25] 594 F.2d 842 (Ct. Cl. 1979).

[26] Owen L. Schwam Constr. Co., ASBCA No. 22,407, 79-2 BCA (CCH) ¶ 13,919 (1979).

[27] FAR 31.205-10.

§ 9.5 —Interest on the Claim in Federal Contracts

For contracts entered into after March 1, 1979, § 12 of the Contract Disputes Act[28] allows the recovery of interest on claims from the date the contracting officer receives the claim until the contractor receives payment. The Act also allows contractors with pre-March 1, 1979 contracts to elect to proceed under the Act with respect to any claim then pending before the contracting officer or initiated after March 1, 1979.[29] If the contractor makes such an election, then the payment of interest on contractors' claims clause is vacated and the Contract Disputes Act is controlling.[30] Section 12 of the Contract Disputes Act[31] provides:

> Interest on amounts found due contractors on claims shall be paid to the contractor from the date the contracting officer receives the claim pursuant to section 605(a) of this title from the contractor until payment thereof. The interest provided for in this section shall be paid at the rate established by the Secretary of the Treasury pursuant to Public Law 92-41 (85 Stat. 97) for the Renegotiation Board.[32]

If the contractor elects to proceed under the Act, it is not necessarily clear when the interest begins to accrue. In one case, the court of claims held that the contractor could recover interest earlier than the date of its election to proceed under the Act but no earlier than the effective date of the Act even though the claim was presented prior to March 1, 1979.[33]

In cases involving contractor elections to proceed under the Act, interest will not be allowed if there was no underlying claim or dispute "pending then" before the contracting officer on March 1, 1979.[34] In *Brookfield Construction Co. v. United States,*[35] the court of claims found that a claim was still pending before the contracting officer although the parties had reached only an oral settlement prior to March 1, 1979 and there was not yet a written agreement or final decision.[36] In another case, the board ruled in the contractor's favor in 1977 and 1978 concerning entitlement and

---

[28] 41 U.S.C. § 611 (1987).

[29] *Id.*

[30] Arlington Elec. Constr. Co., ENGBCA No. 4440, 81-1 BCA (CCH) ¶ 15,073 (1981).

[31] 41 U.S.C. § 611 (1987).

[32] *Id.*

[33] Brookfield Constr. Co. v. United States, 661 F.2d 159 (Ct. Cl. 1981) (the contractor was entitled to recover interest from March 1, 1979 until Dec. 13, 1979, the date of payment of its claim).

[34] Monaco Enters., Inc., ASBCA No. 24,110, 80-1 BCA (CCH) ¶ 14,282 (1980).

[35] 661 F.2d 159 (Ct. Cl. 1981); *see also* Federal Elec. Corp., ASBCA No. 24,002, 82-2 BCA (CCH) ¶ 15,862 (1982).

[36] *Id.*

remanded the claims to the contracting officer for negotiation of quantum.[37] In an appeal, the court held that the quantum claims were pending before the board, and not the contracting officer, on March 1, 1979, because the contracting officer was the board's representative when negotiating quantum. Interest was not allowed because there was no underlying quantum claim governed by the Act.[38]

§ 9.6 —Claim Certification

A contractor will not be allowed to recover interest on its claim until it has been properly certified.[39] In one case,[40] the United States Claims Court ruled that a claim was not properly certified because the plaintiff failed to establish that the project manager who certified the claim was authorized to do so.[41] Other cases have recognized that the project manager has the authority to certify a claim.[42]

Several board cases have held that a project manager has the requisite authority to certify claims. In *Dawson Construction Co.,*[43] the board determined that an individual functioning either as the official in charge of the location or as a corporate officer could certify a claim. The board reasoned that because the project manager's functions included preparation of change orders and assistance in solving onsite disputes, he was deemed a "senior company official at the location involved." Moreover, because the board would not infer a lack of authority due to the previous conduct of the contractor, the certification was valid.[44]

---

[37] Nab-Lord Assocs. v. United States, 682 F.2d 940 (Cl. Ct. 1982).

[38] *Id.*

[39] Fidelity Constr. Co. v. United States, 700 F.2d 1379 (Fed. Cir. 1983); Vemo Co., ASBCA No. 27,048, 83-1 BCA (CCH) ¶ 16,194 (1982); Luedtke Eng'g Co., ENGBCA No. 4556, 82-2 BCA (CCH) ¶ 15,851 (1982).

[40] Donald M. Drake Co. v. United States, 12 Cl. Ct. 518 (1987).

[41] *Id.*

[42] Dawson Constr. Co., VABCA No. 1967, 84-2 BCA (CCH) ¶ 17,383 (1984); *see also* Christie-Willamette, VABCA No. 1182-16, 85-1 BCA (CCH) ¶ 17,930 (1985); Santa Fe, Inc., VABCA No. 1746, 85-2 BCA (CCH) ¶ 18,069. *But cf.* Ball, Ball & Brosamer, Inc., IBCA Nos. 2103, 2350, 88-3 BCA (CCH) ¶ 20,844 (1988); Whitesell-Green Inc., IBCA No. 1927-1940, 85-3 BCA (CCH) ¶ 18,173 (1985).

[43] VABCA No. 1967, 87-2 BCA (CCH) ¶ 17,383 (1984).

[44] *Id.* at p. 86,604; *see also* Christie-Willamette, VABCA No. 1182-16, 85-1 BCA (CCH) ¶ 17,930 (1985) (project manager had authority to certify because contractor's letter to government designating the project manager as having full authority did not exempt the authority to submit or certify claims); Santa Fe, Inc., VABCA No. 1746, 85-2 BCA (CCH) ¶ 18,069 (1985) (project manager certification valid because the corporation had delegated certification authority to the project manager).

However, in another case the board promoted a narrower view of the certification requirement,[45] stating:

> Since the purpose of the certification requirement is to prevent frivolous or fraudulent claims . . . the certification required by the statute ought to be signed by someone who *clearly* has the authority to bind the corporation or other legal entity involved. Otherwise, the certification requirement of the Act would be meaningless.[46]

In this case the board held that the contractor's chief cost engineer was not a proper person to certify because he was neither an onsite project manager with express authority nor a corporate officer.[47]

§ 9.7   Disputes Clause

As previously discussed, in cases in which there was no dispute as to a contractor's entitlement to payment, there was no basis for allowing interest under the payment of interest on contractors' claims clause. Under the Act, however, a contractor is entitled to interest on both the disputed and undisputed parts of its claim.[48] In *Oxwell, Inc.,*[49] the contractor submitted claims based on direct labor hours as defined in the contract. The government generally criticized the claims because it thought indirect labor hours were included as well. The contractor later resubmitted its claims in exactly the same form as before and requested final decisions on the claims. The contracting officer's final decision allowed only a certain amount of the labor hours yet did not make payment for these hours. The board, on appeal, allowed the remaining labor hours claimed by the contractor. The government argued that interest could not accrue on the amounts allowed by the contracting officer's decision beyond the date of the decision because these amounts were no longer in dispute. The board rejected this argument and allowed interest on the undisputed amounts found due by the contracting officer (undisputed amount) and by the board (disputed amount) from the date the contracting officer received the resubmitted claim until the date of payment.[50]

---

[45] Ball, Ball, & Brosamer, Inc., IBCA Nos. 2103, 2350, 88-3 BCA (CCH) ¶ 20,844 (1988).

[46] *Id.* at p. 105,432.

[47] *Id.*

[48] Oxwell, Inc., ASBCA No. 25,703, 81-2 BCA (CCH) ¶ 15,392 (1981).

[49] *Id.*

[50] *Id.*

The disputes clause, as required by the FAR[51] recognizes that under the Act, interest will be allowed on requests for payments that are not acted upon within a reasonable time. This clause reads in part:

(c) Claim as used in this clause means a written demand or written assertion by one of the contracting parties seeking, as a matter of right, the payment of money, in a sum certain, the adjustment or interpretation of contract terms, or other relief, arising under or relating to this contract. However, a written demand by the Contractor seeking the payment of money in excess of $50,000 is not a claim until certified in accordance with (d)(2) below. A voucher, invoice, or other routine request for payment that is not in dispute when submitted is not a claim under the Act. The submission may be converted to a claim under the Act by complying with the submission and certification requirements of this clause if it is disputed as to liability or amount or is not acted on in a reasonable time.[52]

The General Services Administration Board of Contract Appeals has awarded interest for an unreasonable government delay in making payment on a negotiated settlement.[53] The Board has also allowed interest when the government unreasonably delayed in making final payment,[54] and when the government failed to take timely action with respect to a contractor's invoices.[55] Delays in payment beyond 30 days were held to be unreasonable by the Board.[56]

Contractors should be aware that a routine undisputed payment request, such as a voucher or invoice, is not a claim unless it is later disputed or not acted upon in a reasonable time. A decision in one case, *Patock Construction Co.,*[57] suggests that a contractor should certify its routine payment requests and at the same time request a final decision if the payment request is not acted upon within a stated time, such as 30 days.[58] In this case, the board ruled that the contractor could not recover any interest because the contractor had not certified its voucher at the time of submission.[59] If a routine payment request is not acted upon within a reasonable time, at the

---

[51] FAR 52.233-1 (applies to contracts entered into after April 1, 1984).

[52] *Id.*

[53] Dawson Constr. Co., GSBCA No. 5777, 80-2 BCA (CCH) ¶ 14,817 (1980).

[54] Joseph Fusco Constr. Co., GSBCA No. 5717, 81-1 BCA (CCH) ¶ 14,837 (1980).

[55] Capital Sec. Servs., Inc., GSBCA No. 5722, 81-1 BCA (CCH) ¶ 14,923 (1980).

[56] Joseph Fusco Constr. Co., GSBCA No. 5717, 81-1 BCA (CCH) ¶ 14,837 (1980); Capital Sec. Servs., Inc., GSBCA No. 5722, 81-1 BCA (CCH) ¶ 14,923 (1980).

[57] ASBCA No. 25,345, 81-1 BCA (CCH) ¶ 14,993, *motion for reconsideration denied,* 81-2 BCA (CCH) ¶ 15,184 (1981).

[58] *Id.*

[59] *Id.*

very least, the contractor should submit a formal written demand requesting a final decision and also submit the appropriate certification.[60]

Interest under the Act will be calculated based on the Treasury rates as adjusted every six months.[61] Note that this result differs from the single fixed rate as interpreted under the payment of interest on contractors' claims clause. Interest under the Act is based on simple, not compound, interest.[62]

§ 9.8   State Statutes

There are various state statutes that specifically provide for the recovery of prejudgment interest on claims. Other states have statutes that allow a party to recover postjudgment interest. In many instances, both types of interest are recoverable. Moreover, in the absence of state statutes, a party may recover interest pursuant to an interest provision in its contract.

§ 9.9   —Prejudgment Interest

Prejudgment interest is interest payable on an amount awarded in a judgment by a court with respect to a period of time before the entry of judgment. Contractors seeking prejudgment interest must first determine whether there is a statute which would apply to their contracts. Contractors should familiarize themselves not only with the terms of such a statute but also with court decisions interpreting the statute. State courts may have limited the application of the particular statute and may not uphold what seems readily apparent on the face of the statute.

Contractors may be able to recover interest although their particular contract does not come within the terms of the prejudgment interest statute.[63] Recovery of interest also may be allowed even though there is no statute concerning prejudgment interest.

A generally accepted rule is that prejudgment interest will be allowed on liquidated claims or claims for which the costs are readily ascertainable by mathematical computation or with reference to established standards of

---

[60] *See* Federal Elec. Corp., ASBCA No. 24,002, 82-2 BCA (CCH) ¶ 15,862 (1982) (interest was allowed from the date the contracting office received the contractor's letter which certified the amounts due and requested a final decision).

[61] Brookfield Constr. Co. v. United States, 661 F.2d 159 (Cl. Ct. 1981).

[62] *Id.*

[63] *See, e.g.,* Havens Steel Co. v. Randolph Eng'g Co., 613 F. Supp. 514 (W.D. Mo. 1985); City of Mound Bayou v. Roy Collins Constr. Co., 499 So. 2d 1354 (Miss. 1986).

value which have been codified.[64] The basis of the general rule is that if a person against whom a claim has been asserted knows or can readily ascertain the sum of the indebtedness or claim, then prejudgment interest will be awarded for not making timely payment. Prejudgment interest will be allowed even when the person withholding payment disputes the claim. Generally, construction claims are liquidated if they are based on incurred costs which are readily ascertainable and with little jury discretion.[65]

In California, prejudgment interest is allowed on an unliquidated claim within the discretion of the court.[66] Interest accrues from the date payment is due on claims for "damages certain or capable of being made certain by calculation," whereas interest accrues no earlier than the date the suit was filed on unliquidated claims. On public works projects, California regulations provide for payment of claims "settled or agreed upon," and interest commences within 90 days of submission.[67]

Some statutes allow the recovery of interest in contract cases but do not specify whether interest is allowable on both liquidated claims or unliquidated claims, or whether recovery should be allowed as a matter of right or as a matter within the discretion of the court.[68] In Minnesota state highway contracts, a contractor is entitled to prejudgment interest on amounts due it that are not paid within 90 days after final estimate for the work is made. However, this statute is not applicable if the amount of damages depend upon contingencies or upon the discretion of a jury.[69]

New Mexico allows the recovery of interest "on money due by contract."[70] The New Mexico statute has been interpreted to allow the recovery of interest as a matter of right if a contractor's claim is fixed or determinable. If the claim is not fixed or determinable, then interest could still be allowed but only within the discretion of the trial court.[71]

Alaska's interest statutes have been interpreted as allowing prejudgment interest on damages, whether liquidated or not, from the date the cause of

---

[64] S.D. Codified Laws Ann. § 21-1-11 (1991) (South Dakota's is a typical statute governing interest).

[65] Almont Lumber & Equip. Co. v. Hatzenbuehler, 359 N.W.2d 384 (N.D. 1985); Land Paving Co. v. D.A. Constr. Co., 338 N.W.2d 779 (Neb. 1983); Northwestern Eng'g Co. v. Thunderbolt Enters., Inc., 301 N.W.2d 421 (S.D. 1981) (where a contract contained an itemized list of unit prices, total prices and the tasks involved, the amount of damages was readily ascertainable and prejudgment interest was allowed).

[66] Cal. Civ. Code § 3287 (West 1970).

[67] Cal. Gov't Code § 980 (West 1970).

[68] Minn. Stat. Ann. § 161.322 (West 1991).

[69] Alley Constr. Co. v. State, 219 N.W.2d 922 (Minn. 1974).

[70] N.M. Stat. Ann. § 56-8-3 (Michie 1991).

[71] Shaeffer v. Kelton, 619 P.2d 1226 (N.M. 1980). See also City of Mound Bayou v. Roy Collins Constr. Co., (the Mississippi Supreme Court confirmed the award of interest from the date the A/E certified the project as complete).

action accrues.[72] In Nebraska, if a controversy exists as to either the claim amount or right to recovery, the claim is considered to be unliquidated barring recovery of prejudgment interest.[73]

Ohio allows interest on money which becomes "due and payable."[74] In *Sealey v. Boulevard Construction Co.,* [75] a contractor sued a homeowner for the unpaid balance under a contract for construction of a home. Since the contractor strictly complied with and substantially performed the contract, the unpaid balance became "due and payable." The contractor was awarded the unpaid balance plus prejudgment interest on this amount from the date of substantial completion.

The District of Columbia's statute allows a contractor to recover interest on damages for breach of contract. The statute provides in part, "judgment shall allow interest on the amount for which it is rendered from the date of the judgment only."[76] In *Blake Construction Co. v. C.J. Coakley Co.,* [77] prejudgment interest was allowed for a subcontractor when the contractor, among other things, failed to provide a clear and convenient work area, to properly sequence the work, and to supervise other subcontractors. The District of Columbia's statute was also interpreted to allow recovery of interest on borrowings if necessary to fully compensate the contractor when it could be established that the borrowings fairly represented the cost of financing changed work.[78]

The award of prejudgment interest is not necessarily governed solely by statutes.[79] One court has recognized that the award of the prejudgment interest may be allowed in other situations.[80]

§ 9.10   —Postjudgment Interest

Postjudgment interest is interest payable on an amount awarded in a judgment by a court for a period that begins from the date of the judgment. The recovery of postjudgment interest is governed by state law and applies to the amount of the original judgment. If the original judgment included

---

[72] Fairbanks Builders, Inc. v. Morton DeLima, Inc., 483 P.2d 194 (Alaska 1971).

[73] Land Paving Co. v. D.A. Constr. Co., 338 N.W.2d 779 (Neb. 1983).

[74] Ohio Rev. Code Ann. 1343.03 (Anderson 1991).

[75] 437 N.E.2d 305 (Ohio Ct. App. 1980).

[76] D.C. Code Ann. § 15-109 (Michie Supp. 1991).

[77] 431 A.2d 569 (D.C. 1981).

[78] Rohr Indus., ENGBCA No. 4306, 83-1 BCA (CCH) ¶ 16,299 (1983).

[79] Portage Sch. Constr. Corp. v. A.V. Stackhouse Co., 287 N.E.2d 564 (Ind. Ct. App. 1972).

[80] *Id.*

prejudgment interest, then postjudgment interest will apply to the prejudgment interest as well as the other items of damages.

As discussed in § **9.9**, some state statutes expressly allow the recovery of prejudgment interest against the state.[81] However, in *Brown v. State Highway Commission,*[82] the court ruled that postjudgment interest could not be awarded against the state because the postjudgment interest statute during that time period did not refer to judgments against the state.[83] However, the statute was later amended to include the state.

A Kentucky statute[84] provides that "[a] judgment shall bear . . . interest from its date." In *Commonwealth Department of Highways v. Young,*[85] the state claimed it was immune from paying postjudgment interest and, even if it was not immune, the judgment did not provide for interest on the amount awarded. The court found that the state was not immune from paying postjudgment interest and that postjudgment interest would be allowed although the judgment itself made no provision for interest.[86]

Prior to asserting a postjudgment interest claim, the contractor should first examine the relevant state law concerning postjudgment interest. The contractor should also examine any court decisions concerning the postjudgment interest statute.

§ 9.11   —Absence of Statute

In states without prejudgment interest statutes, the recovery of prejudgment interest is allowed under conditions similar to those states which have statutes.

One court allowed recovery when the amount claimed was capable of ascertainment by mathematical computation or with reference to established standards of value because in such a situation the claim is considered to be "liquidated."[87] Other courts allow recovery if these same conditions are met, even though the claim is regarded as "unliquidated" rather than "liquidated."[88] Another court allowed prejudgment interest on an

---

[81] *See* Cal. Gov't Code § 980 (West); Minn. Stat. § 161.322.

[82] 476 P.2d 233 (Kan. 1970).

[83] Kan. Stat. Ann. § 16-204.

[84] Ky. Rev. Stat. Ann. § 360.040 (Michie/Bobbs-Merrill).

[85] 380 S.W.2d 239 (Ky. 1964) (court's decision was based on a statute other than the postjudgment interest statute).

[86] *Id.*

[87] Zitterkopf v. Roussalis, 546 P.2d 436 (Wyo. 1976).

[88] Krieg v. Union Pac. Land Resources Corp., 525 P.2d 48 (Or. 1974).

"unliquidated" claim when the claim amount due could be determined by referring to a fixed standard contained in a contract.[89]

In some states the award of prejudgment interest is left to the discretion of the trial court.[90]

Prior to any claim preparation, contractors should thoroughly review state statutes or court decisions concerning prejudgment interest. The claim presentation should contain the most detailed claim information possible and set forth applicable unit prices, rental rates, or wage rates to preclude the possible argument that the amount of the claim was not ascertainable prior to trial. The areas of dispute should also be narrowed so that interest will at least be allowed on undisputed amounts.

§ 9.12 AIA Contracts

AIA Document A201 has contained an interest provision since 1967 under which amounts owed to either party accrue interest at the "legal rate" in the jurisdiction in which the project is constructed. The 1987 version of AIA Document A201[91] states that interest will accrue from the payment due date at a rate agreed upon by the parties or the "legal rate."[92]

If the parties agree by contract to the recovery of interest on money not paid when due, interest is allowed regardless of whether or not the amount claimed is liquidated.[93] Interest should also be allowed as a matter of right and should not be left to the discretion of the trial court. In Louisiana, the court held that a contractor's interest accrued from the date of the arbitration award rather than at the substantial completion date.[94]

---

[89] North Pac. Plywood, Inc. v. Access Road Builders, Inc., 628 P.2d 482 (Wash. Ct. App. 1981) (interest allowed); Lester N. Johnson Co. v. City of Spokane, 588 P.2d 1214 (Wash. Ct. App. 1978) (interest not allowed).

[90] E.I. DuPont de Nemours & Co. v. Lyles & Lang Constr. Co., 219 F.2d 328 (4th Cir.), *cert. denied,* 349 U.S. 956, 75 S. Ct. 882 (1955) (contractor was allowed to recover prejudgment interest although the court did not consider the claim to be liquidated or determinable with sufficient certainty prior to trial); A&A Masonry Contractors, Inc. v. Polinger, 269 A.2d 566 (Md. 1970); Charles Burton Builders, Inc. v. L&S Constr. Co., 271 A.2d 534 (Md. 1970); *see also* Atlantic States Constr. Co. v. Drummon & Co., 246 A.2d 251 (Md. 1968).

[91] General Conditions, AIA Document A201-1987.

[92] *Id.*

[93] R.E. Bean Constr. Co. v. Middlebury Assocs., 428 A.2d 306 (Vt. 1980).

[94] St. Tammany Manor, Inc. v. Spartan Bldg. Corp., 499 So. 2d 616 (La. Ct. App. 1986).

§ 9.13 Federal Jurisdiction Interest Statute

Federal law now provides for interest in "any judgment in a civil case recovered in a district court" at a floating rate determined by the coupon yield of the United States Treasury bills.[95] It is important to note that no exemption is made for actions based on diversity of citizenship. Thus, several courts have applied the federal interest statute over conflicting state statutes.[96] In *Weitz Co. v. Mokan Carpet, Inc.,*[97] the court provided an interesting solution by applying prejudgment interest according to state law and postjudgment interest pursuant to federal law.

§ 9.14 Prompt Payment Act

The Prompt Payment Act of 1982[98] requires the government to pay an interest penalty on any overdue payments for complete delivered property or services.[99] Although the 1982 version of the Prompt Payment Act is applicable to construction contracts,[100] it was not until the 1988 amendments to the Act that provisions were specifically directed toward construction matters.[101]

Prior to the 1988 amendments, there was some confusion as to the applicability of the Act's interest penalty to late progress payments under construction contracts.[102] However, the 1988 amendments explicitly eliminated any question as to the applicability of the Act to progress payments. The Act now provides for the payment of interest on progress payments and retained amounts under construction contracts.[103] Payment requests under this new section must be accompanied by a substantiation of the amounts requested and a certification by the contractor.[104]

---

[95] Federal Court Improvement Act, 28 U.S.C.A. § 1961(a) (West 1982) as amended, effective Oct. 1, 1982.

[96] Rose Hall, Ltd. v. Chase Manhattan Banking Corp., 566 F. Supp. 523 (D. Nev. 1983); Interstate Fire & Casualty Co. v. Hartford Fire Ins. Co., 548 F. Supp. 1185 (E.D. Mich. 1985).

[97] 723 F.2d 1382 (8th Cir. 1983).

[98] 31 U.S.C. §§ 3901–3906 (1982).

[99] *Id.* § 3902.

[100] *See, e.g.,* Ricway, Inc., ASBCA No. 30,205, 86-1 BCA (CCH) ¶ 18,539 (1985); Consolidated Constr., Inc., GSBCA No. 8871, 88-2 BCA (CCH) ¶ 20,811 (1988).

[101] *See* 31 U.S.C. § 3902 (Supp. 1988).

[102] *See, e.g.,* Batteast Constr. Co., ASBCA No. 34,420, 87-3 BCA (CCH) ¶ 20,044 (1987); Zinger Constr. Co., ASBCA No. 31,858, 87-3 BCA (CCH) ¶ 20,043 (1987).

[103] 31 U.S.C. § 3903 (Supp. 1988).

[104] *Id.*

The 1988 amendments also contain provisions relating to payments by and to subcontractors and suppliers.[105] The Act requires that every prime contract must contain a provision requiring the prime contractor to place in each subcontract (including one with a material supplier) a provision obligating the prime contractor to pay the subcontractor for satisfactory performance within seven days out of funds paid by the agency.[106] The subcontract must also include a provision requiring the prime contractor to pay an interest penalty to the subcontractor for failure to comply with that provision.[107] Subcontractors are also required to place in their lower-tier subcontracts a payment clause and a penalty clause.[108]

---

[105] *See id.* § 3905(b)(1).

[106] *Id.*

[107] *Id.*

[108] *Id.* § 3905(c).

CHAPTER 10

ATTORNEYS' FEES AND CLAIM PREPARATION COSTS

§ 10.1 Introduction

The prevailing party is ordinarily not entitled to an award of attorneys' and consultants' fees from the losing party unless statutorily or contractually authorized. However, there are exceptions which permit an award to the prevailing party if the opponent has acted fraudulently or in bad faith in either bringing or maintaining the litigation.[1] In these situations the purpose of "fee shifting" is punitive, and attorneys' fees are recovered as damages. The majority of jurisdictions allow the attorneys' and consultants' fees of the prevailing party to be taken into consideration in assessing punitive or exemplary damages; other jurisdictions do not allow counsel fees to be computed as part of the exemplary damages but do allow them as part of the compensatory damages. A few states disallow the recovery of attorneys' and consultants' fees as an element of damages altogether.

In fraud actions against building contractors, most courts regularly award attorneys' and consultants' fees to owners. These cases typically involve situations in which construction defects exist, the owner was not advised of their existence, and the contractor is deemed to have either actual or constructive knowledge of them. Moreover, the court may properly award the owner's attorneys' fees on the basis that the contractor fraudulently misled the owner into believing that the project was properly constructed.[2]

---

[1] Hall v. Cole, 412 U.S. 1 (1973); Universal Oil Prods. Co. v. Root Refining Co., 328 U.S. 575 (1946).

[2] *See* Clark v. Aenchbacher, 238 S.E.2d 442 (Ga. Ct. App. 1977).

Contractors have also been allowed to recover attorneys' and consultants' fees in light of another party's wrongful act, such as a breach of its contract with others (for example, subcontractors). In such cases, the courts have treated the attorneys' fees incurred by the contractor as part of the legal consequences of the other party's original wrongful act and have allowed the contractor to recover the amount of fees incurred as part of the damages.[3]

In *Norin Mortgage Corp. v. Wasco, Inc.*,[4] the contractor tried to recover from the owner's lender attorneys' fees incurred in defending suits for payment brought by subcontractors after the lender breached its contract by failing to pay the contractor the full amount due. The court reasoned that the contractor's actions were merely delaying tactics because the contractor knew it owed money to the subcontractors but incurred legal fees in defending against the suits in the hope that by the time judgments were obtained, it would have received its payment from either the owner or the owner's lender. The court held that because the contractor knew it had no defense against the subcontractors, it was neither necessary nor reasonable for the contractor to defend against the suits. Consequently, recovery of attorneys' fees was denied.

Attorneys' and consultants' fees are not recoverable when incurred in the prosecution of a claim against the government.[5] In pursuing such claims, costs incurred by contractors in seeking relief before the boards of contract appeals and in court have uniformly been disallowed regardless of whether the matter has arisen out of an affirmative contractor claim for relief or a government-initiated claim against the contractor.[6] However, a few cases have allowed the contractor to recover the cost of attorney and consultant services incurred in asserting and defending against claims before the contracting officer.[7]

---

[3] *See, e.g.,* Waldinger Corp. v. Ashbrook-Simon-Hartley, Inc., 564 F. Supp. 970 (C.D. Ill. 1983) (third party guilty of intentional interference with contract is liable for attorneys' fees). *See also* Murray First Thrift & Loan Co. v. N-L Paving, 576 P.2d 455 (Wyo. 1978) (subcontractor breached its contract with prime contractor by abandoning project before it had completed all its work; court awarded prime attorneys' fees it had incurred in making necessary arrangements to have someone else complete subcontract work); Campbell Hardwares, Inc. v. R.W. Gregor & Sons, Inc., 516 N.E.2d 150 (Mass. 1987) (attorneys' fees allowed when prime contractor was forced into litigation with supplier because owner refused to issue change order); Department of Transp. v. Arapaho Constr., Inc., 349 S.E.2d 196 (Ga. Ct. App. 1986); David C. Olson, Inc. v. Denver & Rio Grande W. R.R., 789 P.2d 492 (Colo. 1990).

[4] 343 So. 2d 940 (Fla. Dist. Ct. App. 1977).

[5] FAR 31.205-33.

[6] J.E. Robertson Co. v. United States, 437 F.2d 1360 (Ct. Cl. 1971).

[7] *See, e.g.,* Allied Materials & Equip. Co., ASBCA No. 17,318, 75-1 BCA (CCH) ¶ 11,150 (1975).

Some states have statutes which govern the award of attorneys' and consultants' fees. Typically, such statutes include mechanics' lien actions, indemnity, bad faith, fraud, and similar actions. Contractors should consult counsel on the applicability and effect of these state laws.[8] In some instances, attorneys' fees are awarded in arbitration proceedings.[9]

§ 10.2   Provisions

The rule in most jurisdictions as to the validity of a contract provision for attorneys' and consultants' fees is that such a provision is valid if the contract is enforceable and not against public policy or another statutory enactment to the contrary.[10] If the contract contains a fixed sum or percentage constituting the fee, it will be enforced if the fee is reasonable and the services were actually rendered.

Some state courts have refused to enforce contractual provisions for attorneys' fees, holding that these provisions are penalties and against public policy.[11] In *First Atlantic Building Corp. v. Neubauer Construction Co.,*[12] the contract contained a provision that, in the event of a suit brought by either party, the party bringing suit would be responsible for the other's attorneys' fees. The court held that such a clause was unconscionable and would not apply to situations in which the party claiming the right to attorneys' fees had necessitated the suit by breaching the contract.

A common provision for attorneys' and consultants' fees found in construction contracts is an indemnity clause. The prevailing rule in all states is that a contract may validly provide for the indemnification of one against its (or its employees and agents) future acts of negligence, provided the indemnity against such negligence is made unequivocally clear in the contract.

---

[8] *See, e.g.,* Mission Hardwood Co. v. Registrar of Contractors, 716 P.2d 73 (Ariz. Ct. App. 1986) (attorneys' fees allowed under an Arizona equivalent to the federal EAJA); Sime Constr. Co. v. Washington Pub. Power Supply Sys., 621 P.2d 1299 (Wash. Ct. App. 1981) (attorneys' fees allowed in lien foreclosure); Marshall v. Karl F. Schultz, Inc., 438 So. 2d 533 (Fla. Dist. Ct. App. 1983) (owner awarded attorneys' fees for successfully defending against mechanics' lien suit). *See also* Harris v. Dyer, 637 P.2d 918 (Or. 1981).

[9] Harris v. Dyer, 637 P.2d 918 (Or. 1981) (contractor awarded attorneys' fees for arbitration proceedings conducted pursuant to standard AIA contract affording "rights and remedies otherwise imposed or available by law").

[10] United States *ex rel.* Micro-King Co. v. Community Science Technology, 574 F.2d 1292 (5th Cir. 1978).

[11] *See* Missouri Pac. R.R. v. Winburn Tile Mfg. Co., 461 F.2d 984 (8th Cir. 1972).

[12] 352 So. 2d 103 (Fla. Dist. Ct. App. 1977).

§ 10.3   Equal Access to Justice Act

Contractors working under federal construction contracts may be able to recover attorneys' fees and other litigation costs from the government pursuant to the Equal Access to Justice Act (EAJA).[13] The Act was originally enacted for a three-year period, effective October 1, 1981. It amended Title II of the Small Business Act, and provided for the award of attorneys' fees and other related expenses to certain parties who prevailed in adversarial administrative and judicial proceedings brought by or against the United States. Award was to be made when the position of the government in the litigation was not "substantially justified." The purpose of the Act was to provide relief to small business litigants who otherwise might be deterred from seeking review of, or defending against, unreasonable government action because of the expense of litigation and the "greater resources and expertise of the United States."[14]

The original Act expired on October 1, 1984, and was not in effect for a period of several months. It was reenacted on a permanent basis in August 1985 and was applied retroactively to the expiration of the original Act.

To be eligible to recover litigation costs under the Act, a small business must not have a net worth in excess of $7 million or more than 500 employees at the time the action is commenced. In the case of a subcontractor pass-through claim, the size determination is based on the prime contractor, not the subcontractor. Thus, if a subcontractor qualifies but the prime does not, the subcontractor cannot recover under the EAJA.[15]

The Act does not apply to tort actions brought by or against the United States. It does apply to all other civil actions which were "pending" on or commenced on or after October 1, 1981. In *Berman v. Schweiker,*[16] a federal district court held that a case is "pending" for purposes of the Act if the losing party's right to appeal has not yet been exhausted or expired.

A party seeking attorneys' fees under the EAJA must file an application within 30 days after final disposition of the case. The application must contain an itemized statement of fees and costs and must allege that the position of the government was not "substantially justified."

After a prevailing party has submitted an application for an award, the burden of proving that a fee award should not be made rests with the government. The test of whether the government's position is substantially justified is essentially one of reasonableness in law and fact.

---

[13] Pub. L. No. 96-481, 5 U.S.C. § 504 (1982); 28 U.S.C. § 2412 (1982). *See* Pachter & Howartz, *Recovering Legal Fees under EAJA,* 82-2 Briefing Papers Collection (Apr. 1982).

[14] Pub. L. No. 96-481, 94 Stat. 2321 (West 1980).

[15] Teton Constr. Co., ASBCA No. 27,700, 87-2 BCA (CCH) ¶ 19,766 (1987).

[16] 531 F. Supp. 1149 (N.D. Ill. 1982), *aff'd,* 713 F.2d 1290 (7th Cir. 1983).

Certain types of case dispositions may indicate that the government action was not substantially justified. A court will look closely at cases, for example, when there has been a judgment on the pleadings, when there has been a directed verdict, when a prior suit on the same claim has been dismissed, or when there is a substantial difference between the amount or content of the government's original pleadings and the settlement agreed to.

The United States Claims Court has denied an award for attorneys' fees and costs under the Act in a case involving litigation with the Internal Revenue Service. In finding that the government's position was substantially justified, the court concluded:

> The U.S. Court of Appeals for the Federal Circuit has held that, in determining whether or not the position of the United States was substantially justified in a particular case, it is the position taken by the Government in litigating a cause of action before the courts that is determinative and not the position of the administrative agency which caused the dispute to arise. *Broad Avenue Laundry and Tailoring v. United States,* 693 F.2d 1387, 1390–91 (Fed. Cir. 1982).[17]

Thus, it is the conduct of the government in litigating the dispute that forms the basis for an award under the EAJA.

In *Ellis v. United States,*[18] a former civil fire chief sought to recover his litigation expenses in seeking reinstatement of his retirement pay. The court awarded fees and costs for the liability phase of the litigation and denied the same for the damages phase:

> [B]ecause the EAJA's primary purpose is to eliminate legal expense as a barrier to challenges of unreasonable governmental action, it is proper for us to assess attorney's fees and costs against the government for a separate phase or portion of the litigation in which its position lacks substantial justification—even though the government may have adopted wholly reasonable positions in other facets of the case. See *Goldhaber, supra,* 698 F.2d at 196–97; *cf. Electronics Modules Corp. v. United States,* 702 F.2d 218, 219–20 (Fed. Cir. 1983).[19]

Therefore, the courts will scrutinize all aspects of the government's position in determining awards under the EAJA.

In *Kay Manufacturing Co. v. United States,*[20] an earlier award of attorneys' fees and expenses by the Court of Claims was reversed by the Circuit Court of Appeals for the Federal Circuit, finding the government's position

---

[17] Hill v. United States, 3 Cl. Ct. 428 (1983).

[18] 711 F.2d 1571 (1983).

[19] *Id.* at 1576.

[20] 699 F.2d 1376 (Fed. Cir. 1983).

at trial to have been substantially justified. The court found that a reasonable belief by the government in the position asserted, if not entirely without a valid supporting factual and legal basis, precludes a finding that the government's litigation position was substantially unjustified. However, the court reasoned that it is not necessary to prove that the government's position was reprehensible in order to recover under the Act. A secondary issue was also settled in which the court found that fees and expenses generated prior to October 1, 1981, the effective date of the Act, are to be included in awards made pursuant to the Act.

At least one case has held that a contractor can recover attorneys' fees even if the case settles prior to a final resolution by the board of contract appeals.[21] Moreover, attorneys' fees incurred in the negotiation of quantum after a board of contract appeals' favorable decision on entitlement are considered fees incurred as part of the adversarial process and thus recoverable.[22]

The prevailing party, however, might not recover the full amount of its attorneys' fees.[23] When a contractor is only partially successful, that is, prevails on some but not all of its claims, the court or board may apportion the claim for attorneys' fees.[24]

Finally, attorneys' fees are limited to $75 per hour unless the appellant can show a lack of qualified attorneys available at this rate.[25] This limitation is difficult to overcome.[26]

---

[21] PetroElec Constr. Co., ASBCA Nos. 32,999–33,000, 33,417–23, 33,696–97, 34,095, 34,096, 87-3 BCA (CCH) ¶ 20,111 (1987).

[22] B&A Elec., Inc., ASBCA No. 30,721(R), 87-2 BCA (CCH) ¶ 19,879 (1987).

[23] PetroElec Constr. Co., Inc., ASBCA Nos. 32,999–33,000, 33,417–23, 33,696–97, 34,095, 34,096, 87-3 BCA (CCH) ¶ 20,111 (1987).

[24] T.H. Taylor, Inc., ASBCA No. 26,494-O, 83-1 BCA (CCH) ¶ 16,310 (1983).

[25] 5 U.S.C. § 504(b)(1)(A) (1982).

[26] *See, e.g.,* Ken Rogge Lumber Co., AGBCA No. 85-510-10, 87-1 BCA (CCH) ¶ 19,341 (1987).

CHAPTER 11

PRESENTATION OF DAMAGES

§ 11.1 Summary of Damages

A damages presentation, whether in trial or in a claim submission, can be both confusing and tedious. As a result, it is necessary to present damages in a clear, simple, and easily understandable format. A damages presentation should begin with a summary of damages that is keyed or referenced to a series of supporting schedules or exhibits that detail the actual calculations. An example of a summary of damages for a complex construction claim is shown in **Table 11–1**.

As depicted in the example, a claim can have many parts, each of which should be separately scheduled and separately calculated. This summary provides the roadmap to each and every element of the claim.

The damages claimed should, whenever possible, reference and tie out to the contractor's accounting documents and records. This provides a trail by which the calculation can be verified and the source documents accessed. Damages which cannot be traced to accounting records are immediately suspect no matter how reasonable the amount claimed. Each individual damage calculation should be explained briefly. The goal in damages presentation is to facilitate an easy understanding by the reviewers.

§ 11.2 Use of Graphs

Providing raw numerical data can be mind-numbing to the reader and observer of a claim. Whenever possible, charts and graphs should be used. For example, when presenting a labor productivity claim, a graph showing the as-planned labor curve with manhours versus time contrasted with the

Table 11-1

Summary of Amounts Due Contractor

A. Contract Balance Due—Exhibit 29		$ 820,771.00
B. Additional Contractor Field Costs:		
1. Additional Concrete Costs—Exhibit 3	$136,361.00	
2. Additional Cost of Concrete Form Rental—Exhibit 5	$ 78,245.00	
3. Additional Cost of Winter Conditions—Exhibit 6	$ 54,860.00	
4. Additional Cost of Dewatering—Exhibit 7	$ 20,952.00	
5. Extended Equipment Costs—Exhibit 8	$275,430.00	
6. Additional Small Tools Cost—Exhibit 9	$ 67,250.00	
7. Additional Cost of Hiring Consultants—Exhibit 11	$ 67,378.00	
8. Increase in Labor Burden—Exhibit 10	$ 31,214.00	
9. Extended Field Overhead—Exhibit 13	$310,154.00	
10. Acceleration Costs—Exhibit 14	$174,277.00	
Subtotal:		$1,216,121.00
C. Exhibit 15 Additional Cost of Specially Contracted Machinery and Millwright Work		$ 941,898.00
D. Overhead Allocable to Claim		
1. Branch Office—Exhibit 20	$331,240.00	
2. Corporate Office—Exhibit 21	$123,751.00	
Subtotal:		$ 454,991.00
E. Profit on Additional Revenue—Exhibit 28		$ 267,405.00
Subtotal:		$3,701,186.00
F. Additional Bond Cost—Exhibit 29		$ 13,957.00
G. Claim Preparation Cost—Exhibit 27		$ 164,117.00
Subtotal:		$3,879,260.00
H. Submitted but Unresolved Changes—Exhibit 22(a)		$ 479,251.00
I. Interest:		
On Unpaid Contract Balance—Exhibit 30	$132,583.00	
On Equitable Adjustment—Exhibit 30	$517,773.00	
		$ 650,356.00
Total Due Contractor:		$5,008,867.00

as-built labor curve can show the dramatic impacts of labor inefficiencies. One such example is shown in **Figure 11-1**. Entitlement and damages can sometimes be illustrated with one exhibit. **Figure 11-2** compares planned drawing releases and manpower with actual drawing releases and manpower. It makes the point that the drawings were released late, changed often, and overlapped the installation work. This presentation ties entitlement (the late drawing releases) with damages (the increased labor).

When presenting a delay claim, illustrating the impact of delay on jobsite overhead costs graphically can be dramatic. A chart such as the one in

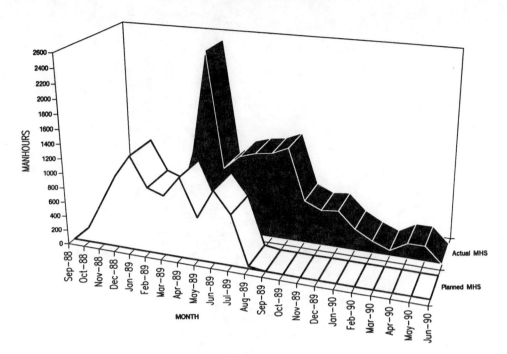

Figure 11–1. Comparison of planned and actual manhours.

Figure 11–3, which compares the as-bid durations for jobsite personnel with the actual durations, can be tied readily to both the contractor's as-planned durations and the cost records for the actual duration. Such a graph helps convey both the shift in time and the extended duration of the project.

Charts can also be used to illustrate concepts such as labor productivity. **Figures 11–4** and **11–5** illustrate productivity losses on a project in two different formats. **Figure 11–4** shows manhours per square foot of contact area of forming on a periodic basis. This format shows the change in productivity from period to period. The same data is presented in **Figure 11–5** in two graphs, one showing manhours and the other showing square feet of contact area installed. Production drops in the impacted time period, but manhours rise. **Table 11–2** contains the raw data for **Figures 11–4** and **11–5**. The raw data, although telling the same story, is much less effective than either **Figure 11–4** or **Figure 11–5**.

When dealing with critical path method (CPM) scheduling issues, it is particularly important to use simplified graphic illustrations. Presenting CPM scheduling data in computer printout tabular form can be both mind-numbing and ineffective because it is hard to follow. Material that is hard to follow is generally ignored. Using charts such as **Figure 11–6**, showing the schedule impacts for specific time periods, can help a nonscheduler understand what happened to the schedule.

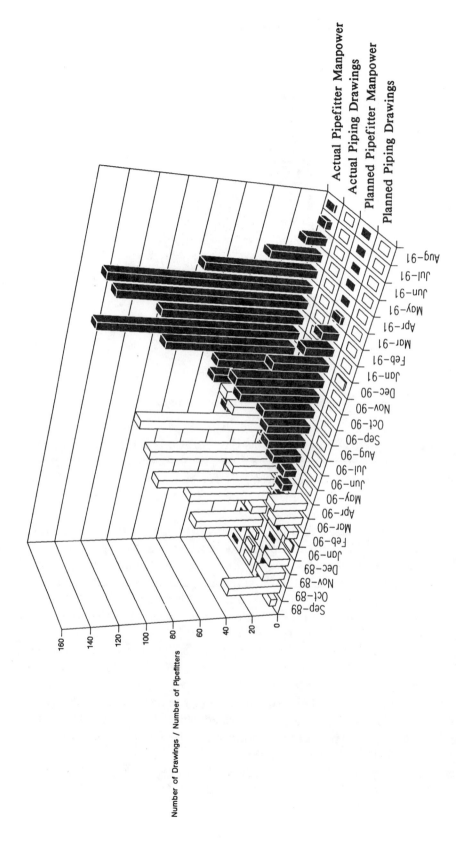

Figure 11-2. Planned versus actual drawing releases and planned versus actual pipefitter manpower.

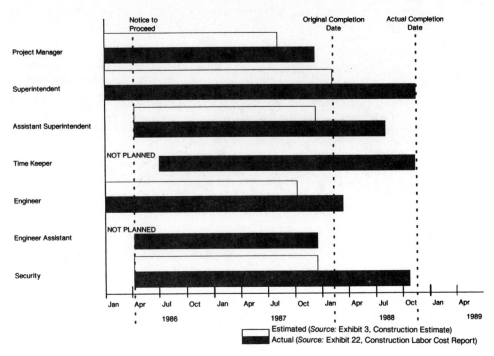

Figure 11–3. Comparison of planned and actual jobsite overhead personnel.

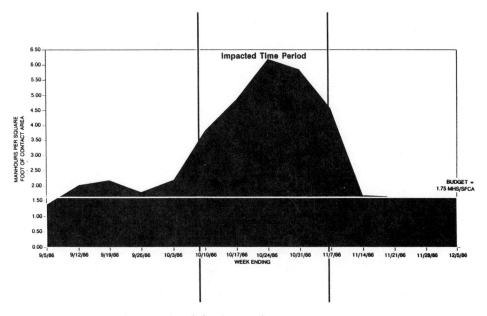

Figure 11–4. Forming productivity by week.

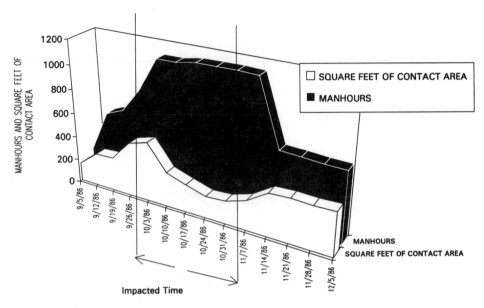

Figure 11–5. Forming manhours and forming production by week.

Table 11–2

Manhours and Production by Week

Week Ending	MHS	SFCA	MHS/SFCA
9/05/86	216	154	1.40
9/12/86	559	274	2.04
9/19/86	623	283	2.20
9/26/86	821	452	1.82
10/03/86	1101	497	2.22
10/10/86	1102	287	3.84
10/17/86	1128	231	4.88
10/24/86	1130	182	6.21
10/31/86	1132	193	5.87
11/07/86	1126	246	4.58
11/14/86	606	355	1.71
11/21/86	598	364	1.64
11/28/86	587	357	1.64
12/05/86	584	362	1.61

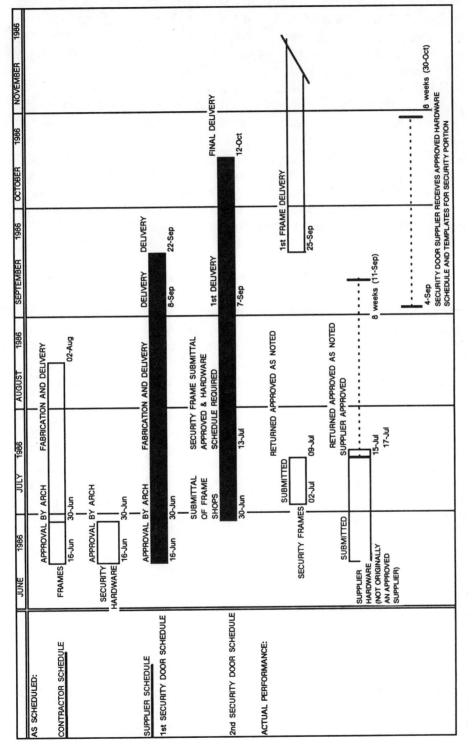

Figure 11–6. Security frame schedule comparison.

With microcomputers, laser printers, and software, charts such as those shown can be turned out quickly at a low cost. This ease of production is both a curse and a blessing. Because charts can be turned out quickly, they may be produced without sufficient review. It is extremely important when using computer-generated graphs to verify that the supporting data is correct. After checking the accuracy of the data, it is equally important to make sure that the presentation of the data is accurate. Such things as the scale of the X and Y axes should be checked to make sure that changes in scale do not prove the other side's point. It has been said, there are three kinds of liars: liars, damned liars, and statisticians. Graphics can lie, and the effect can be strongly negative. A good case can be devastated by testimony from the other side demonstrating bias or skewing of data. For example, if the other party shows that a change in an axis or a statistical method produces a significantly different answer, it will damage your credibility.

§ 11.3   Expert Analysis

When presenting damages that rely heavily on productivity analysis, it may be appropriate to include a productivity expert's report as part of the damage analysis. Although the preparation of a productivity analysis using source documents can be time-consuming and expensive, it can validate significant productivity losses when a measured mile or other comparative analysis cannot be done.

Similarly, when the claim and the damages asserted rely heavily on schedule impact, it may be appropriate to include a detailed schedule analysis with the damages presentation. Such an analysis should include the causal linkages between the damages and the schedule analysis. To the extent possible, the expert report should include graphic presentation of the delay and the effects on the schedule. Without such graphic information, the value of the analysis is significantly reduced.

CHAPTER 12

OWNERS' CLAIMS AGAINST CONTRACTORS

§ 12.1   Introduction

All parties to construction contracts anticipate that the projects will be completed by the date set in the contract and that projects can and will be built in conformance with the plans and specifications. When projects are completed late or not at all, or when the work is not done in accordance with the contract documents, owners as well as contractors suffer significant additional costs. Owners seek to recover these added costs from contractors, construction managers, architects, engineers, and other design professionals. The claims of an owner can be enormous when added financing costs and lost revenues resulting from delayed completion are considered. The claims that are often asserted by an owner against a contractor fall into three broad categories:

1. The contractor has failed to complete a project or portion of a project
2. The project was not completed in accordance with the contract documents, that is, the work is defective or nonconforming
3. The project or a portion of it was completed late.

All three areas of damages may exist on the same project.

§ 12.2   Failure to Complete

When the contractor fails to complete the project, the measure of damage is the reasonable cost of completing the project less the unpaid contract

145

balance at the time work ceased. Such cost would include the charges paid to the completing contractor, additional costs paid to the architects and engineers, and any other additional costs that the owner directly sustained as a result of having to reprocure the project and familiarize a new contractor with the project.

When calculating the cost of completing the work, it is important to include only the cost of completing work that was in the defaulting contractor's contract. If work is added or deleted from the contract, it is necessary to calculate these additions and deletions and properly to adjust the completion cost to the cost which would have been incurred under the prior contractor's scope of work. If multiple contractors are working on one site and the completion work is awarded to one of these contractors, segregating the completion cost from other costs that are not part of the contract can be difficult. Thus, it is extremely important that the contract be administered in a way that allows the original scope of work to be segregated from the additional work.

When the remaining work is procured on a different basis than the prior contract, it is important to calculate the revenues that would have been received by the defaulting contractor. An example of this would be a contractor on a unit price contract who ceases performance, and the owner reprocures on a cost-plus basis. The owner's damages would be the cost of completing the work minus the value of the work performed by the completing contractor at the original contractor's unit prices. In other words, the original contractor is entitled to a credit against the completion cost for the units of work performed by the completing contractor at the original contract price. Therefore, it would be important to keep track of the units of work performed by the completion contractor. Failure to compile adequate documentation of the units of work performed and to credit the completion costs charged against the prior contractor could prevent the owner from receiving compensation for any additional cost.

§ 12.3   Cost of Correcting Nonconforming Work

The owner is entitled to recover the reasonable and necessary cost of correcting defective work or work that does not conform with the contract documents. It is important to analyze alleged defects to verify that they are not merely changes in the work. If items are nonconforming but the cost of correcting them would constitute economic waste, the owner must act with caution. The owner who proceeds with the correction may be left "holding the bag" in litigation.

The measure of damages can be calculated either as the cost of correcting or repairing the nonconforming work, or as the diminution in value of the property. The first measure of damages, the cost of correction, is simply the cost to repair or replace the nonconforming work. The calculation of the second measure of damages, the diminution of value, is more difficult. *Diminution in value* is the amount by which the market value of the property is reduced by the nonconforming work. If the nonconforming work, although large in absolute terms, is small in value relative to the overall project, such a measure may be difficult or impossible to determine. Furthermore, on public works projects such as roads or dams, it may be impossible to determine the market value, let alone the difference in market value. The diminution of value method should not be used when the actual cost of correction can be reasonably calculated.

The courts have held that when the contractor has deliberately or intentionally performed the nonconforming work, the appropriate measure of damages is the corrective cost and not the diminution of value. In *Shell v. Smidt*,[1] the court held that because the contractor had intentionally deviated from the construction plans for a series of tract homes, it was liable for the cost of repairs to bring those homes into conformance with the plans and specifications. The court specifically ruled that the contractor was not entitled to the benefit of relying upon a calculation of diminution of market value because he had willfully and intentionally deviated from the contract.

However, some courts have held that when repairs would result in economic waste, the diminution of value test is appropriate. In *Bayuk v. Edson*,[2] a judgment of damages to a homeowner for nonconforming construction was affirmed. The court ruled that the damage calculation based on a diminution of market value was proper under the circumstances because it was economically unreasonable to repair the defects.[3]

§ 12.4 Cost of Delay

To assess delay damages against a contractor, an owner must first prove not only that the project was late but that the contractor was responsible for the late completion and that there were no concurrent owner-caused delays. Such an analysis may require extensive critical path method studies, which can be the source of significant disagreement between the contractor and the owner. Once the delay has been determined and contractor responsibilities have been established, the owner can assert one of two delay damages. The owner may assert liquidated damages if liquidated damages are provided in the contract, or the owner may assert actual damages. The assessment of both liquidated and actual damages is not normally permitted.

---

[1] 164 Cal. App. 2d 350, 300 P.2d 817 (1958).

[2] 236 Cal. App. 2d 309, 46 Cal. Rptr. 49 (1965).

[3] *Id.*

Many construction contracts, particularly public works contracts, contain provisions for the payment of liquidated damages. These damages are usually set at a specific dollar amount per day of delay. The purpose of such provisions is to set a limit in advance for the damages that the owner will sustain from late completion. When specifying liquidated damages, it is important that they be reasonably related to the actual costs sustained as a result of the delay. Courts may not allow liquidated damages if they have little relation to the actual damages suffered, so that the effect of the damages would be a penalty. In *Massman Construction Co. v. City Council,*[4] a liquidated damages provision was not enforced when a bridge was completed late because the access roads to the bridge were not completed. Moreover, the court found that there could be no damage because the bridge had been completed on time. Therefore, liquidated damages could not be assessed because the bridge could not have been used for its intended purpose. Recovery of liquidated damages, although precluding recovery of actual delay damages, does not preclude recovery of other types of damages, such as the cost of correcting defective work.[5]

Actual delay damages may be recovered by an owner when the project has been delayed if the actual damages claimed were foreseeable by both parties and the amount of the damages can be proven with reasonable certainty.[6]

The costs of delayed completion are varied and substantial. They can include the following:

1. Extended construction interest and fees for extending the construction loan
2. Increased interest on both the construction loan and on the permanent financing if the permanent financing rate increases as a result of the delay
3. Extra licensing costs
4. Lost revenues and profits from the project
5. Extended costs for owner's personnel
6. Costs of owner's personnel hired to operate the facility who cannot be put to work
7. Additional or extended architect and engineer fees
8. Claims by follow-on or fit-up contractors
9. Storage charges or delayed shipment charges from manufacturers of equipment that cannot be installed
10. Extended insurance premiums, particularly builder's risk premiums

---

[4] 147 F.2d 925 (5th Cir. 1945).

[5] Northern Petrochem. Co. v. Thomsen & Thorschov, Inc., 297 Minn. 118, 211 N.W.2d 159 (1973).

[6] Hadley v. Baxendale, 156 Eng. Rep. 145 (Ex. 1854).

11.   Additional utility costs at the site
12.   Escalation in costs of owner-furnished equipment
13.   Rental of substitute facilities during the delay period
14.   Diminished market value as a result of a lost tenant
15.   Attorneys' fees and costs of litigation with third-party contractor's or consultants.

The nature of the project can have a significant impact on the amount of these damages. For example, a two-month delay in opening one retail store may have little meaning if the delay occurs from March to June. On the other hand, a two-month delay to a retail store selling ski wear and located at a ski resort has substantial impact if the delay is from November 1 to January 1. Rather than losing one-sixth of a year, the store may well have lost over half of its selling season for the year. Similarly, the contractor on a large commercial office building may face enormous damages if the owner of the building has a financing commitment for a loan that is now below market rate, but because interest rates have risen, the commitment will be lost if the loan is not closed by a certain date. The damages could be 30 years of increased interest on a large loan.

In *Roanoke Hospital Ass'n v. Doyle & Russell, Inc.,*[7] a significant award was made on behalf of an owner for additional interest cost incurred as a result of late completion of a project. Because the project was completed later than contemplated, the owner's loan commitment expired in the meantime and it had to obtain a new commitment at a significantly higher rate. The trial court awarded significant damages to the owner for the increased cost of the interest. The Virginia Court of Appeals reversed the award of damages and remanded the case to the trial court with instructions to the jury to determine whether, at the time the contract was executed, the parties contemplated "special circumstances" which would justify an award of consequential damages. In this case, the court distinguished between additional interest costs as a result of the extended construction period, which it considered to be direct damages, as opposed to added interest costs due to a higher interest rate during the extended construction period and additional interest costs due to higher interest rates on the permanent loan, both of which the court considered to be consequential damages. The court stated:

> Increases in interest rates are not caused by delays in completion of construction contracts. Rather, they are caused by variable pressures and counter-pressures affecting supply and demand in the money market. . . . For that reason, increases in interest rates are "special circumstances" and damages resulting therefrom are consequential and not compensable unless the circumstances were within the contemplation of the parties.[8]

---

[7] 215 Va. 796, 214 S.E.2d 155 (1975).

[8] *Id.*

The court concluded that the additional interest paid on the construction loan because of the additional time of construction was a direct damage and hence properly recoverable.[9]

In commercial properties, lost rents can be a significant area of damages. The right of the owner to recover lost rents against a contractor has been upheld in California.[10] In *Camper v. W.J. McDermott*,[11] the court concluded that lost rents constitute recoverable damages.[12] However, in this case the developer who was pursuing the action because of late completion of a swimming pool, could not clearly establish the linkage between the causation and the damages. If the developer of the apartment complex in *Camper*[13] had been able to show significant rentals by neighboring or competing complexes with swimming pools and an absence of rental activity in its complex during the period the swimming pool was not available, the causation against the contractor may have been sufficiently established. Causation may have been more readily apparent if the developer had established that neighboring rental activity increased as soon as their swimming pools were completed.

When asserting a claim for lost rental revenues, it is important that there not be an overlap with a claim for financing costs. Even when a project is completed on time, the owner/developer typically incurs financing costs for the project, with the payment for these costs coming from the revenue stream of projected rents. Therefore, if full costs of carrying a project during a delay period are claimed as an interest loss, there would be an overlap if lost revenues are also claimed for the same period.

Costs of additional personnel such as superintendents, project managers, and foremen make up a significant portion of most contractor delay claims. Owners frequently suffer the same costs. Hiring a staff for a large manufacturing facility starts prior to completion of the project due to the needs for special training, to transfer people from other sites and to increase gradually the hiring of personnel. When a project is completed late, the owner may suffer significant added costs as a result of having to carry a substantial workforce longer than originally anticipated. Such costs are properly recoverable. In a commercial project, additional costs of sales offices, leasing staff, on-site personnel, maintenance personnel, and security personnel are all appropriate damages. Similarly, when a construction project is delayed, owners frequently incur additional costs for their architects, engineers, and other consultants.

---

[9] *Id.*

[10] *Id.*

[11] 266 Cal. App. 2d 41, 71 Cal. Rptr. 590 (1968).

[12] *Id.*

[13] *Id.*

APPENDIXES

APPENDIX A

COST ACCOUNTING SYSTEMS

Appendix A contains examples taken from actual contractor cost accounting systems. All three of these examples come from general building contractors with annual volumes between $100 and $200 million. These examples show the types of data that can normally be found in a contractor's cost accounting system. Cost accounting systems vary widely from contractor to contractor. Even though the three contractors from whose cost accounting systems these examples were adapted were similar in size, volume, and type of work, the systems differ significantly in the level of detail and in format. None of the systems is necessarily better. They are presented as examples of the types of source documents from which damage calculations must start. In addition to the work in process or cost report, most contractors also have weekly labor reports, subcontractor status reports, payroll registers, and detailed transaction reports listing each transaction that is posted into a specific cost code or account. All of these documents can be useful in claim preparation.

Table A–1 is a simple report with almost no detail. This report does not project costs; it merely collects them and compares cost-to-date to original budget. Change orders are entered into the system at the end of the report in a lump sum.

Table A–2 is a tiered report with both a summary of the project and detailed line item costing. This report has line item projection and line item updates for changes.

Table A–3 is reprinted only in part because of its length. (The actual report was 63 pages for a $25,000,000 project.) The report lists in great detail each budgeted revision and includes cost projections.

Table A-1
Cost Report

JOB 277: TAMPA OFFICE BUILDING

Code	Description	Cat	Budget	Total Purchased	Variance
0140110	Bond	S	131,499	162,924	-31,425
0150110	General Conditions	M	19,141	21,726	-2,585
0150110	General Conditions	E	2,300	4,200	-1,900
0150231	Crane	E	14,840	8,137	6,703
0150246	Concrete Pump	E	0	4,055	-4,055
0150260	Water Pump	E	848	0	848
0150270	Trucks	E	5,936	0	5,936
0150150	Survey Crew	G	848	10,333	-9,485
0150211	Equipment Maintenance	G	54,000	112,561	-58,561
0150250	Rubbish Chutes	G	4,452	2,388	2,064
0150280	Small Tools	G	7,102	49,656	-42,554
0150311	Owner's Office	G	5,936	10,390	-4,454
0150315	Field Office	G	5,936	20,550	-14,614
0150320	Sheds	G	2,650	81	2,569
0150332	Telephone	G	7,632	27,082	-19,450
0150333	Electricity	G	15,264	10,380	4,884
0150334	Toilet Rental	G	13,118	22,481	-9,363
0150335	Fire Protection	G	2,862	2,836	26
0150412	Builders Risk	G	28,000	49,490	-21,490
0150426	Construction Signs	G	371	143	228
0150430	First Aid	G	1,776	17,038	-15,262
0150440	Record Drawings	G	212	0	212
0150441	Contract Drawings	G	10,600	5,925	4,675
0150443	Surveyor - Sitework	G	8,000	12,634	-4,634
0150511	Travel Expenses	G	3,612	0	3,612
0150514	Miscellaneous	G	17,754	52,737	-34,983
0150613	Safety Barricades	G	1,272	697	575
0150630	Clean Windows	G	318	8,073	-7,755
0150631	Final Clean Up	G	2,290	15,185	-12,895
0150640	Hauling	G	32,101	85,949	-53,848
0151103	Profit Sharing	G	0	19,633	-19,633
0151105	Hospitalization	G	0	14,032	-14,032
0151106	Warehouse Charges	G	0	341,000	-341,000
0150110	General Conditions	S	0	0	0
0150110	General Conditions	L	459,270	930,593	-471,323
0214130	Form Materials	M	5,825	2,260	3,565

154

Code	Description	Unit			
0214165	Polyethylene	M	0	565	-565
0214166	Gravels	M	0	2,425	-2,425
0214365	Forming Accessories	M	743	902	-159
0214366	Rough Hardware	M	401	215	186
0214370	Ready Mix	M	0	0	0
0214414	Expansion Joint Filler	M	0	50	-50
0214429	Perimeter Insulation	M	0	0	0
0214470	Dowels	M	0	0	0
0214504	Summer Concrete	M	0	0	0
0214508	Test Cylinders	M	743	0	743
0214526	Floor Hardener	M	0	0	0
0214530	Membrane Cure	M	0	2,424	-2,424
0215020	All Other Material	M	0	2,676	-2,676
0214110	Concrete Site	E	254	5,106	-4,852
0214110	Concrete Site	L	104,955	289,656	-184,701
0220120	Backhoe	E	35,000	148,776	-113,776
0220110	Earthwork	S	171,000	182,176	-11,176
0220120	Backhoe	S	0	8,592	-8,592
0220110	Earthwork	L	185,000	359,316	-174,316
0235110	Piles	S	70,000	74,683	-4,683
0254110	Paving Bituminous	S	84,000	63,500	20,500
0260110	Underground Utilities	S	0	0	0
0282110	Fountains	S	3,000	8,750	-5,750
0290110	Landscaping	S	255,000	256,000	-1,000
0330130	Formwork	M	17,199	52,458	-35,259
0330165	Polyethylene	M	0	722	-722
0330166	Gravels	M	33,542	70,041	-36,499
0330365	Forming Accessories	M	2,120	15,914	-13,794
0330366	Rough Hardware	M	785	12,422	-11,637
0330370	Ready Mix Concrete	M	330,230	403,286	-73,056
0330414	Exp. Joint Filler	M	0	0	0
0330429	Perimeter Insulation	M	0	0	0
0330454	Anchor Bolts	M	3,169	71,504	-68,335
0330470	Dowels	M	86	89	-3
0330504	Summer Concrete	M	0	0	0
0330508	Test Cylinders	M	7,059	0	7,059
0330526	Floor Hardener	M	17	1,746	-1,729
0330530	Membrane Cure	M	4	635	-631
0331020	All Other Materials	M	20,766	56,135	-35,369
0330110	Building Concrete	E	4,881	218	4,663
0330614	Rebars	S	410,000	400,927	9,073
0330110	Building Concrete	L	392,221	1,137,820	-745,599
0420110	Masonry	S	40,000	49,080	-9,080
0423110	Copings/Keystones/Precast Con	S	2,000	0	2,000

Table A–1 (continued)

JOB 277: TAMPA OFFICE BUILDING

Code	Description	Cat	Budget	Total Purchased	Variance
0510110	Structural Steel	S	1,289,000	1,240,000	49,000
0530110	Metal Decking	S	63,000	62,000	1,000
0610110	Carpentry	S	860,794	860,794	0
0620110	Millwork	S	378,000	348,680	29,320
0625110	Carpentry - Finish	M	0	506	-506
0625110	Carpentry - Finish	L	0	5,576	-5,576
0710110	Waterproofing Membrane	S	58,000	50,000	8,000
0711610	Fluid Appl.Elast.	S	0	0	0
0720110	Building Insulation	S	100,000	52,024	47,976
0722110	Concrete Insulation - L Wgt	S	36,000	42,000	-6,000
0746110	Metal Wall Panels	S	0	153	-153
0758110	Roofing	S	130,000	145,420	-15,420
0758610	Roof Tiles	S	0	0	0
0759110	Sheet Metal	S	0	406	-406
0770110	Roof Accessories	S	0	0	0
0780110	Skylights	S	360,000	358,500	1,500
0790110	Caulking & Sealants	M	6,663	3,513	3,150
0790110	Caulking & Sealants	E	375	0	375
0790110	Caulking & Sealants	L	54,962	1,676	53,286
0810110	Hollow Metal	M	59,000	67,318	-8,318
0810110	Hollow Metal	L	33,000	47,435	-14,435
0820110	Wood Doors	M	90,000	94,429	-4,429
0820110	Wood Doors	L	60,000	129,914	-69,914
0833110	Coiling Doors	S	38,000	39,500	-1,500
0837111	Special Doors	M	5,200	2,173	3,027
0837110	Folding Doors	L	1,800	144	1,656
0840010	Entrance Store Front	S	970,000	964,195	5,805
0845110	Sectional Doors	S	11,000	14,400	-3,400
0849110	Rolling Fire Doors	S	0	0	0
0870110	Finish Hardware	M	145,000	196,622	-51,622
0882110	Steel Windows	S	0	0	0
0915110	Lath and Plaster	S	1,195,000	1,135,000	60,000
0925110	Metal Stud and Drywall	S	1,155,000	1,146,839	8,161
0930110	Tile Ceramic	S	490,000	487,847	2,153
0935110	Marble	S	10,000	7,425	2,575
0950110	Acoustical Ceilings	S	34,000	30,000	4,000
0952110	Metal Ceiling Systems	S	0	0	0
0962110	Flooring Resilient	S	215,000	216,000	-1,000

156

Code	Description	Type			
0969110	Carpet	S	0	0	0
0990110	Painting	S	200,000	199,000	1,000
1010110	Chalk and Tackboards	M	1,700	2,457	-757
1010110	Chalk and Tackboards	L	800	0	800
1015110	Toilet Partitions	S	95,000	98,475	-3,475
1021110	Louver Exterior	S	0	0	0
1030110	Fireplaces	S	3,500	1,450	2,050
1050110	Metal Lockers	S	2,000	2,200	-200
1052110	Fire Extinguishers	M	7,500	8,059	-559
1052110	Fire Extinguishers	L	1,500	1,099	401
1057110	Mail Chute	M	9,000	8,055	945
1057110	Mail Chute	L	1,000	1,160	-160
1057120	Accessories Toilet	S	70,000	74,000	-4,000
1140110	Food Service	S	525,000	525,000	0
1145110	Residential Equipment	M	28,000	30,580	-2,580
1145110	Residential Equipment	L	2,000	1,417	583
1252110	Shades	S	24,000	25,000	-1,000
1267110	Entrance Mats/Rugs	M	3,000	5,538	-2,538
1267110	Entrance Mats/Rugs	L	500	822	-322
1400110	Conveying Systems	S	131,000	124,205	6,795
1410110	Dumb Waiters	S	0	0	0
1500110	Mechanical	S	2,775,000	2,821,173	-46,173
1502110	Fire Sprinkler	S	265,000	263,000	2,000
1600110	Electrical	S	1,320,000	1,537,484	-217,484
1650110	Signage	S	0	0	0
9999998	Owner C/O's	M	0	749	-749
9999998	Owner C/O's	G	0	15,491	-15,491
9999998	Owner C/O's Thru CO#5	S	1,022,569	476,907	545,662
9999999	Profit	P	1,018,431	1,018,431	0

JOB 277 TOTALS:
TAMPA OFFICE BUILDING

	Type			
	S	14,992,362	14,555,709	436,653
	M	796,893	1,138,194	-341,301
	E	64,434	170,492	-106,058
	G	226,106	906,765	-680,659
	L	1,297,008	2,906,628	-1,609,620
	P	1,018,431	1,018,431	0
TOTAL		18,395,234	20,696,219	-2,300,985

Table A-2

Job Summary

Job 3012 State Office

G/L No.	Description	C	T	Original Estimate	Current Budget	Actual This Month	Actual To Date	Projected MGR Final Cost	Projected	Over/Under Budget	% Exp	Revenue To Date	Revenue This Year
Job #	State Office			PROJ. MGR - MGR	START DATE-		2/1/86 COMPLETION DATE -		12/1/86		REVENUE TYPE		PERCENT 5%
5001	Contract Thru C.O. #13			5,221,806	5,444,222	66,660	5,417,115		5,444,222		100%	5,119,654	230,801
5101	Labor		L	376,412	401,182	6,766	408,200		459,571	58,389	102%		
5102	Material		P	114,865	108,134	4,906	107,612		151,484	43,350	100%		
5103	Subcontract		S	3,668,371	4,099,369	95,609	4,125,541		4,215,074	115,705	101%		
5104	Material Contract		M	389,388	194,632	7,805	208,454		215,888	21,256	107%		
5105	Equipment		E	203,880	203,659	1,146	192,652		245,940	42,281	95%		
5106	Expense		X	169,049	197,012	529	121,466		200,535	3,523	62%		
	Total Costs			4,921,965	5,203,988	116,761	5,163,925	0	5,488,492	284,504	99%	5,163,924	119,478
	Margin			299,841	240,234	-50,101	253,190	0	-44,270	-284,504	105%	-44,270	350,279
											Over/Under Billed		297,461

158

Table A-2 (continued)

Job 3012 - State Office

Pay Cd/Cd	Description	Original Estimate	Current Budget	Cost This/Month	Cost To Date	Actual Qty	Budget Qty	U/M	Act/Unit Cost	Projected
001670	E Concrete Buckets	500	461		1,133 *				*	1,133
001690	E Vibrators	500	500		1,533 *				*	1,533
001710	E Concrete Pump	3,000								
002200	E Earthwork SM Tools	10,000	2,943	360	4,992 *				*	4,992
002605	E Curb & Gutter Forms	2,000	2,000		5,544 *				*	5,544
003001	E Pump Conc Caissons		4,700		4,700					4,700
003100	E Form Rental	3,000	3,000	-21	9,632 *				*	9,632
001150	E Job Office	2,380	2,380		1,373					2,380
001170	E Tool Trailer	2,100	2,100		1,500					2,100
001250	E Temp Roads	2,000	2,000							2,000
001290	E Job Communications	2,800	2,800		1,125					2,800
001310	E Unload & Haul	1,500	1,500							1,500
001350	E Temp Power Cords	1,200	1,200		3,536 *				*	3,536
001380	E Temp Heat	500	500		620 *				*	620
001400	E Pumping Casual	1,000	1,000		455					1,000
001410	E Printing, Post & Supp	1,200	1,200		814					1,200
001450	E Office Equipment	36,000	34,000		9,589					34,000
001480	E Handhats	600	600		27					600
001510	E Periodic Cleanup	1,000	1,000		280					1,000
001610	E Mobilization & Off	2,000	2,000	175	657					2,000
001650	E CPM Schedule	600	600							600
001660	E Small Tools	25,000	25,000	4	21,934					25,000
001710	E Concrete Pump	8,000	6,300		6,620 *				*	6,620
001720	E Survey Equipment	6,000	6,000	379	5,538					6,000
001740	E Pickups & Autos	10,000	10,000		6,858					10,000
001750	E Flatbed Truck	3,500	3,500		1,169					3,500
001760	E Compressor & Airtool	2,500	2,500		4,830 *				*	4,830
001790	E Crane	23,000	23,000		28,116 *				*	28,116
001800	E Loader	6,000	14,875		14,728 *				*	14,875
001830	E Fork Lift	9,000	9,000		14,341 *				*	14,341
001840	E Backhoe	20,000	20,000		32,318 *				*	32,318
001850	E Scaffold	3,000	3,000		3,468 *				*	3,468
001860	E Fuel, Oil, Grease	14,000	14,000	246	5,220 *				*	14,000
		203,880	203,659	1,143	192,650				*	245,938

Table A-2 (continued)

Job 3012 - State Office

	Description	Original Estimate	Current Budget	Cost This/Month	Cost To Date	Actual Qty	Budget Qty	U/M	Act/Unit Cost	Projected
					25*					25*
000001	L Assist CTL Per JB									
001790	L Loader Operator	12,000	12,000	395	11,600	27	24	WKS	429.629	11,600
002225	L Hand Excavation	5,765	2,765	2,215	2,581	87	100	PCT	29.666	2,967
002230	L Hand Backfill	9,609	5,609		12,297*	2095	1500	CY	5.869	12,296
002240	L Fine Grade	11,059	7,059		5,401	25520	25000	SF	0.211	5,401
002456	L Manhole Rework				2,429*	1			2429.000	2,429
002457	L Light Pole Bases			326	1,344*					1,344
002500	L Drain Lines	8,587	8,587		2,334	581	600	LF	4.017	2,411
002544	L Pipe Sleeves				1,893*					1,893
002550	L Roof Drains	325	325		1,225*	6	6	EA	204.166	1,225
002551	L Site Drainage	3,822	3,822		1,831	544	1500	LF	3.365	5,048
002553	L Subdrains	4,300	4,300		1,827	1080	1100	LF	1.691	1,861
002601	L Drain Pans	5,000	5,000			115	1500	SF		4,617
002605	L Curb & Gutter	5,000	5,000	220	21,792*	5310	5000	LF	4.103	21,792
002610	L Sidewalk	12,988	12,988	426	8,164	10907	20000	SF	0.748	14,971
003010	L Caisson Dowels & Bolt	500	500		1,163*	100	100 c	PCT	11.630	1,163
003110	L Form Grade Beams	5,900	5,900		14,140*	12859	7375	SF	1.099	14,140
003130	L Form Walls	4,000	4,000		7,865*	6651	8300	SF	1.182	9,815
003135	L Form 5th Curbs	8,076	8,076		3,970	3190	4500	SF	1.244	3,970
003145	L Form SOG	1,825	1,825		1,457	500	500	SF	2.914	1,457
003165	L Form Susp Slab	600	600		226	400	400 c	SF	0.565	226
003170	L Form Stairs	600	600		357	260	400	SF	1.373	548
003180	L Form Topping	14,607	14,607		6,000	4200	3600 c	SF	1.428	6,000
003190	L Set Topping Screeds	1,825	1,825		337	1180	22000	LF	0.285	2,064
003200	L Install Mesh Bldg	2,000	2,000		3,759*	138100	120000	SF	0.027	3,759
003201	L Install Rebar	500	500		513*	51	100	PCT	10.058	1,006
003202	L Backcharge S&S				117*					117
003310	L Place Cong Gr Beams	521	521		1,332*	233	136	CY	5.716	1,331
003311	L Caisson Concrete	1,000	1,000		636	459	1000 c	CY	1.385	636
003330	L Place Conc Walls	467	467		304	76	102	CY	4.000	409
003335	L Place Conc 5th Curb	533	533		246	41	83 c	CY	6.000	245
003345	L Place Conc SOG	1,643	1,643	137	1,789*	351	305	CY	5.096	1,790
003365	L Place Conc Susp Slab	200	200		15	5	5 c	CY	3.000	14
003370	L Place Conc Stairs	609	609		56	9	30	CY	6.222	186
003380	L Place Topping	3,591	3,591		4,398*	944	1000 c	CY	4.658	4,398
003400	L Trowel Finish	9,860	9,860		14,308*	124429	120000	SF	0.114	14,308
003415	L Curing	1,339	1,339		356	131336	160000	SF	0.002	434
003430	L Rub Walls	668	668		3,650*	105	100	PCT	34.761	3,650
003600	L Grouting	11,379	28		651*	1	1	PCT	651.000	651
005500	L Catwalk Rails			225	225*	11			20.454	225
006000	L Rough Carpentry	28,694	28,794	370	8,630	6662	28000	BF	1.295	36,271

160

Code	Item									
008110	L H-M Frames	3,462	3,462		4,418 *	91	60	EA	48.549	4,418
008200	L Doors, Hrdwr	7,675	7,675		1,236	91	60	EA	13.582	1,236
012690	L Install Pedimat		508	81	757 *	2	2	EA	378.500	757
		190,529	168,786	4,395	157,654 *					205,104
002001	L Clean Rubbish		545		560 *	11			50.909	560
002002	L PSCO Grade West 26		746		1,272 *	20			63.600	1,272
002003	L Grading North & East		107		3,178 *					3,178
			1,398		5,010 *					5,010
002500	L Fine Grade & Compact				636 *					636 *
002505	L Backfill & Compact				1,050 *	80			13.125	1,049 *
003110	L Form Footing				1,913 *	424			4.511	1,914 *
003130	L Form Walls				2,826 *	3400			0.831	2,826 *
003310	L Place & Fin Footing				639 *	56			11.410	639 *
003330	L Place Walls				689 *	95			7.252	689 *
003400	L Rub Walls				323 *					323 *
					8,076 *					8,076 *
001150	L Job Office	300	300	1	187	8	7	MOS	23.375	187
001250	L Temp Road Maintain	3,000	3,000		1,983 *	70	100	PCT	28.328	2,832 *
001300	L Drinking Water	700	700		972 *	7	7	MOS	138.857	972 *
001310	L Unload & Haul	5,949	3,900		4,469 *	45	45	WKS	99.311	4,469 *
001320	L Weather Protection	750	750		2,653 *	55	10	WKS	48.236	2,653 *
001321	L Extra Labor 4-3Storm		1,226		1,226	75	100 c	PCT	16.346	1,226
001330	L Install Temp Power	1,000	1,000		83	2	2 c	EA	41.500	83
001400	L Pumping	2,000	2,000		638	80	100 c	PCT	7.975	637
001490	L Safety, Rails, Scaffol		6,000		5,624	99	100	PCT	56.808	5,681
001510	L Periodic Cleanup	15,840	15,840		14,397 *	7	6	MOS	2056.714	14,398
001515	L Clean Forms				1,543 *		c			1,543 *
001610	L Mobilization	2,000	7,521	133	6,785	78	100	PCT	86.987	8,698 *
001620	L Initial Layout	3,000	3,000		12,581 *	706	200	HRS	17.820	12,582 *
001640	L Parking Layout	250	250		286 *	86	100	PCT	3.325	332 *
001870	L Supervision	40,000	74,400	288	71,572	32	30	WKS	2236.625	71,572
001920	L Job Secretary	7,200	7,200		8,186 *	39	24	WKS	209.897	8,187 *
		81,989	127,087	422	133,185 *					136,052 *

161

Table A-2 (continued)

Job 3012 - State Office

	Description	Original Estimate	Current Budget	Cost This/Month	Cost To Date	Actual Qty	Budget Qty	U/M	Act/Unit Cost	Projected
017600	L Payroll Taxes	34,286	30,418	656	28,422	99	100	PCT	287.090	28,709
017700	L Workmen's Comp Ins	12,468	38,072	805	40,014 *	99	100	PCT	404.181	40,418 *
017800	L Union Fringes	57,140	35,421	489	35,840 *	99	100	PCT	362.020	36,202 *
		103,894	103,911	1,950	104,276 *					105,329 *
		376,412	401,182	6,767	408,201 *					459,571 *

Job 3012 - State Office

Cat/Cd	Description	Original Estimate	Current Budget	Contract Amount	Cost This/Month	Cost To Date	Projected
003000	M Concrete	120,000	112,830	145,818	7,805	138,472	145,818
003200	M Supply Reinforcing	34,581	16,514	13,096		13,095	13,096
005400	M Struct & Misc Steel	200,000					
006400	M Doors & Millwork	10,303	23,925	16,861		16,861	16,861
008110	M Hollow Metal	7,337	7,337	6,087		6,000	6,087
008710	M Finish Hardware	17,167	31,585	31,585		31,585	31,585
012690	M Pedimats		2,441	2,441		2,441	2,441
		389,388	194,632	215,888	7,805	208,454	215,888
		389,388	194,632	215,888	7,805	208,454	215,888

Job 3012 - State Office

	Description	Original Estimate	Current Budget	Cost This/Month	Cost To Date	Actual Qty	Budget Qty	U/M	Act/Unit Cost	Projected
002200	P Earthwork Materials	10,000		17	3,565 *				*	3,565
002700	P Prkg Lot Temp Stripe			700	700 *				*	700
002710	P Subdrainage System	20,000	19,972	103	14,156					19,972
002711	P Landscape Drainage	8,500	8,500		6,225					8,500
003101	P Form Material	2,500	2,500		3,670 *				*	3,670
003103	P Form Lumber	5,000	5,000	75	4,289					5,000
003104	P Misc Concrete Acc	1,750	1,750	38	5,916 *				*	5,916
003105	P Sawcut Slabs		1,658		3,183 *				*	3,183
003200	P Mesh		7,027		7,427 *				*	7,427
003415	P Curing Compound	750	750		1,470 *				*	1,470
003600	P Grout	10,000			557 *				*	557
005500	P Metal Fabrications	24,837	26,500		8,562					26,500
006000	P Rough Carpentry Mat'l	15,000	17,000		8,189					17,000
007112	P Damp Proof G-Beams		1,796		1,796					1,796
007571	P Foot Traffic Topping	1,844								
007720	P Roof Access Skylite	1,838	1,837							1,837
007820	P Metal Frame Skylite	1,967	1,966		2,322 *				*	2,322
008305	P Access and Doors	689	688							688
008411	P Column Clad		1,000		1,492 *				*	1,492
009678	P Base	940	940							940
		105,615	98,884	933	73,519					112,535
002500	P Drainage Mat'l				428 *				*	428
003000	P Concrete				10,566 *				*	10,566
003101	P Form Lumber				2,827 *				*	2,827
003102	P Form Hardware				293 *				*	293
003103	P Form Accessories				208 *				*	208
003104	P Misc Accessories				698 *				*	698
003200	P Tie Reinforcing				2,923 *				*	2,923
003205	P Furnish Reinforcing				2,145 *				*	2,145
005000	P Handrail			3,900	4,303 *				*	4,303
				3,900	24,391 *					24,391
001150	P Job Office	200	200		135					200
001170	P Tool Trailer	50	50							50
001250	P Temp Roads	3,000	3,000		-42					3,000
001400	P Pumping Casual	500	500							500
001610	P Mobilization & Off	2,000	2,000		801					2,000
001620	P Initial Layout	250	250		413 *				*	413
001630	P Layout by Engineer	3,000	3,000	70	7,351 *				*	7,351
001640	P Road & Lot Layout	250	250		1,043 *				*	1,043
		9,250	9,250	70	9,701 *				*	14,557
		114,865	108,134	4,903	107,611				*	151,483

163

Table A-2 (continued)

Job 3012 - State Office

Cst/Cd	Description	Original Estimate	Current Budget	Contract Amount	Last C/O#	Cost This Month	Cost To Date	Projected
001111	S Unallocated Costs				999			
000112	S Unallocated Dirt				999			
002201	S Rework Pad and Exc	10,000	44,962	99,434	7	45,889	99,331	99,434
002202	S Overlot Grading/Ames		50,000	51,615	1		50,000	51,615
002203	S Frontier Storm Sewer		17,128	51,825	1		51,825	51,825
002371	S Drill Caissons	13,309	16,168	16,168	916		16,101	16,168
002513	S Asphaltic Paving	198,381	188,571	195,670	1	55,556	162,544	195,670
003200	S Install Reinforcing	15,144			913			
003210	S Place Reinforcing	14,897	14,857	7,209	2		7,217	7,217
003400	S Precast Concrete	1,007,190	834,060	827,639	4	-6,221	827,639	827,639
003600	S Grouting		12,500	12,825	1		12,365	12,825
005400	S Erect Struct & Misc	75,408	212,048	217,061	3		217,061	217,061
005500	S Metal Stairs	69,163	36,739	39,480	2		38,476	39,480
007120	S Fluid Applied Wp	4,918			906			
007200	S Insulation		12,780	12,780	910		12,780	12,780
007320	S Concrete Roof Tiles	116,065	99,455	99,455	5		99,455	99,455
007413	S Soffit Panels	144,747	165,980	169,117	6		169,019	169,117
007600	S Flashing & Sht Metal	31,093	22,680	23,528	2		23,152	23,528
007900	S Joint Sealers	2,507	9,375	9,514	2	139	9,514	9,514
008410	S Alum Ent & Str Front	269,950	251,900	253,069	1		251,900	253,069
008411	S Handrail & Lobby Fin		63,842	64,112	1		57,701	64,112
009260	S Drywall & Studs	212,958	260,450	258,036	5		258,036	258,036
009310	S Ceramic Tile	23,331	24,908	25,153	1	245	25,153	25,153
009900	S Paint & VWC	27,005	25,590	29,750	1		25,600	29,750
010160	S Toilet Ptn & Acc	13,114	15,201	17,223	2		17,223	17,223
010270	S Lobby Pavers	88,235	141,466	142,911	901		142,911	142,911
012690	S Floor Mats	2,951			910			
014200	S Elevators	211,474	236,890	231,178	6		231,177	231,178
014450	S Elev Cab SS-Scherer			16,500			16,500	16,500
015000	S Mechanical	535,365	837,342	837,936	6		837,936	837,936
015500	S Fire Protection	122,524	96,390	95,696	5		95,696	95,696
016000	S Electrical	399,892	362,126	363,951	4		350,000	363,951
		3,609,621	4,053,408	4,168,835		95,608	4,106,312	4,168,843
001200	S Temp Fence	5,000	4,623	4,863	2		4,622	4,863
001250	S Temp Road & Lot	17,030	7,030	7,030	902		6,982	7,030
001341	S Install Temp Electric	10,000	7,625	7,625	902		7,625	7,625
001520	S Final Clean	8,400	8,400					8,400
001530	S Clean Glass	7,500	7,500					7,500
		47,930	35,178	19,518			19,229	35,418
		3,657,551	4,088,586	4,188,353		95,608	4,125,541	4,204,261

164

Job 3012 - State Office

	Description	Original Estimate	Current Budget	Cost This/Month	Cost To Date	Actual Qty	Budget Qty	U/M	Act/Unit Cost	Projected
002001	X Clean Rubbish		1,970		1,970					1,970
002002	X Rings Raise Manhole		135		135					135
			2,105		2,105					2,105
001000	X P & P Bond	36,298	37,137		35,944					37,137
001010	X Sub Bonds	37,986	40,047		27,366					40,047
001050	X All Risk Ins	17,996	18,356		18,414 *				*	18,414
001111	X Maintenance	14,000	34,206		395					34,206
001180	X Chemical Toilets	1,260	1,260		1,918 *				*	1,918
001190	X Signs	500	500		1,401 *				*	1,401
001210	X Barricades	500	500		399					500
001270	X Dust Control	1,000	1,000							1,000
001300	X Drinking Water	175	175	35	666 *				*	666
001320	X Winter Conditions	1,500	750		160					750
001340	X Temp Power Monthly	950	950		1,368 *				*	1,368
001341	X Install Temp Pwco	2,050	2,050		2,045					2,050
001360	X Temp Water Install	200	200							200
001370	X Temp Water Monthly	2,000	2,000	40	392					2,000
001390	X Telephone	1,950	1,950		2,310 *				*	2,310
001410	X Printing, Post, & Supp	1,200	1,200		1,839 *				*	1,839
001411	X Messenger Service		2,000		1,310					2,000
001440	X Photographs	500	500		126					500
001470	X First Aid & Safety	1,500	1,500		260					1,500
001490	X Guardrails	1,500	1,500							1,500
001510	X Periodic Cleanup	1,000	1,000		111					1,000
001550	X Dumpster	8,750	8,750	200	2,317					8,750
		132,815	157,531	275	98,741					161,056
017900	X Liability Ins	36,234	37,376	254	20,623					37,376
		36,234	37,376	254	20,623					37,376
		169,049	197,012	529	121,469				*	200,537

Table A-3

Detailed Costing

JOB 214 - PRISON

Cost Code	Cost Type	Cost Description	Estimated Quantity	U/M	Cost Unit Cost	Quantity Reported J-T-D	Pct Cmp	Unit Cost J-T-D	Act. Cost Current J-T-D	Projected Act. Cost & U/O
309.10	L				0 0 0	0	0.0	0.000	0 39	39 ** -39
1011.00	L	Project Manager		78 Wk 84	95175 105175 1252.083	83	100.0	1,258.422	0 104,449	104,449 ** 726
C6001		Changes/Revisions			10000					
1012.00	L	Proj Supt		78 Wk 80	90180 96213 1202.663	79	100.0	1,459.232	0 115,279	115,279 ** -19,066
C6001 C6017 R7234		Changes/Revisions			3100 1629 1304					
1013.00	L	Proj Administrator		78 Wk 83	81650 88284 1063.663	82	100.0	1,192.061	0 87,749	97,749 ** -9,465
C6001		Changes/Revisions			6634					
1014.00	L	Masonry Administration			0 33557	0	100.0	0.000	0 0	0 33,557
R7027 R7029		Changes/Revisions			53691 -20134					
1016.00	L	Secretary		78 Wk 80	34120 35220 440.25	79	100.0	544.411	0 43,008	43,008 ** -7,788
C6001		Changes/Revisions			1100					
1019.00	L	Cost Engineer			0 0 0	0	0.0	0.000	0 2,134	2,134 ** -2,134
1021.00	L	Sub Superintendent		78 Wk 84	90180 97980 1166.429	81	100.0	1,441.852	0 116,790	116,790 ** -18,810

Code		Description	Quantity					
C6001		Changes/Revisions		7800				
3040.00	L	F&S Sq & Rect. Column	3,408 SFC 3,408	10574 10574 3.103	3408 C 100.0	1.560	0 5,315	5,315 5,259
3041.00	L	F&S Round Column	595 LF 595	4708 4708 7.913	595 C 100.0	17.625	0 10,487	10,487 ** -5,779
3042.00	L	F&S Stair Walls	127 SFC 127	598 598 4.709	127 C 100.0	11.566	0 1,469	1,469 ** -871
3045.00	L	F&S Irreg Columns	4,764 SFC 4,764	18481 18481 3.879	4764 C 100.0	5.250	0 25,010	25,010 ** -6,529
3049.00	L	Cont. CJ	2,855 LF 2,855	3616 3616 1.267	2855 C 100.0	0.392	0 2,546	2,546 1,070
3055.00	L	F&S Hu Roof Slabs	26,512 SF	43347 0 0	0 C 0.0	0.000	0 0	0 0
C6001		Changes/Revisions	-26,512	-43347				
3056.00	L	F&S Balcony Cells	51,560 SF 60,000	79550 151800 2.53	55056 C 100.0	2.893	0 159,285	159,285 ** -7,485
C6009 R7035 R7075		O.C.O. #9 Changes/Revisions Form Housing Units Additions to 3056	8,440	3268 45854 23128				
3057.00	L	F&S Elevated Slabs	15,035 SF 6,261	25932 6045 0.966	6261 C 100.0	2.320	0 14,528	14,528 ** -8,483
R7035 R7075		Changes/Revisions Form Housing Units Additions to 3056	-8,744 -13488 -6399					
3061.00	L	F&S Edge Em Elev Slab	2,157 SF 365	4345 564 1.545	356 C 100.0	9.396	0 3,430	3,430 ** -2,866
R7035		Changes/Revisions Form Housing Units	-17,921	-3781				

167

Table A-3 (continued)

JOB 214 - PRISON

Cost Code	Cost Type	Cost Description	Estimated Quantity	U/M	Estimated Cost Unit Cost	Quantity Reported J-T-D	Pct Cmp	Unit Cost J-T-D	Act. Cost Current J-T-D	Projected Act. Cost & U/O
9250.00	S	Paint/Drywall/Dryvit			1,989,165 2,044,644 0	0	0.0	0.000	0 2,049,323	0 2,049,323 *** -4,679
		Changes/Revisions								
C6001		CO#3 Misc. CP-13,28,29,36,38			42,439					
C6003					2,016					
C6006		NVE C.O. 6			-1,492					
C6008		O.C.O 8			9,758					
C6010		OCO #10			10,110					
R6011		OCO #11			-13,695					
C6012		OCO #12			-4,713					
C6014		OCO #14			1,701					
C6015		OCO #15			3,557					
R7024					-950					
R7064		Printing Contract			-320,000					
R7089		V#0055-82590-88702-84399-8800			-15,000					
R7123		Paint Cell Ceilings			15,561					
R7127					-134					
C7139		Furr Fire Pipe @ H.O.'s			1,671					
C7144		Paint Light STDs			909					
R7169		Space Frame			11,005					
R7185		Finish Dryvit @ Dock			-600					
R7196		Solari Firedamage			2,335					
R7197		Set-Up 2 Subcontracts for glass			641					
R7198		Hold down clips			-289					
R7200		Solari to RDA			-1,674					
R7211		Solari to RDA			-652					
R7212		Solari Clean Out Drains			-327					
R7217		Solari to Valley Fix Bunk Fin			-3,360					
R7224		Lens Correction Only			319,433					
R7229		Glidden Paint			-2,881					
9300.00	S	Tile Work			120,996 129,443 0	0	0.0	0.000	0 129,443	129,443 0
		Changes/Revisions								
C6008		O.C.O. 8			240					
C6009		O.C.O. #9			2,128					
R7089		V#0055-82590-88702-84399-8800			-1,250					
C7095		Hu Waterproofing			1,428					
R7109		Add Ceramic Tile			5,145					
R7195		Quality Tile			756					
9500.00	S	AC Ceilings			197,072 246,488 0	0	0.0	0.000	0 246,488	246,488 0
		Changes/Revisions								
C6001					34,440					
C6012		Change Order OCO #12			211					
R7041		Value Engr. Correction			12,560					
R7089		V#0005-82590-88702-84399-8800			-2,000					
R7165		Repair Ceiling			489					

APPENDIX B

SAMPLE DAMAGE CALCULATIONS

§ B.1　Introduction

Appendix B is a sample claim, with the entitlement presented in **§§ B.3** through **B.13**, followed by a detailed presentation of damages (see **§ B.14**, Exhibits 1 through 15). Included with the presentation of damages are examples of the cost reports and financial statements (see **§§ B.15** and **B.16**) from which the damages were, in part, derived. Copies of all the supporting reports that would be used in preparation of such damage claims are not included because of their voluminous nature. However, sufficient backup is provided to demonstrate how damages can be tied to cost reporting data.

Although the documents that would support the calculations in the various exhibits are omitted, each exhibit attempts to reference the appropriate documents. In an actual claim presentation, these documents would either be included in the claim or be available for examination in support of the calculations.

In the case of small tools, Exhibit 5, and extended overhead, Exhibit 10, alternate calculations using different methods are included. Which method is more appropriate must be determined from the specific factual situation.

Not all the claim elements presented in this sample would be found in a single claim. The sample calculations were adapted from a number of separate, actual claims. They are included not as an endorsement of any method of calculation or format but as examples of how claims can be presented.

§ B.2   Statement of Facts

Prime Contractor is a contractor that specializes in the construction of power plants, dams, hydroelectric facilities, and similar heavy engineering projects. Prime Contractor has contracted with Owner for the construction of an expansion of an existing hydroelectric facility (Project) in the state of Columbia. Prime Contractor is a national contractor, headquartered in Metropolis, which is in an adjoining state. Prime Contractor also maintains a branch office in Utopia, Columbia. It was this branch office that chose to bid upon the Project.

Owner independently contracted with a major engineering firm to prepare the plans and specifications for the expansion of the hydroelectric facility. Additionally, Owner directly purchased the major equipment for installation in the expanded hydroelectric plant, including the turbines, generators, major electrical switch gear, values, and similar long lead-time, major items. Owner had originally contracted with Engineer to provide construction management of the Project. However, after the design was complete but prior to the Project being put out to bid, Owner decided to perform construction administration with its own personnel. Owner put the Project out for bid without changing the contracts and specifications prepared by Engineer, with the exception of designating Owner as Engineer. Owner solicited proposals from several contractors. Prime Contractor was the low bidder, but its bid was within 2 ½ percent of the second bidder's proposal. Owner interviewed both Prime Contractor and the second lowest bidder, because Owner was concerned about schedule as well as price. Owner selected Prime Contractor because it was the low bidder and because of Prime Contractor's 502-day schedule for constructing the Project.

The contract documents were executed in January of 1990 and Notice-to-Proceed was given with an effective date of March 17, 1990. The Project was located in the coastal mountains of Columbia. As a result, winter conditions were severe, with heavy snows and severe cold weather. Prime Contractor's schedule, which was submitted at the time Notice-to-Proceed was issued in January of 1990, contemplated the major concrete work being completed during the summer months due to the extreme costs of winter work. Prime Contractor's schedule contained milestone dates referencing Owner's delivery of major equipment items. Although the Contract required schedule approval, Owner did not approve or reject the schedule.

In March 1990, Prime Contractor began performing the initial excavation and blasting work to remove the significant quantities of rock and overburden. Almost immediately, Prime Contractor was delayed in its work when Owner implemented new and unanticipated restrictions on blasting work. Owner implemented these restrictions when it decided that it did not want blasting done during the operation of the existing hydroelectric plant. No such restriction was contained within the contract documents nor had any such restriction been mentioned previously. Owner refused to grant a time extension, stating that such a restriction should have been obvious to Prime Contractor. Owner refused to advise Prime Contractor in advance as to when the plant would be operating because Owner wanted to operate the plant as a peaking plant, selling power at the highest possible rate only when peaking power was needed. As a result, in addition to delaying Project, Prime Contractor was forced to work in a stop/start manner with little advance notice regarding when worktime would be available.

Owner's contract documents, which were written by Engineer in anticipation that Engineer would provide construction management services, provided that the construction manager would provide survey and layout for the Project. When Owner designated itself as Engineer and construction manager, it did not make any changes in the contract documents. However, Owner was not prepared to provide survey and control on-site and was consistently late in providing requested control; it also provided control and survey that were inaccurate. Owner required Prime Contractor to bear all costs of correcting survey errors, on the basis that Prime Contractor had an obligation to verify the survey and control.

Prime Contractor found numerous problems with the contract documents. Particularly, the mechanical, electrical, and civil drawings were not coordinated and were inconsistent. In accordance with the contractual procedure, contractor would issue a request for information (RFI) to Owner, who was designated as construction manager/engineer. Owner, however, refused to deal with such problems in a timely manner and would not respond to Prime Contractor's RFIs.

Because Owner did not have the manpower to also act as construction manager, the review of shop drawings, submittals, and lift submittals for concrete was substantially delayed. Prime Contractor's requests for additional time and compensation for the delays were rejected by Owner. Further, Owner notified Prime Contractor's surety that Prime Contractor was in default and demanded that Prime Contractor accelerate its work and finish the Project. After an investigation Surety declined to intervene and Owner allowed Prime Contractor to complete. Project ultimately was finished more than 15 months late. The major causes for the delay were the late delivery of Owner-furnished major equipment, which was more than one year late, and Owner's failure to provide timely engineering information. Moreover, Owner did not deliver turbine generator to the site until six months after the original completion date of the Project. In spite of this, Owner has maintained that any delay resulted from the actions or inactions of Prime Contractor. As a result, Prime Contractor has prepared a detailed claim with damages and has submitted it to Owner under the contract provisions. Prime Contractor anticipates that this claim will form the basis of its lawsuit, which it intends to file 31 days after submitting the claim. Under the terms of the contract, Owner has 30 days in which to accept or deny the claim.

§ B.3 Prime Contractor's Claim

Prime Contractor has recently completed the civil portion of the enlargement of a hydroelectric powerplant. That work included more than 100,000 cubic yards of excavation, construction of a reinforced concrete and steel frame powerplant, installation of tailrace gates, penstock piping, as well as mechanical and electrical work. The contract for the work was awarded to Prime Contractor in the amount of $6,125,120. A notice to proceed was issued in January 1990, with an effective date of March 17, 1990; the contract allowed 502 calendar days for completion, making the original contract completion date August 1, 1991.

During the performance of its work, Prime Contractor encountered problems not of its own making which extended its time of performance and increased its costs. These difficulties included:

1. Owner's unjustified denial of an excavation permit, which delayed the start of Prime Contractor's excavation work.

2. Owner's failure to provide survey and layout in an accurate and professional manner, thereby causing delay and disruption to the progress of Prime Contractor's work.

3. Defective contract documents. Prime Contractor issued more than 50 RFI's indicating that a discrepancy, conflict, or omitted information had been discovered in the contract documents. During the course of construction, Owner issued numerous changes to the work. Specific defects in the contract documents include:

   a. Significantly larger boulders than indicated by Owner's geologic reports were found during the powerplant excavation. Such unforeseen conditions delayed and disrupted excavation.

   b. Owner's field directives changed the elevation and centerline of
       an access road, thereby substantially increasing the quantities of
       work beyond that set forth in the contract documents.

   c. The Owner changed the elevations and grades for certain struc-
       tural work.

   d. Rock pockets occurred in some concrete placements as a result of
       Owner's congested rebar design, Owner's use of a harsh, unsuit-
       able concrete mix, and Owner's refusal to permit the use of small-
       diameter concrete vibrators.

4. The Owner's contract administration practices were faulty and con-
   tributed to the delay and disruption Prime Contractor experienced in
   its field work. Examples of Owner's poor contract administration procedures include:

   a. The Owner returned approximately 45 percent of Prime Contrac-
       tor's submittals later than the 30 days allowed by the specifica-
       tions.

   b. Although Owner's notations on the documents indicate that
       Owner had completed its review, Owner kept 40 submittals at
       least 10 extra days before returning them to Prime Contractor.

   c. In its review of Prime Contractor's submittals, Owner sometimes
       noted defects or required resubmittal for minor and insignificant
       reasons.

   d. Changes were issued when the affected construction activity was
       already underway, resulting in disrupted work.

   e. For the 20 change directives having accompanying drawings, the
       time period between the date of the drawing revision and the date
       the change directive was issued averaged 45 days. This means
       that, on the average, Owner took more than six weeks to prepare
       each change directive's boilerplate and to distribute the change
       directive.

   f. Owner failed to grant justified time extensions for days when un-
       usually severe weather conditions caused critical aspects of Prime
       Contractor's work to be shut down.

5. Throughout the course of the Project, Prime Contractor performed
   considerable extra work not specified by the contract documents, extending its time of performance and increased its costs. In addition,
   Prime Contractor was forced to accelerate due to extra work and
   Owner-caused delays.

   As a result of the many problems encountered by Prime Contractor during the construction of the powerplant, problems for which Owner is responsible, Prime Contractor is entitled to a time extension of 509 calendar

days. In addition, Prime Contractor is entitled to the contract balance of $780,711 and additional compensation in the amount of $2,259,495.76, for a total of $3,040,206.76.

§ B.4 Additional Compensation Due

An explanation of each direct cost item follows.

Labor Cost

Prime Contractor's cost reports have been used as the base data from which most of the calculations of additional labor cost have been developed. The Job Cost Type Status Reports and the Combined Project Quantity and Manhour Cost Reports provide raw data on direct labor, overtime premium, and benefit expenses associated with the labor which Prime Contractor has spent on this project to date. The specific data source for each area is referenced in the individual discussions.

Labor Burden

Prime Contractor's labor burden for the original schedule for the power-plant project is 17.68 percent. The factor was determined as set forth in Exhibit 6. Prime Contractor's cost reports provide data from which its labor burden was developed. The Job Cost Type Status Report provides the raw data for the labor burden expenses associated with direct labor. The labor burden on straight-time wages during the extended schedule was determined to be 27.94 percent as shown in Exhibit 6. The increase in labor burden due to extended project duration is set forth in Exhibit 6.

Small Tools and Supplies

Cost Code 1600M in Prime Contractor's cost reports contains the small tools costs incurred throughout the Project. Direct labor costs are recorded in Prime Contractor's cost report. An increase in either labor expenditures or schedule will directly increase small expenditures. The additional expense to which the contractor is entitled to is $74,966. The calculations are set forth in Exhibit 5.

Home Office Overhead on Additional Work

Prime Contractor's time of performance on the Project was *extended* by events for which Owner was responsible. Prime Contractor also performed work during the Contract performance period which was not included in its bid.

Prime Contractor incurred home office overhead expense when it performed this additional work. Prime Contractor has not been compensated for its additional home office overhead cost. Exhibit 11 of this claim addresses the home office overhead expense associated with the additional work performed by Prime Contractor during the period of extended performance.

Additionally, Prime Contractor is entitled to the added home office expenses it incurred as a result of *any* added, non-bid item work performed during the original contract period. (Bid item work should be excluded because home office overhead expense is already included in the contract prices.) The total extended overhead that Prime Contractor is entitled to is $165,587.88. (See Exhibit 11.)

Profit

A standard profit percentage rate of 5 percent has been used throughout the calculation of the additional compensation owed to Prime Contractor. This rate is typical for construction work that has been changed, accelerated, and disrupted in a manner not contemplated at the time of bid.

Bond

Upon completion of this project, Prime Contractor's surety and subcontractor's surety's will require the payment of bond premiums based upon revenues received. Prime Contractor is entitled to collect the increase in premium for the 10-month additional time period after the 24-month base period according to Prime Contractor bond premium schedule in Exhibit 12.

Cost of Funding

Whenever the duration of a construction project is extended beyond the original completion date, or additional work is required outside the scope of work contained in the original contract, Prime Contractor's costs increase and Prime Contractor is entitled to reimbursement by Owner for these additional costs if the extended duration and extra work are caused by events for which Owner is responsible. If compensation for these additional costs is not made at the time they occur, Prime Contractor must carry the financial burden of funding the additional costs until such time that compensation is received. The cost of funding these additional expenses is not part of the cost of performing the original contract work as it was bid, and Prime Contractor is due reimbursement for these extra financial costs.

Prime Contractor carried the burden of funding these additional costs, experienced as a consequence of Owner's actions, and is therefore due reimbursement for the use of its funds. Because no compensation for these additional work efforts has been received, these funds are still committed to the Project and are continuing to incur financing costs.

The average prime interest rate from the effective date of the Notice to Proceed, March 17, 1990, and projected through December 1992 was determined as 9.83 percent as shown in Exhibit 13 using the established rates. Prime Contractor borrows money at an annual rate of 0.5 percent over the prime rate. The sum of these interest rates, 10.33 percent (9.83% + 0.5%) per year, has been used in Exhibit 14 to calculate the cost of funding the additional monies Prime Contractor has been compelled to commit to the Project. Exhibit 14 lists each of the additional cost items which Prime Contractor has experienced on this job, the extra cost of each item (net of bond), and the duration over which the additional cost was incurred. The As-Built Schedule has been used to determine when each unforeseen added expenditure started and ended. For each item, the base amount due Prime Contractor plus other markups when they are appropriate (for example, labor burden, small tools, and supplies), but excluding bond costs (which will be paid only when the additional revenue is received) and profit, have been uniformly distributed over the months in which they were incurred. Certain items, costs could not be identified with a given period of time and were, therefore, distributed in accordance with the percent completed each month as established in Owner's Construction Estimates. A cumulative amount for each item was also calculated. The average interest rate, 0.8608 percent per month (10.33% divided by 12 months), has been multiplied by the prior month's cumulative amount in order to calculate the current month's cost of funding the additional work performed by Prime Contractor.

The cost of funding for each item of additional cost, as set forth in Exhibit 14 has been calculated on the amounts due Prime Contractor exclusive of profit or bond. The cost of funding has been calculated through an anticipated settlement date of December 31, 1992, and has been included with each calculation of additional compensation. The cost of funding to which Prime Contractor is entitled will increase or decrease dependent upon the time Prime Contractor actually receives payment.

§ B.5 Acceleration

When Prime Contractor prepared its bid for the Project, it planned to work in an orderly sequence without disruption and thus make the most efficient use of its work force and other resources. As described in the previous sections of the Change Order Request, Prime Contractor's work was delayed and disrupted by events for which Owner was responsible throughout the duration of the Project. Owner's offered time extension was late and was insufficient to cover the disruption and additional efforts experienced by Prime Contractor. Thus, throughout the course of this project, Prime Contractor has been constructively accelerated in its work in an attempt to try to meet milestones and the completion date of the contract.

During the performance of the Project, Prime Contractor experienced excusable delays for which time extensions were justified. Prime Contractor requested time extensions in a timely manner but Owner did not grant sufficient time extensions; nevertheless, Owner imposed liquidated damages and otherwise acted to compel contractor to complete the project within the originally scheduled period. As a consequence, Prime Contractor incurred substantial additional costs. Prime Contractor is entitled to reimbursement for the expenses it sustained in complying with Owner's direction. **Section B.6** sets forth *some* of the correspondence between Prime Contractor and Owner which illustrates that Prime Contractor's work was constructively accelerated.

§ B.6 Acceleration Correspondence

By its letter dated August 9, 1990, Prime Contractor requested a 21-day time extension because the access road excavation quantities had increased from what was indicated on the Bid Schedule. Owner replied on August 24, 1990. Owner stated that the access road excavation quantities had not increased significantly; Owner denied Prime Contractor's time extension request.

Prime Contractor's letter dated January 26, 1991 (letter #76) noted that additional excavation of the powerplant foundation was required due to the discovery of fractured bedrock, the removal of which was directed by change directive #5. Prime Contractor requested a time extension for the additional work. By its letter dated February 16, 1991 (letter #55), Owner denied Prime Contractor's request for a time extension because it did not believe that the work directed by change directive #5 delayed Prime Contractor. In its letter dated January 28, 1991, Prime Contractor stated that the additional excavation of the powerplant foundation directed by change directive #5 had delayed Prime Contractor's progress and that either the plant shutdown scheduled for January 1991 would have to be extended or Owner would have to order that the project be accelerated. Owner replied on March 6, 1991 (letter #69). Owner said that the work added by change directive #5 had not delayed the job and refused Prime Contractor's request for an order to accelerate. In a subsequent letter dated June 9, 1991 (letter #97), which also dealt with the work added by change directive #5, Owner stated, "Owner agrees that Prime Contractor should make every effort to return to their original schedule but does not and will not agree that this is to be considered 'acceleration,' in any shape or form."

Owner forwarded Contract Change Order #3 (Revised) with its letter dated July 25, 1991 (letter 4112). The change order included a 21-day time extension for overexcavating and shaping the powerplant foundation. Owner stated that because the 21 days were concurrent with batch plant setup and establishment of adequate dewatering, the contract time would be extended but no monetary compensation would be allowed. Prime Contractor replied in its letter dated August 22, 1991 (letter #147), denying that either the batch plant or dewatering were concurrent delays, and refused to sign the change order.

These examples, drawn from the parties' correspondence, illustrate that on many occasions throughout construction of the Powerplant, Prime Contractor advised Owner that Owner's actions would require Prime Contractor to expend additional time. These examples illustrate that Owner routinely failed to act expeditiously to address the issue of additional time. These examples also show that on only one occasion did Owner offer a time extension and because it was conditioned on being non-compensable, Prime Contractor rejected it. The examples cited are typical of the entire job: Owner added or changed work so as to increase Prime Contractor's time of performance; Prime Contractor advised Owner that its time of performance would increase; Owner routinely failed to address the added time requirements; and Prime Contractor was forced to try to meet the original contract completion dates. In attempting to adhere to the specified intermediate milestone and final contract completion dates, Prime Contractor sustained expenses not foreseen when it prepared its bid for the work. Owner, having constructively accelerated Prime Contractor, is responsible for these costs. These additional costs include premium time labor costs and loss of labor productivity due to working extended overtime.

Premium Labor Cost

Prime Contractor was forced to accelerate the work in an attempt to meet intermediate milestones and the Project completion date. During the course of the Project, Prime Contractor worked a considerable amount of scheduled overtime and has incurred additional costs which were not anticipated at the time of bid. These additional premium costs are a direct result of problems beyond Prime Contractor's control for which Owner is responsible.

Prime Contractor planned to work a single eight-hour shift per day, Monday through Friday, and made no allowance in its bid to work overtime on the Project. As recorded in Prime Contractor's Job Cost Type Status Reports, a substantial amount of overtime was worked through November 18, 1991. A portion of the overtime manhours Prime Contractor worked—and, therefore, a portion of the premium costs which Prime Contractor incurred to accelerate the work—are Owner's responsibility. The overtime manhours and the associated premium labor costs experienced by Prime Contractor through November 18, 1991, are set forth in Prime Contractor's Job Costs Type Status Reports and are summarized in Exhibit 9.

Loss of Labor Productivity—Overtime

Apart from the additional premium costs incurred in accelerating the work, Prime Contractor also incurred a loss of labor productivity. Three different methods were used to calculate productivity loss. These methods are: the total cost approach, the Leonard method, and industry standards. Prime Contractor has elected to use the average of the three methods as illustrated in Exhibit 10.

As a result of Owner-caused problems encountered throughout the Project, Prime Contractor was forced to work overtime in an attempt to meet various milestones and the completion date established by the Contract. The additional costs due to loss of labor productivity as a result of working extended overtime were beyond Prime Contractor's control; therefore, the costs are Owner's responsibility and Prime Contractor should be compensated for loss of productivity in the amount of $564,220.80.

§ B.7 Delay Costs

Many time-related costs are incurred during a construction project in support of direct labor, material, and service costs. These costs are typically classified as indirect costs and construction support equipment costs. Actions for which Owner is responsible have increased the overall duration of the project by 509 calendar days, all of which are compensable. As a result of the increased duration, Prime Contractor's supervisory and support personnel costs, jobsite expenses, jobsite support equipment expenses, and rental expenses of support equipment, yard services, and miscellaneous items have increased. Owner is responsible for these increased costs. Additional material costs are calculated in Exhibit 2. Escalation of material costs is calculated in Exhibit 3.

In addition to the costs already discussed, there were many other indirect, time-related costs incurred by Prime Contractor. These costs included construction support equipment costs, yard services, and other miscellaneous items. These costs are calculated in Exhibit 4.

§ B.8 —Allocation of Delay

The delay can be allocated by reviewing the As-Built Schedule which is discussed in the Schedule Analysis section of the Change Order Request.

The initial excavation phase of the Project was completed on March 17, 1991, with the completion of the activity entitled, "Structure Excavation." This activity could have been completed on December 30, 1990; therefore, 77 days of delay occurred during this initial phase. A review of the Schedule Analysis section indicates that the noncompensable delay due to interference by a governmental entity, 5 days, occurred during this initial phase; therefore, 72 compensable days of delay occurred during the initial phase. The middle phase of the work (structural concrete) was actually finished on August 23, 1991, with the completion of the pour for the activity entitled, "Concrete Activities." This activity could have been completed on February 5, 1991; therefore, the completion of this phase was delayed by 198 calendar days. Deducting the initial phase's delay, 27 days, establishes that the total compensable delay for the middle phase is 171 calendar days. The remaining Project delay, 311 calendar days, has been allocated to the third phase of the Project.

Because the daily time-related costs and the compensable days of delay for each phase have been established, the increase in time-related costs for which Owner is responsible can be determined by totaling the products of each phase's daily cost, then multiplying by days of delays. Prior to adding burdens, a final adjustment is necessary. As discussed elsewhere in this Claim, variations in contract quantities, primarily in the earthwork and reinforcing steel quantities, caused a portion of the total compensable delay. Because compensation for these variations in quantities at Prime Contract's unit prices included some allowance for jobsite overhead or indirect costs, the previously paid jobsite overhead and indirect costs have been removed from the additional compensation now due.

The jobsite overhead costs compensated as a result of variations in quantities were subtracted from the increase in time-related costs previously calculated. Burdens were then applied to determine the total compensation due. Calculations of the total time-related costs and the total compensation due can be found in Exhibit 8.

§ B.9 —Cost of Funding the Retention

It is normal in construction contracts for the owner to retain a percentage of the payment owed to the contractor until the work covered by the contract is substantially complete. The cost of funding this amount during the planned duration of the job is part of the contractor's costs figured at the time of bidding. If the duration of the project is extended, the cost of funding the retention increases. Moreover, if the value of the work increases, thus increasing the amount of retention, the cost of funding the retention also increases. If the extended duration of the job is prolonged due to actions or inactions for which the owner is responsible, the cost of funding the retention during the period of extended duration for which the owner is responsible should be borne by the owner.

Had there been no delays to construction for which Owner was responsible, the contract work would have been substantially complete on August 1, 1991, which was Prime Contractor's expected completion date as determined elsewhere in this claim. Therefore, the cost of funding the retention from the August 1, 1991, billing through the projected settlement date must be assumed by Owner.

Because an August 1991 billing would be due and payable by the end of the following month, the interest on an unpaid August billing would start to accrue on October 1, 1991. The interest rate to be used for funding the retention, therefore, is the average rate at which Prime Contractor could borrow money during the period from October 1, 1991, through December 31, 1991. Prime Contractor's average cost-of-funding rate for this period is the average prime rate of interest plus 0.5 percent. The actual amounts of retention at each month's end, beginning with the expected project completion date through December 1991, were used in Exhibit 14 to determine the cost of funding the retention.

The retention money withheld each month was multiplied by the monthly average cost-of-funding rate and the costs, so obtained, were added to determine the total cost to Prime Contractor of funding the retention during this period.

§ B.10   —Labor Escalation

Construction costs increase yearly and experienced contractors allow for this in their bid prices. If there are no increases in overall project time for which the owner is responsible, these escalation costs must be absorbed by the contractor. However, when the project duration is extended due to events for which the owner is responsible and if that extension requires the use of labor at a time when the hourly cost of labor has increased, additional compensation is owed for that increase in cost.

As discussed in § B.7, the contract duration has been increased by 509 calendar days due to events for which Owner is responsible. Of these 509 days, three are noncompensable weather days which occurred during the original period of contract performance and have been retained in the collapsed schedule. Five other days of prolongation also occurred during the original period of contract performance, but were caused by actions of another governmental entity and also are not compensable. However, these five days are potential workdays and are included in the 506 calendar days of delay. For the purpose of calculating labor escalation, the full period over which the escalation occurred—506 calendar days—has been used. However, a credit has been given for that portion of the escalation attributable to the five noncompensable days included in this period. Thus, labor escalation costs have been requested for the 501 calendar days of compensable delay.

Hourly labor costs have increased during this contract period. The increase in construction labor costs resulting from the delays for which Owner is responsible are for Owner's account.

Prime Contractor's labor forces were subject to collective bargaining agreements and the timing and amount of the labor rate increases varied by craft. The monthly employment utilization reports prepared by Prime Contractor and submitted to Owner were used to determine the labor hours for each craft by month. The Project's actual completion date has been taken as December 23, 1992, which is when Prime Contractor substantially completed its demobilization from the site. The labor escalation analysis is shown in Exhibit 7.

In order to determine the cumulative manhours by craft which had been expended immediately prior to the dates that the wage rates changed, the cumulative manhours were linearly interpolated from the cumulative manhours for the dates immediately preceding and succeeding the desired date.

The wage increases are summarized in supporting documents to Exhibit 7 and were determined from the labor rates provided in Prime Contractor's Craft Labor Breakdown reports. Some of the reports did not provide labor rates for certain apprentices; however, because wage rate increases typically apply to all members of a craft or a collective bargaining agreement, the apprentice wage rate increases were assumed to be 60 percent of the journeymen's increases when no specific labor rates were available for the apprentices. This factor, 60 percent, was used because most apprentice wage rates range from 40 to 80 percent of the journeyman's rates.

The additional costs due to the labor rate increases for which Owner is responsible have been calculated as follows:

1. For each date immediately prior to a labor rate increase, the actual cumulative manhours by craft and the expected cumulative manhours by craft have been determined by linearly interpolating between the cumulative totals.

2. At the time of each wage rate increase, the actual cumulative manhours were deducted from the expected cumulative manhours. Each difference represents the manhours which were actually expended after the labor rate increases, but which could have been expended before the labor rate increases had Owner delays not occurred.

3. Each manhour difference was then multiplied by the appropriate hourly wage rate differentials to determine the labor escalation costs Prime Contractor incurred due to Owner delays.

4. The products of the manhours and the differentials were summed and appropriate burdens were applied to determine the total labor escalation costs due.

5. As discussed in the Schedule Analysis section of this claim, five calendar days of delay are due to interference by a governmental entity and are noncompensable. In order to correct the labor escalation cost for this noncompensable event, the cost has been reduced by the ratio of 501 days to 509 days, or 1.79 percent.

§ B.11 —Home Office Overhead

During the course of the Project, Prime Contractor provided home office support. The home office provided services for payroll preparation, cost accounting, and a variety of other tasks necessary to maintain the field operation. The powerplant project was extended for an additional 509 calendar days, of which 501 calendar days are compensable. Because of this prolongation, the home office overhead support costs were extended.

A widely used method of calculating extended home office overhead is the method set forth in the *Eichleay* decision, a landmark ruling of the Armed Services Board of Contract Appeals. The *Eichleay* decision allocated extended home overhead according to the ratio of the Project's billings to the total company billing during the contract period. The contract period included delay time. The method of application is expressed in the following formula:

$$\frac{\text{Total contract billings}}{\substack{\text{Total company billings} \\ \text{for contract period}}} \times \substack{\text{Total home office overhead} \\ \text{for contract period}} = \substack{\text{Overhead allocable} \\ \text{to contract}}$$

$$\frac{\text{Allocable overhead}}{\text{Total days of performance}} = \substack{\text{Daily contract} \\ \text{overhead}}$$

$$\text{Daily contract overhead} \times \text{Days of delay} = \text{Amount recoverable}$$

The actual period of construction was from January 1, 1990, through December 23, 1992. Prime Contractor financial data necessary to apply *Eichleay* cover the period from January 31, 1990, through December 31, 1992. The calculations presented here have been prepared on a cost rather than a billing basis. The critical factor in applying the *Eichleay* concept is to always compare apples with apples. In Prime Contractor's situation, a pure cost basis (rather than an anticipated revenue basis) is clearer. Subjective judgments regarding pending changes and potential claim recoveries are eliminated and therefore require no justification.

§ B.12   Unpaid Work

Exhibit 1 of this claim requests payment for certain work which Prime Contractor performed but which have not been fully paid for at the unit price rates established in the contract. Work which has not been paid for includes general and structure excavation, pit liner and structural steel, compacted backfill at the construction road, structure excavation at the construction road, and riprap. Exhibit 15 sets forth the additional compensation to which Prime Contractor is entitled as a result of Owner's failure to pay. Because these quantities should be paid at contract prices, neither profit nor bond has been added to the amount due Prime Contractor because these markups are already included in the unit prices. However, because Prime Contractor has improperly been denied the use of its money, cost of funding has been added.

§ B.13   Summary of Claim

During the construction of the powerplant project, Prime Contractor experienced many problems for which it was not responsible. These problems included:

1. Governmental interference with the work
2. Defective contract administration
3. Defective plans and specifications
4. Extra work.

As a result of these difficulties, Prime Contractor experienced delay and disruption to its work as well as substantial additional costs. Prime Contractor seeks an equitable adjustment to its contract. This claim sets forth the time extension to which Prime Contractor is entitled and quantifies the additional compensation owed as a result of actions for which Owner is responsible. Exhibit 1 summarizes the additional compensation to which Prime Contractor is entitled.

§ B.14 Summary of Amounts Due Contractor

A. Contract Balance Due - Exhibit 1 $780,711.00

B. Additional Contractor Field Costs:

1. Additional Concrete Costs/Material Escalation - Exhibit 2	$5,312.95	
2. Escalation of Miscellaneous Material - Exhibit 3	$40,840.03	
3. Extended Equipment Costs - Exhibit 4	$179,530.32	
4. Additional Small Tools Cost - Exhibit 5	$74,866.00	
5. Increase in Labor Burden - Exhibit 6	$52,738.00	
6. Labor Escalation - Exhibit 7	$122,829.00	
7. Extended Field Overhead - Exhibit 8	$428,578.00	
8. Acceleration Costs/Premium Time - Exhibit 9	$78,335.15	
9. Productivity Loss - Exhibit 10	$591,205.00	
Additional Field Costs Subtotal:		$1,574,234.45

C. Overhead Allocable to Claim - Exhibit 11 $165,587.88

    Subtotal: $2,520,533.33

D. Profit on Additional Field Costs at 5% $78,711.72
    Subtotal: $2,599,245.05

E. Additional Bond Cost due to Extended Time - Exhibit 12 $5,094.00
F. Additional Bond Cost due to Additional Revenue - Exhibit 12 $13,067.00

    Subtotal: $2,617,406.05

G. Interest:

On Unpaid Contract Balance - Exhibit 13	$126,111.56	
On Equitable Adjustment - Exhibit 13	$296,689.15	
		$422,800.71

Total Due Contractor: **$3,040,206.76**

EXHIBIT 1

CALCULATION OF REMAINING CONTRACT BALANCE DUE

The contract amount initially was $6,125,120. It was amended by six executed change orders and one agreed-upon but unexecuted change order. Additionally, the quantity of several unit price items varied from the original allowance quantities. The agreed net change in unit price items totals $14,382.50. The total agreed-upon adjusted contract amount is $6,443,210. This figure is calculated as follows:

Original Contract Price		$6,125,120.00
Approved Change Orders 1 through 6		$201,437.00
	Change Order 1	($881,628)
	Change Order 2	$51,027
	Change Order 3	$287,117
	Change Order 4	$317,943
	Change Order 5	$197,048
	Change Order 6	$229,930
Agreed-Upon But Unexecuted Change		$102,271.00
Agreed-Upon Unit Price Adjustment		$14,382.00
Total Agreed-Upon Contract Amount		$6,443,210.00
Payments to Date—Pay Applications 1 through 17		$5,662,499.00
Contract Balance Due		**$780,711.00**

Source: Pay Applications 1 through 17
         Change Orders 1 through 6
         Unit Price Reconciliation 1-21-91

EXHIBIT 2

ADDITIONAL CONCRETE COST—MATERIAL ESCALATION

A firm price purchase order for concrete delivered through December 31, 1990, was entered into with Speedy Concrete. All concrete was anticipated to be placed by September 15, 1990, based on the original approved schedule. After December 31, 1990, 1715 yards of concrete were placed at the higher price. Based on the actual pour tickets, the price per yard increase is as follows:

	Price through 12/31/90	Price after 12/31/90	Increase
2500 PSI concrete	$48.44	$51.30	$2.86
3000 PSI concrete	$51.25	$54.20	$2.95
4000 PSI concrete	$56.50	$60.00	$3.50

The increased price based on yards poured after December 31, 1990, is:

420 yards	2500 PSI	2.86	=	1,201.20
765 yards	3000 PSI	2.95	=	2,256.75
530 yards	4000 PSI	3.50	=	1,855.00

Total Concrete Cost Escalation Claim: **5,312.95**

Source: Delivery Tickets
Speedy Concrete Contract
Speedy Concrete Purchase Order

EXHIBIT 3

Escalation of Miscellaneous Material

Because of Owner-caused delay, completion of the project was pushed from August 1991 to December 1992. Much of the miscellaneous material that would have been purchased during the project's original schedule in 1990 and 1991 was in fact purchased during 1991–1992. This was a time of significant price escalation. The reasonable measure of this damage is computed by taking the average material price index for the original schedule and comparing it with the average price index for the extended period.

ORIGINAL SCHEDULE		EXTENDED SCHEDULE	
	Utopia City Matl		Utopia City Matl
Date	Price Index*	Date	Price Index*
7/15/89	286.82	9/14/91	355.39
8/12/89	298.79	10/12/91	355.39
10/14/89	302.98	11/16/91	355.39
11/11/89	305.47	12/14/91	355.39
2/10/90	305.36	1/11/92	355.39
3/17/90	308.57	2/15/92	357.28
4/4/90	309.15	3/15/92	356.03
5/12/90	307.19	4/12/92	351.76
6/16/90	300.29	5/17/92	348.19
7/14/90	312.85	6/14/92	361.09
8/4/90	318.90	8/16/92	380.76
9/15/90	336.00	9/13/92	398.57
12/15/90	330.12	11/15/92	392.12
1/12/91	333.46	12/6/92	393.47
2/16/91	333.06		
3/16/91	337.55		
4/13/91	338.03		
5/11/91	344.09		
6/15/91	345.33		
7/13/91	349.70		
8/17/91	350.63		

Average for Period 07/89 to 08/91 = 321.64
Average for Period 08/91 to 12/92 = 365.44

The average index for the originally scheduled period is 321.64 and for the extended period 365.44. The increase, therefore is 43.80 (365.44 – 321.64 = 43.80), which is 13.62 (43.80/321.64 = 13.62%).

From the Job Cost Status Report, it can be seen that miscellaneous material, that is, material not subject to lump sum purchase contracts or subcontracts, is $350,000. The index increase is 13.21, dividing 1.1321 into $350,000 produces $309,159.97. Subtracting $309,159.97 from $350,000 gives the amount of escalation suffered during the delay period ($350,000 – 309,159.97 = $40,840.03).

Total Miscellaneous Material Escalation Cost Claim: $40,840.03

* ENR (*Engineering News Record*) based on city's 1967 Average = 100

EXHIBIT 4

EXTENDED EQUIPMENT COSTS

The schedule for the concrete work was substantially extended by action of the Owner. This is demonstrated by the Schedule Analysis. This additional time required additional equipment time. This computes the additional cost of the equipment.

EQUIPMENT	OWNERSHIP & REPAIR EXPENSES ($/MONTH)	AS-PLANNED DURATIONS (MONTHS)	AS-BUILT DURATIONS (MONTHS)	ADDITIONAL TIME REQUIRED (MONTHS)	ADDITIONAL COST	C.O. ADJUSTMENT*	ADJUSTED ADDITIONAL COST
CONCRETE PUMP	$3,420.00	6.15	8.90	2.76	$9,430.56	($1,222.20)	$8,208.36
FORKLIFT	$2,988.00	4.05	11.73	7.67	$22,931.16	$0.00	$22,931.16
FLATBED TRUCK	$1,846.00	4.05	11.73	7.67	$14,166.98	$0.00	$14,166.98
AIR COMPRESSOR	$2,760.00	5.75	9.34	3.59	$9,902.99	$0.00	$9,902.99
SKIP LOADER	$2,299.00	5.75	9.34	3.59	$8,248.90	($1,069.06)	$7,179.85
WATER TRUCK	$1,336.00	15.55	26.58	11.03	$14,735.95	$0.00	$14,735.95
4 PICKUPS	$4,836.00	15.55	26.58	11.03	$53,340.60	$0.00	$53,340.60
STORAGE VAN	$347.00	15.55	26.58	11.03	$3,827.38	$0.00	$3,827.38
BACKHOE	$3,974.00	5.32	9.44	4.12	$16,371.30	($2,121.72)	$14,249.58
BOBCAT	$1,593.00	5.32	9.44	4.12	$6,562.52	($850.50)	$5,712.02
DRUM ROLLER	$1,332.00	5.32	9.44	4.12	$5,487.31	($711.16)	$4,776.15
3 WACKERS	$1,458.00	5.32	9.44	4.12	$6,006.38	($778.43)	$5,227.95
FRONTEND LOADER	$3,707.00	5.32	9.44	4.12	$15,271.36	$0.00	$15,271.36
TOTAL:					$186,283.39	($6,753.06)	$179,530.32

Total Extended Equipment Costs Claim: $179,530.32

Source: Equipment rates derived from *Contractors' Equipment Cost Guide* (Dataquest 1991).

*Credit for additional amounts allowed on change orders 1 through 6.

   Source: Equipment Usage Report
        Original Estimate
        Change Order Estimate

EXHIBIT 5

ADDITIONAL SMALL TOOLS COST

Small tools costs vary directly with both schedule length and labor expenditures. An increase in either labor expenditures or schedule length will directly increase small tool expenditures. This effect is mathematically represented as follows:

$$\frac{\text{Actual Labor}}{\text{Budget Labor}} \times \frac{\text{Actual Schedule}}{\text{Budget Schedule}} \times \text{Budget} = \frac{\text{Predicted}}{\text{Expense}}$$

The application of this calculation to this project follows:

Budgeted Small Tools	$24,240
Budgeted Labor	$821,297
Budget Schedule	16 Months

$$\frac{\text{Actual Labor}}{\text{Budget Labor}} \times \frac{\text{Actual Schedule}}{\text{Budget Schedule}} \times \text{Budget} =$$

$$\frac{1,685,992}{821,297} \times \frac{33}{16} \times 24,240 \quad = \quad 102,632$$

= Predicted Expense

This closely compares with $99,106, the actual expense as shown in cost code 1660M of the Job Cost Status Report.

The actual expenses closely track the predicted expense. This validates the approach. The underrun is due to contractor's careful management being able to keep small tools costs down.

The additional expense to which contractor is entitled to be compensated is the difference between the actual cost and the estimated cost. This is $74,866 ($99,106 − $24,240 = $74,866).

Total Small Tool's Cost Claim: **$74,866.00**

Source: Job Cost Status Report

EXHIBIT 5—ALTERNATE

Additional Small Tools Costs

Small tools costs are a function of labor. This project required additional labor, as shown in Exhibit 10, Productivity Loss. Additional labor requires additional small tools. The Contractor is entitled to be compensated for the additional small tools costs. This cost is calculated as follows:

Productive Labor =

Actual Total Labor Cost – Labor Escalation – Premium Time Cost =

$$\$1,685,992 \quad - \quad \$122,829 \quad - \quad \$78,338 \quad = \$1,484,825$$

The small tools rate is equal to:

$$\frac{\text{Actual Small Tools Costs}}{\text{Actual Productive Labor}} = \frac{\$99,106}{1,484,825} = 6.67\%$$

This is the actual small tools rate. This rate should be applied to the additional labor cost due to lost productivity, or $591,205. This calculation is as follows:

$$6.67\% \times \$591,205 = \$39,433.37$$

This is the amount the Contractor is entitled to, or the additional small tools cost.

Source: Job Cost Status Report

EXHIBIT 6

INCREASE IN LABOR BURDEN DUE TO EXTENDED PROJECT DURATION

Labor burden consists of state and federal UCF, FICA, workers' compensation insurance, fringe benefits, and subsistence. These costs are a function of both the amount of labor dollars expended and the rates required for the various charges. These rates over the past several years have increased dramatically. The actual labor burden applicable to this project through the originally scheduled contract completion date of November 30, 1990, was 17.68%. This is calculated as follows:

Cost: $$\frac{\text{Fringes} + \text{FICA} + \text{Workers' Comp.} + \text{Federal/State UCA}}{\text{Total 11/30/90 Labor (Net of Burden)}} =$$

$$\frac{40,390 + 61,521 + 45,344 + 7,602}{875,818} = 17.68\%$$

Because of increases in state and federal UCF, FICA, and workers' compensation, on labor expended after November 30, 1990, the labor burden was 27.94%, an increase of 10.26%. This is calculated as follows:

$$\frac{\text{Total Burden Cost} - \text{Burden Cost as of 11/30/90}}{\text{Total Labor} - \text{Total 11/30/90 Labor}} =$$

$$\frac{298,433 - 154,857}{1,389,605 - 875,818} = 27.94\%$$

Added labor burden is 27.94% − 17.68%   =   10.26%

Contractor is entitled to be paid the additional labor burden expended. Had the project not been extended, Contractor would not have expended labor on the project at those higher rates. The labor expended after November 30, 1990, is $513,787.

Applying the 10.26% additional labor burden rate to this amount produces an additional cost of $52,738. Contractor is entitled to be paid this additional amount.

Total Increase in Labor Burden Claim: **$52,738.00**

Source: Job Cost Status Report

EXHIBIT 7

LABOR ESCALATION

This project was delayed as shown on the Schedule Analysis. As a result, much of the labor was expended during higher wage rate periods. The original labor distribution was taken from the estimate, as shown below.

	1989	1990	1991	1992
Original Anticipated Wage Rate	$10.00	$10.50	$11.25	$12.25
Estimated Percentage of Labor Expended	15%	60%	25%	0%

Using the original distribution, the actual manhours of 122,452 are distributed using the estimated percentage distribution. This is compared with the actual distribution.

	1989	1990	1991	1992
Actual labor hours using anticipated distribution	22,500	90,000	37,500	0
Actual labor hours Distribution	8,007	15,095	66,000	33,350

The labor escalation for this project is calculated as follows:

	1989	1990	1991	1992
Anticipated hours based on original schedule	22,500	90,000	37,500	40,000
Labor hours actually expended	8,007	15,095	66,000	33,350
Hours escalated from prior period	0	12,500	77,500	0
Total hours to be escalated to next period rate	12,500	77,500	40,000	
Period differential	0.50	0.75	1.00	
Escalated wages	$6,250	$58,125	$40,000	=

Total escalated wages	$104,375
Labor burden (at original rate) 17.68%	$18,454
Total Wage Escalation Claim:	**$122,829**

EXHIBIT 8

EXTENDED FIELD OVERHEAD

Due to Owner's inaction, Contractor was forced to man and support the project beyond the anticipated completion date. The total cost of the field overhead is $850,794, which was spent over the course of 1,011 days. This results in a per day cost of $842. This calculation is shown below.

Cost Code	Cost Type	Description	Total Cost	Credit for Appd CO	Adjusted Total Cost
001150	L	Job Office	316		316
001160	L	Engineer Office	782		782
001170	L	Tool Shed	11		11
001190	L	Signs	189		189
001260	L	Storage of Materials	10,054		10,054
001300	L	Drinking Water	91		91
001310	L	Unload and Haul	17,678		17,678
001490	L	Guard Rails	1,202		1,202
001510	L	Clean Up - Periodic	38,292		38,292
001520	L	Clean Up - Final	36,255		36,255
001610	L	Move On - Off	143		143
001630	L	Layout	22,851		22,851
001860	L	Maintenance	11,477		11,477
001870	L	Superintendent	163,176		163,176
001880	L	Asst. Superintendent	88,989		88,989
001890	L	Field Engineer	49,690		49,690
001910	L	Timekeeper	13,424		13,424
010400	L	Subsistence	56,018		56,018
017600	L	Payroll Taxes	38,006		38,006
017700	L	Workers' Comp Ins	27,532		27,532
017800	L	Fringes	11,348		11,348
001040	M	Subsistence	525		525
001150	M	Job Office	3,550		3,550
001160	M	Engineer Office	5,181		5,181
001170	M	Tool Shed	3,750		3,750
001180	M	Chemical Toilets	8,124		8,124
001190	M	Signs	668		668
001204	M	Repairs	106		106
001260	M	Storage of Materials	16,014		16,014
001290	M	Job Communications	5,822		5,822
001300	M	Drinking Water	612		612
001310	M	Unload & Haul	19,824		19,824
001315	M	Unload & Haul Equip.	1,312		1,312
001330	M	Temp. Power - Install	8,552		8,552
001350	M	Temp. Power - Cords	7,157		7,157
001360	M	Temp. Water - Install	6,095		6,095
001390	M	Telephone	12,635		12,635
001410	M	Printing - Supplies	624		624
001420	M	Blueprinting	896		896
001440	M	Photographs	223		223
001450	M	Office Equipment	9,324	($1,360)	7,964
001460	M	Arch. Office Equip.	2,403		2,403
001470	M	First Aid	1,547		1,547
001480	M	Hard Hats	1,921		1,921
001500	M	Fire Extinguishers	1,481		1,481

Cost Code	Cost Type	Description	Total Cost	Credit for Appd CO	Adjusted Total Cost
001520	M	Clean Up - Final	2,822		2,822
001590	M	Travel & Entertain	5,087		5,087
001610	M	Move On-Off	4,018		4,018
001620	M	Layout	379		379
001630	M	Layout - Reg. Engineer	263		263
001680	M	Portable Generators	9,564	($1,600)	7,964
001720	M	Survey Equipment	6,101		6,101
001740	M	Pickup Trucks	17,532		17,532
001750	M	Flatbed Trucks	8,990		8,990
001850	M	Scaffold	808		808
001860	M	Fuel Oil and Grease	70,460	($310)	70,150
001870	M	Superintendent	14,776		14,776
010400	M	Subsistence	3,817		3,817
017800	M	Fringe Benefits	318		318
000900	X	Misc. Cost	2,749		2,749
		TOTAL COST			$850,284
		TOTAL NUMBER DAYS			1,011
		TOTAL COST PER DAY			842

    502 Days in Original Contractor Schedule
    <u>509</u> Days Overrun Due to Owner

    1,011 Total Project Days

Because the project continued 509 days past the reasonably anticipated completion date, Contractor is entitled to 509 days × $842 per day, or $428,578 for extended field overhead.

Total Extended Field Overhead Claim: **$428,578.00**

    Source: Job Cost Status Report
             Approved Schedule and Update

EXHIBIT 9

ACCELERATION COSTS—PREMIUM TIME

On August 23, 1990, the Owner directed Contractor and its subcontractors to accelerate the project. This exhibit details the premium cost that Contractor directly incurred
as a result of the Owner's directive. This acceleration coupled with the Owner's general attitude toward the contractor had a major impact on labor productivity. The
negative input on productivity is included with the costs requested in Exhibit 10.

The Labor Cost Summary (not included) shows the labor costs Contractor incurred per
cost code by week from August 23, 1990, until November 18, 1991. The column labeled
"Premium Cost" is the difference between the cost at the regular rate of pay and cost at
the premium rate. This cost, $66,566.24, was the bare cost labor during that period.
Therefore, burden at the original rate of 17.68% was added, for a total of $78,335.15.

Summary of Costs:

Labor Cost:	$66,566.24
Burden at 17.68%:	$11,768.91
TOTAL:	$78,335.15

Total Premium Time Cost Claim: **$78,335.15**

Source: Payroll Register

EXHIBIT 10

PRODUCTIVITY LOSS

Contractor suffered a severe productivity loss from the acceleration of the project in August 1990 and from the many changes which were made to the project. The cost of this productivity loss has been calculated using 3 different methods: the total cost approach, the Leonard method and industry studies. The loss, as calculated by all these methods, is in the same range. Contractor has elected to use the average of the three methods. The average is calculated below.

Loss of Productivity

1. Total Cost Approach	=	$564,221
2. Leonard Method	=	$592,499
3. Industry Studies	=	$616,894
Average Methods 1 through 3	=	$591,205

Total Loss of Productivity Cost Claim: **$591,205**

With the total cost approach, the cost of the productivity loss is calculated by subtracting the cost of change orders from the total cost to determine the actual cost of base contract work. From this is subtracted the estimated hours for the base contract work to determine the productivity loss. This calculation is shown below.

Calculation of Labor Productivity Loss Using Total Cost Approach

Total Actual Manhours		122,452
Change Order Hours Added to Contractor Work		
Change Order No. 1	451	
Change Order No. 2	1,450	
Change Order No. 3	6,790	
Change Order No. 4	9,417	
Change Order No. 5	6,157	
Change Order No. 6	6,941	
Subtotal	31,206	
Additional Manhours Pending Change	3,455	
Additional Manhour Unit Price Adjustment	479	
Total Change Order Hours		(35,140)
Actual Hours for Base Contract Work		87,312
Estimated Hours Base Contract Work		(63,200)
Unproductive Hours		24,112
Hourly Billing Rate - Original Project		$23.40
Lost Productivity Cost Claim:		**$564,220.80**

Calculation of Labor Productivity Loss Using Leonard Model

Change orders can cause a loss of productivity in unchanged work. Change orders issued during a construction project create disruptions in the flow of the project, preventing the contractor from performing the work in an orderly and planned sequence. Estimating the effects of such changes on the balance of the work is difficult. An extensive study was done by Charles A. Leonard in his thesis entitled, *The Effects of Change Orders on Productivity.* This thesis was presented by Mr. Leonard to Concordia University, Montreal, Quebec, in February of 1988. The study is a quantitative analysis of empirical data from 90 cases involving 57 different projects that sets forth the effects of change orders on productivity. Based upon a statistical analysis, Leonard developed a model that can be used to estimate productivity losses resulting from change orders on a project.

The Leonard analysis divides construction projects into two types, building and industrial, and each type is divided into civil/architectural and mechanical/electrical categories. A different analysis was done for each type and category. Leonard's conclusion is that the major variable for determining the impact of change orders is the percentage of change order labor to all labor incurred. The greater the percentage of change order labor to total labor, the greater the impact felt. The Leonard study indicated that when change order labor was less than 10% of all labor incurred, the effects were minimal. Above 10%, there were substantial impacts to the unchanged work. Leonard's study further determined that other major causes occurring at the same time on a project with significant change orders resulted in significant additional productivity loss. Such additional major causes include:

1. Inadequate scheduling and coordination by owners and general contractors
2. Acceleration
3. Changes in sequence
4. Late supply of information, equipment, or material
5. Increased complexity of the work
6. Ripple effect of change orders issued to other prime contractors.

Leonard's study isolated the effects of change orders, change orders plus one other major cause, and change orders plus two other major causes.

In addition to change orders on the project, there was one other major cause of labor productivity loss: the acceleration of the work. Therefore, the appropriate chart and algorithm to use in calculating the productivity loss is the change orders plus one major cause chart for civil/architectural work on an industrial project. The productivity loss factor is applied against the actual "contract" hours to determine the actual productivity loss.

The calculation is as follows:

Total Actual Manhours	122,452
Change Order Hours	35,140
Actual Hours of Base Contract Work	87,312
Change Order Hours as a Percentage of Base Contract Hours	40.25%

Leonard Model for Civil/Architectural Work on an Industrial Project, Based on One Additional Cause: 29% Inefficiency

Calculation of Unproductive Hours:

Contract Craft Hours Impacted	87,312
Multiplied By:	
Leonard Inefficiency Factor (One Additional Cause)	29%
Equals:	
Unproductive Hours Caused By Owner	25,320

Calculation of Impact Costs:

Unproductive Hours	25,320
Multiplied By:	
Hourly Rate (Original Project Average)	$23.40
Lost Productivity Cost Claim:	**$592,499**

Calculation of Labor Productivity Loss Using Industry Studies

There are many industry studies for estimating productivity losses caused by various factors. Two major factors present on this project were prolonged overtime and crew overcrowding. Two studies were used to calculate the effect of the factors on productivity. These studies are:

Modification Impact Evaluation Guide
EP 415-1-3
United States Department of the Army,
Office of the Chief of Engineers (COE Guide) (July 1979)

Owner's Guide on Overtime, Construction Costs and Productivity
American Subcontractors
Association, the Associated General Contractors of
America and the Associated Specialty Contractors,
Inc. (includes Business Roundtable Study) (1979)

Productivity Loss Due to Overtime, Using the Business Roundtable Study

Overtime was worked between August 23, 1991, and November 18, 1992, a total of 65 weeks. The Business Roundtable Study has a table to estimate productivity losses. This table follows:

Relationship of Hours Worked, Productivity, and Costs
(40 Hours versus 50 Hours)

50 Hour Overtime Work Weeks	Productivity Rate		Actual Hr. Output for 50 Hr. Week	Hour Gain Over 40 Hr. Week	Hour Loss Due to Productivity Drop
	40 Hr. Week	50 Hr. Week			
0-1-2	1.00	.926	46.3	6.3	3.7
2-3-4		.900	45.0	5.0	5.0
4-5-6		.870	43.5	3.5	6.5
6-7-8		.800	40.0	0.0	10.0
8-9-10		.752	37.6	- 2.4	12.4
10-11-12 & up		.750	37.5	- 2.5	12.5

Using the table from the Business Roundtable Study and time-weighting the weekly factors produces a total inefficiency factor of 0.766.

Applying the inefficiency factor of .234 (1-0.766) to the 77,415 hours worked during the overtime period produces inefficient hours of .234 × 77,415 = 18,115.

Productivity Loss Due to Crew Overloading, Using COE Modification Impact Evaluation Guide.

Crew Overloading - January 28, 1991 through June 30, 1991.

Optimum Peak Crew	=	20 men
Peak Actual Crew	=	47 men

First Shift	=	40 men
Second Shift	=	5 men
Third Shift	=	2 men

Crew Overloading Factor	=	
47 divided by 20	=	2.35
	=	134.23% Increase

COE Guide - Figure 4-3d

Percentage Crew Size Increase	=	134.23%
Percent Labor Loss	=	30%

Crowding:

COE Guide - Activity Stacking and Congested Working Space (p. 4-7 to 4-8)

Manhours worked between January 28, 1991, and June 30, 1991	=	35,740
Productive Hours	=	

$$\frac{35,740}{1.3} \quad = \quad 27,492$$

Non-Productive Hours (due to overcrowding)	=	
Total Hours - Productive Hours	=	
35,740 - 27,492	=	8,248

Combined Loss of Labor Efficiency

Overtime Impact	18,115
Crew Overloading	8,248
Total Hours	26,363 Hrs.
Billing Rate	$23.40
Lost Productivity Cost Claim:	**$616,894**

APPENDIXES

EXHIBIT 11

CALCULATION OF EXTENDED OVERHEAD COSTS
ON PROJECT USING *EICHLEY* METHOD

Annual Revenues of Contractor During Contract Period

Year	Total Corporation	Branch Office	Project
1990	164,911,421	43,511,728	3,025,661
1991	126,808,743	16,398,683	2,533,238
1992	153,432,518	27,431,157	758,434
Total	445,152,682	87,341,568	6,317,333

Overhead During Contract Period

Year	Total Corporation	Branch
1990	1,196,120	1,294,577
1991	1,285,743	1,301,716
1992	1,250,225	1,233,920
Total	3,732,088	3,830,213

502 days in the original schedule.

509 days of delays.

Eichleay Method:

$$\frac{\dfrac{\text{Project Revenue}}{\text{Corporate (Branch) Revenues}} \times \text{Corporate Overhead}}{\text{Total Days of Performance}} = \begin{array}{l}\text{Daily Rate of}\\ \text{Overhead Allocable}\\ \text{to Project}\end{array}$$

$$\text{Daily Rate} \quad X \quad \text{Number of Days of Delay} \quad = \begin{array}{l}\text{Overhead Allocable}\\ \text{to Delay}\end{array}$$

This must be computed for both corporate and branch overheads. These calculations are:

Corporate

$$\frac{\dfrac{\$6,317,333}{\$455,152,682} \times \$3,737,088}{1,011} = \$51.30 \text{ per Day}$$

Branch

$$\frac{\dfrac{\$6,317,333}{\$87,341,568} \times \$3,830,213}{1,011} = \$274.02 \text{ per Day}$$

$$
\begin{aligned}
\text{Total per-day overhead cost} &= \text{Corporate} + \text{Branch} \\
&= \$51.30 + \$274.02 \\
&= \$325.32
\end{aligned}
$$

$$
\begin{aligned}
\text{Total additional cost} &= \text{Overrun days} \times \text{Daily Rate} \\
&= 509 \text{ days} \times \$325.32 \text{ per day} \\
&= \$165,587.88
\end{aligned}
$$

Total Extended Overhead Cost Claim: **$165,587.88**

Source: Audited Financial Statement 1990–1992

EXHIBIT 11—ALTERNATE

OVERHEAD ALLOCABLE TO THE CLAIM

Contractor maintains a corporate office in Metropolis which provides general services for each of its various branch and subsidiary offices. The various branch offices are responsible for the supervision and management of projects within certain areas. This project was the responsibility of the Utopia branch office.

The overhead costs, which are detailed herein, originate in two offices: the corporate headquarters (hereinafter Corporate Office) and the Utopia branch office (hereinafter Branch Office). A portion of the overhead expenses incurred by these two offices has been allocated to the project and is part of the excess cost arising from the Owner's actions. This allocation is computed using field labor (direct labor dollars) as an allocation base. Field labor is the appropriate base for allocating overhead costs because labor is the stock-in-trade of a construction company. The material costs and other cost items may vary greatly between two projects which utilize the same quantity of labor, without significantly affecting the overhead costs related to the two projects. It is the business of construction companies, such as Contractor, to sell and manage its labor services. The overhead expenses incurred are most directly related to, and vary in proportion to, the quantity of field labor performed by the company. Thus, the field labor (direct labor dollar) method of allocating such expenses provides the most accurate and the most appropriate allocation of overhead expenses to this contract.

Contractor
Total Field Payroll
1990, 1991, & 1992

Year	Total Contractor Including all Subsidiaries	Branch Office	Project Land and Job
1990	23,142,470	7,258,563	513,125
1991	16,778,144	2,961,049	683,990
1992	20,193,385	4,142,803	451,085

The following tables list all field labor expended on the project, first as a percentage of the total field labor expended by the corporation and its subsidiaries on all projects for the year, and then as a percentage of the total field labor expended by the branch office on projects for which it was responsible each year.

Project Field Labor as a
Percentage of Companywide Field Labor

	1990	1991	1992
Project Field Labor	513,125	683,990	451,085
Total Companywide Field Labor	23,142,470	16,778,144	20,193,385
Project as a Percentage of Total Field Labor	2.2%	4.08%	2.23%

	Project Field Labor as a Percentage of Branch Office Field Labor		
	1990	1991	1992
Project Field Labor	513,125	683,990	451,085
Total Branch Field Labor	7,258,563	2,961,047	4,142,803
Project as a Percentage of Total Branch Field Labor	7.07%	23.1%	2.23%

Contractor geared up to perform and support the performance of the projected amounts of field labor for 1990. When the project was delayed and the actual amount of field labor performed on the project in 1990 turned out to be substantially less than the projected amount, Contractor was required to absorb its overhead costs over a lower volume of work.

Overhead costs, although perhaps variable in the long run, are fixed in the short run. The lowered volume of work available to absorb the overhead cost was a direct result of the Owner's unreasonable delay of the work at the project. The project would have absorbed 9.35% of the branch office overhead in 1990 because 9.35% of the field labor performed out of the branch office was to be performed at the Project. Similarly, 2.98% of the corporate office overhead expenses would have been absorbed by the project, based on the ratio of projected field labor to total companywide field labor. This calculation is as follows:

	Branch	Companywide
Actual Total Field Labor	7,258,563	23,142,470
Less Actual Project Labor	(513,125)	(513,125)
Add Projected Project Field Labor	696,000	696,000
Total Projected Field Labor	7,441,438	23,325,345
Projected Project Field Labor as a Percentage of Total Projected Field Labor	9.35%	2.98%
Less Actual Project Field Labor as a Percentage of Total Field Labor	7.07%	2.22%
Unabsorbed Overhead as a Percentage of Total Overhead	2.28%	.76%

The actual overhead amounts absorbed by the project were less than the anticipated amounts, resulting in unabsorbed overhead expenses to the branch office of 2.28% of the total overhead and unabsorbed corporate expenses of 76% of the total overhead.

As a result of the extension of the project, additional overhead costs were incurred during the period of contract performance extending beyond the estimated completion date. These costs were incurred both in 1991 and 1992. No overhead was originally anticipated for 1992.

Calculation of Extended
Overhead During 1991

	Branch	Companywide
Actual Total Field Labor	2,961,047	16,778,144
Less Actual Project Field Labor	(693,990)	(693,990)
Add Projected Project Field Labor	125,000	125,000
Total Projected Field Labor	2,392,057	16,209,154
Actual Project Field Labor as a Percentage of Actual Field Labor	23.44%	4.14%
Less Projected Project Field Labor as a Percentage of Total Field Labor	5.23%	.77%
Additional Overhead as a Percentage of Total Overhead	18.21%	3.37%

The calculation of the unabsorbed and extended overhead is shown below.

Allocation of Branch Office Overhead
Expenses to Contract

	1990	1991	1992
Total Branch Office Overhead Expenses	$1,294,577	$1,301,716	$1,233,920
Percentage of Overhead Expenses Allocable to Project	2.28% (1)	18.21% (2)	10.89%
Branch Office Overhead Allocable To Project	29,516	237,042	134,374
Total Branch Office Overhead Allocable			$ 400,000

Allocation of Corporate Overhead
Expenses to Contract

	1990	1991	1992
Total Corporate Office Overhead Expenses	$1,196,120	$1,285,743	$1,250,225
Percentage of Overhead Expenses Allocable to Project	.78% (1)	3.37% (2)	2.23%
Corporate Office Overhead Allocable to Project	9,330	42,558	27,880
Total Corporate Office Overhead Allocable			$ 80,540

Total Extended Overhead:

Branch	400,932
Corporate	80,540
TOTAL	481,472

(1)   Unabsorbed Overhead Only

(2)   Extended Overhead Only

Source: Audited Financial Statements 1990, 1991, 1992
                 Payroll Register

EXHIBIT 12

ADDITIONAL BOND COST

Contractor is entitled to additional bond premium because the project was extended by the Owner and because the contract value increased. Contractor's base bond rates were based on a project not more than 24 months long. The original schedule was 17 months in duration. The actual schedule as extended was 34 months. Owner's actions, as shown in the Schedule Analysis, are the cause of this extension. Contractor is entitled to the increased premium for the additional 10 months after the 24-month base period. Contractor bond premium schedule is:

$14.40/Thousand Dollars for first $ 500,000
$ 8.70/Thousand Dollars for next $2,000,000
$ 6.90/Thousand Dollars for next $2,500,000
$ 6.30/Thousand Dollars for next $2,500,000
$ 5.76/Thousand Dollars over $7,500,000
Premium increased by 1% for every month over 24 months

Calculating the base premium for the current contract value of $6,443,210 (including change order 1 through 6, pending change and unit price adjustment) gives a premium of $50,942. This is calculated as follows:

Bond premium on total contract amount of $6,443,210:

$$0.0144 \times \$ \ 500,000 = \$ \ 7,200$$
$$0.0087 \times \$2,000,000 = \$17,400$$
$$0.0069 \times \$2,500,000 = \$17,250$$
$$0.0063 \times \$1,443,210 = \$ \ 9,092$$

$50,942

The additional premium because of added time is calculated as follows:

The additional premium for contract duration in excess of 24 months is 1% of the total premium per month for the 10-month extension. The additional cost is:

$$34 \text{ Months} - 24 \text{ Months} = 10 \text{ Months}$$
$$10 \text{ Months} \times 1\%/\text{Month} \times \$50,942 = \qquad \textbf{\$5,094}$$

The additional premium on additional contract value is calculated as follows:
Increase in contract value due
to the equitable adjustment
$$\$1,818,538.05 - \$780,711.00 = \$1,037,827.05$$

Additional premium from rate table
$$0.0144 \times \$500,000$$
$$0.0087 \times \$537,827$$
$$= \qquad \$11,879.10$$

10% increase for 10 additional months
$$\$11,879 \times 10\% \qquad = \qquad \$1,187.91$$

Additional Premium due to Additional Revenue: =   **$13,067.00**

EXHIBIT 13

CALCULATION OF INTEREST DUE

Contract Balance Due—Exhibit 1 $780,711

Interest from December 31, 1992,
to August 23, 1994 (600 days) at
Contractor's Cost of Funding Rate—
(see calculation below):

$$\frac{600 \text{ Days}}{365 \text{ Days}} \times 9.83\% \times \$780,711 \qquad = \qquad \mathbf{\$126,111.56}$$

Equitable Adjustment (Subtotal minus
Contract Balance Due)

   $2,617,406.05 − $780,711.00 = $1,836,695.05

Interest at .0983 simple from December 31, 1992,
to August 23, 1994:

$$\frac{600 \text{ Days}}{365 \text{ Days}} \times 9.83\% \times \$1,836,695.05 = \$296,689.15$$

Total Interest Claim: **$296,689.15**

Cost of Funding Rate

Rate thru Date	Number of Days	Annual Prime Rate *	Days X % per Year
31-Dec-92			
19-Apr-93	109	10.25	1,117.25
12-May-93	23	10.75	247.25
2-Jul-93	51	11.00	561.00
16-Jul-93	14	11.25	157.50
25-Oct-93	101	10.50	1,060.50
20-Dec-93	56	10.25	574.00
30-May-94	161	9.75	1,569.75
23-Aug-94	85	9.62	818.00
Total	600		6,105.25

Average Annual Prime Rate	= 6,105.25 day – % divided by 600 days
	= 9.83%
Cost of Funding** Rate is	= 9.83% plus 0.5%
	= 10.33%

* Prime rate of interest established by National Bank of Columbia
** Contractor's borrowing rate equals the prime rate plus 0.5%.

EXHIBIT 14

COST OF FUNDING RETENTION

PAY ESTIMATE	PERIOD ENDING DATE	FUNDING COST ACCRUES	AMOUNT OF RETENTION	AVERAGE ANNUAL PRIME RATE 0.5% (1)	MONTHLY COST OF FUNDING RATE	MONTHLY COST OF FUNDING RETENTION
35 (3)	25-Jun-91	01-Aug-91	$582,994	9.00%	0.75%	$4,372.46
		01-Sep-91	$582,994 (2)	8.50%	0.71%	$4,127.60
		30-Sep-91	$582,994 (2)	8.50%	0.71%	$4,127.60
		31-Oct-91	$582,994 (2)	8.50%	0.71%	$4,127.60
		30-Nov-91	$582,994 (2)	8.00%	0.67%	$3,888.57
		31-Dec-91	$582,994 (2)	8.00%	0.67%	$3,888.57
		01-Jan-92	$583,992 (4)	7.00%		$41,229.44
				Total		$65,761.83

(1) Prime rate dates are from bank.
(2) Retention amount is assumed to be same as that for Pay Estimate #35.
(3) Last Pay Estimate is assumed to be Pay Estimate #35; settlement is assumed Dec. 31, 1991.
(4) Annual Rate—No change throughout 1992.

EXHIBIT 15

UNPAID WORK

Description	Quantity	Units	Unit Price Bid	Amount	Compensation Due
1. Additional Excavation					
Bid Item #5: General Excavation	548	cy	$3.77	$2,065.96	
Bid Item #7: Structure Excavation	166	cy	$7.65	$1,269.90	
2. Steel					
Bid Item #65: Structural Steel	1,100	lbs	$1.40	$1,540.00	
Bid Item #67: Pit Liner Steel	775	lbs	$1.97	$1,526.75	
3. Compacted Backfill (Bid Item #9)					
Quantity Actually Placed	745	cy	$10.71	$7,978.95	
			Total		$14,382

§ B.15 Job Cost Status Reports

PRIME CONTRACTOR   JOB COST STATUS REPORT AS OF 7/31/91

Cost Code		Description	Original Estimate	Actual cost as of 7/31/91
1150	L	Job Office	470	316
1160	L	Engineer Office	470	650
1170	L	Tool Shed	160	11
1190	L	Signs	160	189
1260	L	Storage of Material	6,300	10,054
1300	L	Drinking Water	1,480	56
1310	L	Unload and Haul	6,060	5,852
1320	L	Winter Conditions	6,380	29,244
1380	L	Temp Heat	1,090	4,316
1400	L	Pumping-Casual	390	3,513
1490	L	Guard Rails	390	812
1510	L	Clean up-periodic	2,370	21,761
1520	L	Clean up-final	720	
1610	L	Move on-off	1,050	143
1630	L	Layout	3,000	22,590
1780	L	Truck Crane-Operator	5,843	6,575
1790	L	Hydro Crane-Operator	3,670	2,240
1830	L	Loader-Operator	1,890	239
1840	L	Backhoe-Operator	630	
1845	L	Operator-Batch Plant	2,640	8,159
1860	L	Maintenance	2,000	9,358
		SUBTOTAL	**47,163**	**126,078**
1870	L	Superintendent	32,420	57,975
1880	L	Asst. Superintendent	66,016	79,643
1890	L	Field Engineer	14,984	36,772
1910	L	Timekeeper		10,129
		SUBTOTAL	**113,420**	**184,519**
1960	L	B/C Mobile Premix		484
1961	L	Repair Culvert	100	54
1962	L	Demo No Wall Switch		132
1963	L	Down-time Block del		30
1964	L	B/C RR Liner		5,109
1966	L	BC Demolition		7,391
1967	L	BC Dust Cont		266
1968	L	B/C Railroad Rebar		337
1969	L	B/C Rebar Shortage		1,105
1970	L	B/C Railroad Epoxy		1,649
1971	L	B/C RR Tunnel R Bol		1,823
1973	L	Portal Gate Transitn		4,641
1974	L	Transformer Cover		414
1975	L	B/C RR Sleeves		351

PRIME CONTRACTOR   JOB COST STATUS REPORT AS OF 7/31/91

Cost Code		Description	Original Estimate	Actual cost as of 7/31/91
1976	L	Insulate Liner		1,724
1977	L	B/C RR Walkway		504
1978	L	B/C RR Temp Roof		554
1979	L	Extra Retaining Wall		6,503
1980	L	Demo Roof	2,400	104
1981	L	Retain Wall Duct #1		957
1982	L	Backfill Duct #1		1,092
1983	L	BC RR Concrete Delay		124
1984	L	Transformer Relocate		0
1985	L	Remove Damper-B/C RR		59
1986	L	Hauling Water-BP		282
1987	L	B/C RR Water Problem		48
1988	L	Demo Duct 2-Lean		150
1989	L	Owner Furn Equipment		757
1990	L	Portal Gate Sills		921
1991	L	Level Indicator		18
1992	L	BC RR Ductwork		2,472
1993	L	BC Joy Dampers		768
1994	L	Elect Change Order		0
1995	L	Weep Holes Clean-up		948
1997	L	B/C Plasterer		733
1998	L	B/C Door Manufacturer		142
1999	L	BC RR Doorway SGGR		203
2001	L	BC Taylor Fence Conc		0
2002	L	BC Scaffold		0
2003	L	BC RR Cover Outage		0
2004	L	BC Multi-coatings		0
2005	L	BC RR Rev Control RM		0
2006	L	BC RR Wattline		0
2011	L	BC RR Waterline		0
2012	L	BC Hoover Backfill		0
2017	L	BC Trans Rework		0
2018	L	BC RR Motorbase Con		0
2019	L	BC RR Zerks		0
2021	L	BC RR Trench Drains		0
		SUBTOTAL	2,500	42,849
2022	L	BC RR Low Roof		0
2110	L	Misc Demo-Generator	2,390	1,162
2111	L	Demo Generator	3,250	2,841
2112	L	Misc. Demo	5,620	1,952
2113	L	Demo Fans	1,500	0
2114	L	Demo Damper	4,090	261

PRIME CONTRACTOR   JOB COST STATUS REPORT AS OF 7/31/91

Cost Code		Description	Original Estimate	Actual cost as of 7/31/91
2115	L	Relocate Fuel Tank	1,030	479
2116	L	Concrete Demolition	15	3,672
		SUBTOTAL	17,895	10,367
2220	L	Misc. Excav		4,408
2225	L	Hand Exc-Rock	1,330	1,049
2240	L	Fine Grade Rock	1,600	1,197
2245	L	Fine Grade Dirt	1,560	984
2250	L	Set Wells	280	79
2251	L	Observe Wells	1,300	499
2260	L	Sand Fill-Gen Room	210	165
2270	L	Dust Control		106
2280	L	Install Rock Bolts		598
2300	L	Sheeting	5,890	0
2501	L	Weep Holes	120	66
		SUBTOTAL	12,290	9,151
3100	L	Concrete Testing	4,970	246
3110	L	Forms-Footings	3,670	5,464
3115	L	Forms-Lean Concrete	1,370	5,062
3130	L	Forms-Infill Walls	11,890	46
3131	L	Forms-Wall-Snow Shed	17,000	15,674
3132	L	Forms-Wall-Air Duct	46,000	43,740
3133	L	Forms-Wall-Portal	62,146	82,525
3134	L	Forms-Wall-Generator	14,740	16,316
3135	L	Forms-Tank Supports	850	634
3136	L	Forms-Walls-Misc.	190	266
3137	L	Forms-Retaining Wall	4,650	6,271
3138	L	Forms-Fan-Motor Bas	5,500	9,299
3139	L	Forms-Duct Piers	8,260	9,559
3140	L	Forms-Wall Fuel Tank	6,810	6,444
3145	L	Forms-Slab on Grade	590	4,197
3146	L	Build Gang Forms	9,925	12,573
3155	L	Forms-Columns	1,240	1,831
3160	L	Forms-Beams	8,380	8,158
3165	L	Forms-Suspended Slab	29,250	36,017
3166	L	Forms-Slab Edge Form	4,570	4,876
3167	L	Forms-Curbs	940	1,370
3170	L	Forms-Stairs	160	0
3185	L	Forms-Bulkheads	10,480	8,684
3187	L	Forms-Transitions	890	4,256
3188	L	Forms-Gate Rest	1,290	1,425
3189	L	Forms-Misc Bases	870	1,788

PRIME CONTRACTOR   JOB COST STATUS REPORT AS OF 7/31/91

Cost Code		Description	Original Estimate	Actual cost as of 7/31/91
3190	L	Screeds	5,040	2,848
3191	L	Standard Keyway	5,240	2,925
3200	L	Place Rebar	62,240	78,913
3201	L	Drill and Set Dowels	7,460	862
3205	L	Unload & Haul Rebar	5,240	5,543
3210	L	Install Mesh	200	388
3250	L	Waterstop	1,080	1,373
3310	L	Place Conc-Footings	1,780	1,473
3315	L	Place Conc-Bases	4,450	3,289
3320	L	Place Conc-Lean	990	5,347
3330	L	Place Conc-Walls	12,360	14,441
3335	L	Place Conc-Infill	1,010	80
3345	L	Place conc-S O G	3,180	4,095
3355	L	Place Conc-Columns	170	183
3365	L	Place Conc-Susp Slab	3,440	6,885
3370	L	Place Conc-Stairs	50	0
3385	L	Place Grout	5,320	422
3386	L	Place Conc-Pads	590	1,244
3400	L	Trowel Finish	1,420	1,558
3410	L	Float Finish	2,750	5,940
3415	L	Cure Concrete	2,430	469
3430	L	Rub Walls	4,390	265
3435	L	Point and Patch	6,140	19,507
3445	L	Expansion Joints	370	1,079
		SUBTOTAL	**393,971**	**445,850**
3446	L	Special Exp Joints	690	3,881
3450	L	Bush Existing Conc	2,150	221
3470	L	Epoxy Bonding	450	276
3510	L	Underslab Visqueen	10	183
3600	L	Precast Coping	370	908
3610	L	Set Precast Gate RS	1,560	0
5400	L	Install Misc Metal	9,960	5,456
5401	L	Remove Trench Drain	760	138
5402	L	Set Trench	730	184
5403	L	Misc Metal-Gate Rest	550	0
5404	L	Misc Anchor Bolts	3,600	2,286
5600	L	Unload Liner	1,370	832
5601	L	Set Liner	12,370	11,684
5602	L	Relocate Liner	1,870	1,677
5603	L	Remove & Load Liner	4,650	4,051
5604	L	Build Car Frame	1,250	566
5606	L	Set Box Liner Form	3,435	6,916
5607	L	Remove Box Liner	1,335	5,233

PRIME CONTRACTOR   JOB COST STATUS REPORT AS OF 7/31/91

Cost Code		Description	Original Estimate	Actual cost as of 7/31/91
5608	L	Seal Airducts		1,267
6140	L	Rough Carp-Blocking	380	0
7150	L	Damproofing	70	0
7200	L	Insulation	90	149
7510	L	Reslet	200	22
8000	L	Airtight Doors	1,280	0
8100	L	Hollow Metal Frames	160	605
8150	L	Hollow Metal Doors	210	16
8500	L	Hollow Metal Windows	30	100
8700	L	Finish Hardware	490	0
10400	L	Subsistence	0	0
10800	L	Toilet Accessories	60	0
13900	L	Millwright Office Work		0
14301	L	Chain Operated Hoist	40	0
15000	L	Install Mechanical	40,000	1,308
15001	L	Misc. Pipe	950	533
15820	L	Unload & Haul Fans	5,050	393
15821	L	Set Fans	13,900	2,867
15822	L	Align Fans & Startup	4,630	0
15823	L	Grout Fan Bases	1,620	0
15824	L	Weld Fan Bases	2,620	0
15825	L	Set Fan Emplates	975	926
16001	L	Drill Ground Rods	580	0
16130	L	Elect. Manholes		2,931
16620	L	Set Main Generator	1,420	506
16621	L	Set Aux Generator	1,420	172
16622	L	Set Temp Generator	61	293
		SUBTOTAL	**123,346**	**56,580**
10400	L	Subsistence	51,520	40,390
17600	L	Payroll Taxes	16,860	61,521
17700	L	Workmen's Comp Ins	16,860	45,344
17900	L	Fringe Benefits	25,472	7,602
		SUBTOTAL	**110,712**	**154,857**
		Prepare Claim		
		GRAND TOTAL	**821,297**	**1,030,251**
1000	M	Performance Bond	41,710	41,592
1010	M	Subcontractor Bond	16,760	8,757

PRIME CONTRACTOR   JOB COST STATUS REPORT AS OF 7/31/91

Cost Code		Description	Original Estimate	Actual cost as of 7/31/91
1040	M	Subsistence		225
1050	M	Builders Risk Ins	18,820	20,822
1060	M	Railroad Insurance	93,870	90,555
		SUBTOTAL	171,160	161,951
1150	M	Job Office	3,215	2,495
1160	M	Engineer Office	3,385	3,605
1170	M	Tool Sheds	3,800	2,550
1180	M	Chemical Toilets	8,270	4,637
1190	M	Signs	410	604
1204	M	Repairs		30
1260	M	Storage of Materials	16,760	16,014
1290	M	Job Communications	1,920	3,984
1300	M	Drinking Water	580	612
1310	M	Unload and Haul	2,745	16,236
1315	M	Unload Haul Equip	2,410	1,000
1320	M	Winter Conditions	2,615	10,517
1330	M	Temp Power-Install		8,552
1350	M	Temp Power-Cords	12,860	6,002
1360	M	Temp Water-Install	4,900	6,018
1380	M	Temp Heat	9,410	13,289
1390	M	Telephone	9,320	7,207
1400	M	Pumping-Casual	500	13,351
1410	M	Printing-Supplies	825	69
1420	M	Blueprinting	770	821
1440	M	Photographs	825	198
1450	M	Office Equipment	590	7,621
1460	M	Arch Office Equip	1,535	2,317
1470	M	First Aid	825	1,137
1480	M	Hard Hats	1,030	1,294
1490	M	Guard Rails	515	0
1500	M	Fire Extinguishers	620	1,385
1520	M	Cleanup-Final	200	0
1550	M	Debris Box	7,920	0
1560	M	Shore Existing Brg.	5,000	0
1590	M	Travel and Entertain		4,272
1610	M	Move on-off	2,100	0
1620	M	Layout	200	379
1630	M	Layout-Reg. Engineer	830	263
		SUBTOTAL	106,885	136,459
1660	M	Small Tools	3,170	66,989
1670	M	Concrete Buckets	2,920	0

PRIME CONTRACTOR   JOB COST STATUS REPORT AS OF 7/31/91

Cost Code		Description	Original Estimate	Actual cost as of 7/31/91
1680	M	Portable Generators	3,000	9,087
1690	M	Vibrators	3,250	9,496
1720	M	Survey Equipment	3,730	5,397
1730	M	Farm Wagons	960	0
1740	M	Pick-up Trucks	8,580	9,104
1750	M	Flatbed Trucks	3,600	6,077
1760	M	Compressors	4,950	12,114
1780	M	Truck Crane	44,000	113,558
1790	M	Hydro Crane	25,900	60,734
1830	M	Loader	13,500	45,200
1840	M	Backhoe	3,210	2,159
1850	M	Scaffold	1,000	0
1860	M	Fuel Oil and Grease	49,525	39,972
		SUBTOTAL	171,295	379,887
1870	M	Superintendent		12,808
1961	M	Repair Culvert		266
1962	M	Demo No Wall Switch		0
1963	M	Down-time Block Delay		0
1964	M	BC Railroad Liner		10,673
1965	M	Blasting Consultant		7,775
1966	M	BC Demolition		1,467
1967	M	BC Dust Cont.		0
1969	M	B/C Rebar Shortage		0
1971	M	B/C RR Tunnel R Bolt		1,212
1972	M	B/C RR Power Outage		1,538
1975	M	BC Railroad Sleeves		240
1976	M	Insulate T Liner		215
1977	M	BCRR Walkway		375
1978	M	BCRR Temp Roof		713
1979	M	Extra Retaining Wall		23,446
1980	M	RR Hydrant		182
1981	M	Retain Wall Duct #1		1,810
1982	M	Backfill Duct #1		2,556
1983	M	BC RR Concrete Delay		0
1984	M	Transformer Relocate		0
1985	M	Remove Damper-B/C RR		0
1987	M	B/C RR Water Problem		0
1988	M	Demo Duct 2-Lean		0
1989	M	Owner Furn Equipment		0
1990	M	Portal Gate Sills		0
1991	M	Level Indicator		0
1992	M	Repairs - Snow Melt		1,917
1993	M	Repair Snowmelt Fird		347

PRIME CONTRACTOR   JOB COST STATUS REPORT AS OF 7/31/91

Cost Code		Description	Original Estimate	Actual cost as of 7/31/91
1994	M	Elect Change Order		0
1995	M	Weep Holes Clean up		0
1996	M	Temp Help		3,844
		SUBTOTAL	0	71,384
1997	M	BC Plasterer		0
1999	M	BC RR Doorway SGGR		0
2001	M	BC Fence Conc		0
2003	M	BC RR Xover Outage		0
2005	M	RC RR Rev Control RM		0
2006	M	BC RR Material		0
2007	M	BC RR Tunnel Rock		0
2008	M	BC Duct Bank		0
2009	M	BC RMMW Misc Metal		0
2010	M	Soil Testing	1,820	996
2011	M	BC RR Waterline		0
2012	M	BC Backfill		0
2017	M	BC RC Trans Rework		0
2019	M	BC PR Zerks		0
2021	M	BC RR Trench Drains		0
2022	M	BC RR Low Roof		0
		SUBTOTAL	1,820	996
2050	M	Rock Bolt Testing	321	1,889
2110	M	Demo	1,880	420
2230	M	Sand Backfill	660	174
2250	M	Observations Wells	660	763
2300	M	Sheeting	23,880	2,748
2301	M	Sheeting Equip.	2,805	0
2501	M	Weep Holes	80	0
2981	M	Rock Bolts		2,356
3000	M	Concrete Material	540,934	615,153
3018	M	BC RC Motor Base Con		0
3050	M	Concrete Testing	12,470	0
		SUBTOTAL	583,690	623,503
3100	M	Form Rental	9,000	76,913
3101	M	Form Plywood	29,626	14,414
3102	M	Form Hardware	13,840	23,299
3103	M	Form Dim Lumber	51,330	37,236
3104	M	Form Ties	14,640	8,961
3190	M	Screeds	6,650	271

PRIME CONTRACTOR   JOB COST STATUS REPORT AS OF 7/31/91

Cost Code		Description	Original Estimate	Actual cost as of 7/31/91
		SUBTOTAL	125,086	161,094
3200	M	Furnish Rebar	160,310	166,317
3201	M	Furnish Dowels	5,770	4,087
3210	M	Furnish Mesh	620	729
3250	M	Waterstop	1,340	5,364
3385	M	Grout	15,650	14,233
3415	M	Cure	3,270	385
3430	M	Point & Patch	4,870	4,127
3445	M	Expansion Joint	640	1,254
3446	M	Special Expansion Jt	30,000	38,415
3470	M	Epoxy Bonding	3,680	374
3510	M	Visqueen	10	362
3511	M	Saw Cutting	1,290	1,290
3600	M	Precast Coping	1,800	40
5400	M	Misc Metal	103,990	47,250
5401	M	Misc Anchor Bolts	2,970	4
5402	M	Misc Steel Items	1,510	11,473
5403	M	Ultrasonic Testing	7,250	0
5600	M	Steel Tunnel Liner	125,169	135,718
5601	M	Misc Liner Material	9,581	6,759
5606	M	Liner Form Material	1,270	25,388
6000	M	Rough Carpentry	430	0
7150	M	Damproofing	150	0
7200	M	Insulation	270	433
7510	M	Reglet	100	0
8100	M	Hollow Metal Dr & Fr	4,220	4,271
8385	M	Airtight Doors	33,205	33,205
8700	M	Hardware	1,500	3,102
10400	M	Subsistence		3,817
10800	M	Toilet Accessories	180	728
13900	M	WI Install RMM Gate		0
13901	M	WI Rework RMM Gate		0
13910	M	WI Fabricate RMM Gate		0
13911	M	WI Rework RMM Gate		0
14301	M	Electric Hoists	1,160	1,231
15000	M	Furnish Mechanical		29,028
15001	M	Pipe Material	2,060	8,629
15869	M	Relief Dampers	40,000	0
15900	M	Controls	317,840	17,105
15950	M	Temp Controls	21,020	0
16001	M	Drill Ground Rods	1,890	2,160
16010	M	Electrical Manholes		6,081
16620	M	Main Generator	645,560	624,988

PRIME CONTRACTOR   JOB COST STATUS REPORT AS OF 7/31/91

Cost Code		Description	Original Estimate	Actual cost as of 7/31/91
16621	M	Stanby Generator	32,130	40,147
17800	M	Fringe Benefits	1,000	318
		SUBTOTAL	1,583,705	1,238,812
		GRAND TOTAL	2,743,641	2,774,086
2005	P	Material CRM Rev		0
2008	P	BC Con Rework		0
3200	P	Extra Rebar		0
5400	P	Extra Misc Metal		0
13900	P	RMM Equipment Buyout	0	0
16010	P	Extra Manholes		0
		GRAND TOTAL	0	0
2000	S	Earthwork	340,739	328,628
2250	S	Well	2,810	0
2700	S	Fence	17,340	0
2850	S	Work Train	4,000	0
3500	S	Core Drilling	1,380	0
3511	S	Saw Cutting	440	0
5605	S	B/C Railroad-Liner		26,052
7100	S	Waterproofing	5,880	2,150
7500	S	Built up Roof	20,160	7,210
7530	S	Elastomeric Roof	9,790	0
7550	S	Foam Roofing	22,464	0
7600	S	Sheet Metal	8,800	167
7601	S	Sheet Metal		0
7900	S	Caulking	16,480	0
8300	S	Telescoping Door	7,070	7,071
8367	S	Vert Lift Door	56,300	0
8850	S	Glass and Glazing	350	0
9100	S	Plaster	9,740	0
9250	S	Drywall	4,950	0
9300	S	Ceramic Tile	1,590	0
9310	S	Ceramic		0
9500	S	Acoustic Ceiling	350	0
9650	S	Resilient Floor	500	0
9900	S	Painting ·	20,000	0
9905	S	Gate Equipment Paint		0
10200	S	Louver	19,800	18,800
13900	S	Portal Gate	415,000	296,882
13910	S	Millwright	0	0
15043	S	Mechanical Contractor	0	0

APPENDIXES

PRIME CONTRACTOR   JOB COST STATUS REPORT AS OF 7/31/91

Cost Code		Description	Original Estimate	Actual cost as of 7/31/91
15180	S	Mech Insulation	12,332	0
16000	S	Electrical Contractor	756,150	532,016
		GRAND TOTAL	1,754,415	1,218,976
900	X	Internal Charges	0	0
1000	X	Legal Expenses	0	0
1100	X	Prepare Claim	0	0
13900	X	Engin Mechanical	0	0
13901	X	Engin Civil	0	0
17900	X	Liability Insurance	0	0
13900	X	Claim	0	0
15000	X	Warranty Work	0	0
		GRAND TOTAL	0	0

PRIME CONTRACTOR   JOB COST STATUS REPORT AS OF 12/31/92

Cost Code		Description	Original Estimate	Cost as of 12/31/92
1150	L	Job Office	470	316
1160	L	Engineer Office	470	782
1170	L	Tool Shed	160	11
1190	L	Signs	160	189
1260	L	Storage of Material	6,300	10,054
1300	L	Drinking Water	1,480	91
1310	L	Unload and Haul	6,060	17,678
1320	L	Winter Conditions	6,380	38,676
1380	L	Temp Heat	1,090	5,212
1400	L	Pumping-Casual	390	9,811
1490	L	Guard Rails	390	1,202
1510	L	Clean up-periodic	2,370	38,292
1520	L	Clean up-final	720	36,255
1610	L	Move on-off	1,050	143
1630	L	Layout	3,000	22,851
1780	L	Truck Crane-Operator	5,843	7,611
1790	L	Hydro Crane-Operator	3,670	2,241
1830	L	Loader-Operator	1,890	556
1840	L	Backhoe-Operator	630	5
1845	L	Operator-Batch Plant	2,640	8,159
1860	L	Maintenance	2,000	11,477
		SUBTOTAL	**47,163**	**211,612**
1870	L	Superintendent	32,420	163,176
1880	L	Asst. Superintendent	66,016	88,989
1890	L	Field Engineer	14,984	49,690
1910	L	Timekeeper		13,424
		SUBTOTAL	**113,420**	**315,279**
1960	L	B/C Mobile Premix		480
1961	L	Repair Culvert	100	54
1962	L	Demo No Wall Switch		132
1963	L	Down-time Block del		30
1964	L	B/C RR Liner		5,110
1966	L	BC Demolition		20,266
1967	L	BC Dust Cont		266
1968	L	B/C Railroad Rebar		337
1969	L	B/C Rebar Shortage		1,105
1970	L	B/C Railroad Epoxy		1,649
1971	L	B/C RR Tunnel R Bol		1,824
1973	L	Portal Gate Transitn		4,641
1974	L	Transformer Cover		414
1975	L	B/C RR Sleeves		352

PRIME CONTRACTOR   JOB COST STATUS REPORT AS OF 12/31/92

Cost Code		Description	Original Estimate	Cost as of 12/31/92
1976	L	Insulate Liner		1,724
1977	L	B/C RR Walkway		1,022
1978	L	B/C RR Temp Roof		554
1979	L	Extra Retaining Wall		6,503
1980	L	Demo Roof	2,400	1,702
1981	L	Retain Wall Duct #1		957
1982	L	Backfill Duct #1		1,093
1983	L	BC RR Concrete Delay		124
1984	L	Transformer Relocate		0
1985	L	Remove Damper-B/C RR		156
1986	L	Hauling Water-BP		283
1987	L	B/C RR Water Problem		48
1988	L	Demo Duct 2-Lean		150
1989	L	Owner Furn Equipment		757
1990	L	Portal Gate Sills		6,870
1991	L	Level Indicator		19
1992	L	BC RR Ductwork		15,363
1993	L	BC Joy Dampers		3,644
1994	L	Elect Change Order	.	0
1995	L	Weep Holes Clean-up		948
1997	L	B/C Plasterer		2,377
1998	L	B/C Door Manufacturer		142
1999	L	BC RR Doorway SGGR		203
2001	L	BC Taylor Fence Conc		30
2002	L	BC Scaffold		156
2003	L	BC RR Cover Outage		75
2004	L	BC Multi-coatings		156
2005	L	BC RR Rev Control RM		252
2006	L	BC RR Wattline		0
2011	L	BC RR Waterline		1,541
2012	L	BC Hoover Backfill		0
2017	L	BC Trans Rework		0
2018	L	BC RR Motorbase Con		1,951
2019	L	BC RR Zerks		2,886
2021	L	BC RR Trench Drains		3,814
		SUBTOTAL	2,500	92,160
2022	L	BC RR Low Roof		916
2110	L	Misc Demo-Generator	2,390	1,163
2111	L	Demo Generator	3,250	3,633
2112	L	Misc. Demo	5,620	2,083
2113	L	Demo Fans	1,500	0
2114	L	Demo Damper	4,090	1,101

PRIME CONTRACTOR   JOB COST STATUS REPORT AS OF 12/31/92

Cost Code		Description	Original Estimate	Cost as of 12/31/92
2115	L	Relocate Fuel Tank	1,030	479
2116	L	Concrete Demolition	15	4,360
		SUBTOTAL	**17,895**	**13,735**
2220	L	Misc. Excav		17,192
2225	L	Hand Exc-Rock	1,330	2,235
2240	L	Fine Grade Rock	1,600	1,276
2245	L	Fine Grade Dirt	1,560	3,834
2250	L	Set Wells	280	79
2251	L	Observe Wells	1,300	500
2260	L	Sand Fill-Gen Room	210	166
2270	L	Dust Control		106
2280	L	Install Rock Bolts		598
2300	L	Sheeting	5,890	77
2501	L	Weep Holes	120	66
		SUBTOTAL	**12,290**	**26,129**
3100	L	Concrete Testing	4,970	246
3110	L	Forms-Footings	3,670	5,464
3115	L	Forms-Lean Concrete	1,370	5,062
3130	L	Forms-Infill Walls	11,890	46
3131	L	Forms-Wall-Snow Shed	17,000	15,674
3132	L	Forms-Wall-Air Duct	46,000	43,740
3133	L	Forms-Wall-Portal	62,146	83,494
3134	L	Forms-Wall-Generator	14,740	16,316
3135	L	Forms-Tank Supports	850	722
3136	L	Forms-Walls-Misc.	190	449
3137	L	Forms-Retaining Wall	4,650	6,271
3138	L	Forms-Fan-Motor Bas	5,500	9,299
3139	L	Forms-Duct Piers	8,260	9,559
3140	L	Forms-Wall Fuel Tank	6,810	6,445
3145	L	Forms-Slab on Grade	590	4,197
3146	L	Build Gang Forms	9,925	13,366
3155	L	Forms-Columns	1,240	1,831
3160	L	Forms-Beams	8,380	8,312
3165	L	Forms-Suspended Slab	29,250	36,362
3166	L	Forms-Slab Edge Form	4,570	4,877
3167	L	Forms-Curbs	940	1,371
3170	L	Forms-Stairs	160	0
3185	L	Forms-Bulkheads	10,480	8,684
3187	L	Forms-Transitions	890	4,655
3188	L	Forms-Gate Rest	1,290	4,879
3189	L	Forms-Misc Bases	870	4,303

PRIME CONTRACTOR   JOB COST STATUS REPORT AS OF 12/31/92

Cost Code		Description	Original Estimate	Cost as of 12/31/92
3190	L	Screeds	5,040	2,848
3191	L	Standard Keyway	5,240	3,126
3200	L	Place Rebar	62,240	81,151
3201	L	Drill and Set Dowels	7,460	1,281
3205	L	Unload & Haul Rebar	5,240	5,543
3210	L	Install Mesh	200	388
3250	L	Waterstop	1,080	1,373
3310	L	Place Conc-Footings	1,780	1,473
3315	L	Place Conc-Bases	4,450	3,332
3320	L	Place Conc-Lean	990	5,347
3330	L	Place Conc-Walls	12,360	14,441
3335	L	Place Conc-Infill	1,010	80
3345	L	Place conc-S O G	3,180	4,095
3355	L	Place Conc-Columns	170	184
3365	L	Place Conc-Susp Slab	3,440	6,885
3370	L	Place Conc-Stairs	50	0
3385	L	Place Grout	5,320	4,157
3386	L	Place Conc-Pads	590	1,481
3400	L	Trowel Finish	1,420	1,558
3410	L	Float Finish	2,750	5,983
3415	L	Cure Concrete	2,430	481
3430	L	Rub Walls	4,390	592
3435	L	Point and Patch	6,140	93,675
3445	L	Expansion Joints	370	4,575
		SUBTOTAL	**393,971**	**539,673**
3446	L	Special Exp Joints	690	14,992
3450	L	Bush Existing Conc	2,150	807
3470	L	Epoxy Bonding	450	276
3510	L	Underslab Visqueen	10	183
3600	L	Precast Coping	370	1,292
3610	L	Set Precast Gate RS	1,560	1,346
5400	L	Install Misc Metal	9,960	25,914
5401	L	Remove Trench Drain	760	138
5402	L	Set Trench	730	184
5403	L	Misc Metal-Gate Rest	550	420
5404	L	Misc Anchor Bolts	3,600	3,027
5600	L	Unload Liner	1,370	832
5601	L	Set Liner	12,370	11,684
5602	L	Relocate Liner	1,870	1,677
5603	L	Remove & Load Liner	4,650	4,051
5604	L	Build Car Frame	1,250	567
5606	L	Set Box Liner Form	3,435	6,916
5607	L	Remove Box Liner	1,335	5,233

PRIME CONTRACTOR   JOB COST STATUS REPORT AS OF 12/31/92

Cost Code		Description	Original Estimate	Cost as of 12/31/92
5608	L	Seal Airducts		1,267
6140	L	Rough Carp-Blocking	380	0
7150	L	Damproofing	70	0
7200	L	Insulation	90	149
7510	L	Reslet	200	22
8000	L	Airtight Doors	1,280	1,204
8100	L	Hollow Metal Frames	160	905
8150	L	Hollow Metal Doors	210	2,236
8500	L	Hollow Metal Windows	30	100
8700	L	Finish Hardware	490	1,334
10400	L	Subsistence	0	0
10800	L	Toilet Accessories	60	200
13900	L	Millwright Office Work		12,874
14301	L	Chain Operated Hoist	40	0
15000	L	Install Mechanical	40,000	41,854
15001	L	Misc. Pipe	950	1,452
15820	L	Unload & Haul Fans	5,050	393
15821	L	Set Fans	13,900	4,005
15822	L	Align Fans & Startup	4,630	2,213
15823	L	Grout Fan Bases	1,620	5,505
15824	L	Weld Fan Bases	2,620	308
15825	L	Set Fan Emplates	975	926
16001	L	Drill Ground Rods	580	0
16130	L	Elect. Manholes		2,998
16620	L	Set Main Generator	1,420	506
16621	L	Set Aux Generator	1,420	259
16622	L	Set Temp Generator	61	293
		SUBTOTAL	**123,346**	**160,542**
10400	L	Subsistence	51,520	56,018
17600	L	Payroll Taxes	16,860	126,767
17700	L	Workmen's Comp Ins	16,860	88,634
17900	L	Fringe Benefits	25,472	27,014
		SUBTOTAL	**110,712**	**298,433**
		Prepare Claim		30,475
		GRAND TOTAL	**821,297**	**1,688,038**
1000	M	Performance Bond	41,710	50,942
1010	M	Subcontractor Bond	16,760	8,757

PRIME CONTRACTOR   JOB COST STATUS REPORT AS OF 12/31/92

Cost Code		Description	Original Estimate	Cost as of 12/31/92
1040	M	Subsistence		525
1050	M	Builders Risk Ins	18,820	18,904
1060	M	Railroad Insurance	93,870	85,802
		SUBTOTAL	**171,160**	**164,930**
1150	M	Job Office	3,215	3,550
1160	M	Engineer Office	3,385	5,181
1170	M	Tool Sheds	3,800	3,750
1180	M	Chemical Toilets	8,270	8,124
1190	M	Signs	410	668
1204	M	Repairs		106
1260	M	Storage of Materials	16,760	16,014
1290	M	Job Communications	1,920	5,822
1300	M	Drinking Water	580	612
1310	M	Unload and Haul	2,745	19,824
1315	M	Unload Haul Equip	2,410	1,312
1320	M	Winter Conditions	2,615	11,245
1330	M	Temp Power-Install		8,552
1350	M	Temp Power-Cords	12,860	7,157
1360	M	Temp Water-Install	4,900	6,095
1380	M	Temp Heat	9,410	19,833
1390	M	Telephone	9,320	12,635
1400	M	Pumping-Casual	500	16,731
1410	M	Printing-Supplies	825	624
1420	M	Blueprinting	770	896
1440	M	Photographs	825	223
1450	M	Office Equipment	590	9,324
1460	M	Arch Office Equip	1,535	2,403
1470	M	First Aid	825	1,547
1480	M	Hard Hats	1,030	1,921
1490	M	Guard Rails	515	0
1500	M	Fire Extinguishers	620	1,481
1520	M	Cleanup-Final	200	2,822
1550	M	Debris Box	7,920	0
1560	M	Shore Existing Brg.	5,000	0
1590	M	Travel and Entertain		5,087
1610	M	Move on-off	2,100	4,018
1620	M	Layout	200	379
1630	M	Layout-Reg. Engineer	830	263
		SUBTOTAL	**106,885**	**178,199**
1660	M	Small Tools	3,170	99,106
1670	M	Concrete Buckets	2,920	0

PRIME CONTRACTOR   JOB COST STATUS REPORT AS OF 12/31/92

Cost Code		Description	Original Estimate	Cost as of 12/31/92
1680	M	Portable Generators	3,000	9,564
1690	M	Vibrators	3,250	9,818
1720	M	Survey Equipment	3,730	6,101
1730	M	Farm Wagons	960	0
1740	M	Pick-up Trucks	8,580	17,532
1750	M	Flatbed Trucks	3,600	8,990
1760	M	Compressors	4,950	19,412
1780	M	Truck Crane	44,000	134,078
1790	M	Hydro Crane	25,900	78,017
1830	M	Loader	13,500	66,084
1840	M	Backhoe	3,210	16,834
1850	M	Scaffold	1,000	808
1860	M	Fuel Oil and Grease	49,525	70,460
		SUBTOTAL	171,295	536,804
1870	M	Superintendent		14,776
1961	M	Repair Culvert		266
1962	M	Demo No Wall Switch		0
1963	M	Down-time Block Delay		0
1964	M	BC Railroad Liner		10,673
1965	M	Blasting Consultant		7,775
1966	M	BC Demolition		17,722
1967	M	BC Dust Cont.		0
1969	M	B/C Rebar Shortage		0
1971	M	B/C RR Tunnel R Bolt		1,212
1972	M	B/C RR Power Outage		1,538
1975	M	BC Railroad Sleeves		240
1976	M	Insulate T Liner		215
1977	M	BCRR Walkway		375
1978	M	BCRR Temp Roof		713
1979	M	Extra Retaining Wall		23,446
1980	M	RR Hydrant		182
1981	M	Retain Wall Duct #1		1,810
1982	M	Backfill Duct #1		2,556
1983	M	BC RR Concrete Delay		0
1984	M	Transformer Relocate		0
1985	M	Remove Damper-B/C RR		0
1987	M	B/C RR Water Problem		0
1988	M	Demo Duct 2-Lean		0
1989	M	Owner Furh Equipment		0
1990	M	Portal Gate Sills		327
1991	M	Level Indicator		0
1992	M	Repairs - Snow Melt		14,245
1993	M	Repair Snowmelt Fird		1,841

PRIME CONTRACTOR   JOB COST STATUS REPORT AS OF 12/31/92

Cost Code		Description	Original Estimate	Cost as of 12/31/92
1994	M	Elect Change Order		1,592
1995	M	Weep Holes Clean up		0
1996	M	Temp Help		9,964
		SUBTOTAL	0	111,468
1997	M	BC Plasterer		356
1999	M	BC RR Doorway SGGR		0
2001	M	BC Fence Conc		2,332
2003	M	BC RR Xover Outage		0
2005	M	RC RR Rev Control RM		0
2006	M	BC RR Material		262
2007	M	BC RR Tunnel Rock		0
2008	M	BC Duct Bank		62,179
2009	M	BC RMMW Misc Metal		6,526
2010	M	Soil Testing	1,820	996
2011	M	BC RR Waterline		1,120
2012	M	BC Backfill		4,981
2017	M	BC RC Trans Rework		0
2019	M	BC PR Zerks		1,179
2021	M	BC RR Trench Drains		2,573
2022	M	BC RR Low Roof		0
		SUBTOTAL	1,820	82,504
2050	M	Rock Bolt Testing	321	2,233
2110	M	Demo	1,880	420
2230	M	Sand Backfill	660	5,510
2250	M	Observations Wells	660	763
2300	M	Sheeting	23,880	2,748
2301	M	Sheeting Equip.	2,805	0
2501	M	Weep Holes	80	0
2981	M	Rock Bolts		2,356
3000	M	Concrete Material	540,934	617,203
3018	M	BC RC Motor Base Con		0
3050	M	Concrete Testing	12,470	122
		SUBTOTAL	583,690	631,355
3100	M	Form Rental	9,000	84,863
3101	M	Form Plywood	29,626	14,414
3102	M	Form Hardware	13,840	23,811
3103	M	Form Dim Lumber	51,330	37,239
3104	M	Form Ties	14,640	8,961
3190	M	Screeds	6,650	271

PRIME CONTRACTOR   JOB COST STATUS REPORT AS OF 12/31/92

Cost Code		Description	Original Estimate	Cost as of 12/31/92
		SUBTOTAL	**125,086**	**169,559**
3200	M	Furnish Rebar	160,310	165,453
3201	M	Furnish Dowels	5,770	4,087
3210	M	Furnish Mesh	620	729
3250	M	Waterstop	1,340	5,364
3385	M	Grout	15,650	31,810
3415	M	Cure	3,270	385
3430	M	Point & Patch	4,870	18,114
3445	M	Expansion Joint	640	1,459
3446	M	Special Expansion Jt	30,000	38,415
3470	M	Epoxy Bonding	3,680	459
3510	M	Visqueen	10	362
3511	M	Saw Cutting	1,290	4,110
3600	M	Precast Coping	1,800	703
5400	M	Misc Metal	103,990	61,259
5401	M	Misc Anchor Bolts	2,970	431
5402	M	Misc Steel Items	1,510	11,583
5403	M	Ultrasonic Testing	7,250	0
5600	M	Steel Tunnel Liner	125,169	135,718
5601	M	Misc Liner Material	9,581	6,759
5606	M	Liner Form Material	1,270	25,388
6000	M	Rough Carpentry	430	0
7150	M	Damproofing	150	0
7200	M	Insulation	270	433
7510	M	Reglet	100	0
8100	M	Hollow Metal Dr & Fr	4,220	4,301
8385	M	Airtight Doors	33,205	33,205
8700	M	Hardware	1,500	3,986
10400	M	Subsistence		3,817
10800	M	Toilet Accessories	180	891
13900	M	WI Install RMM Gate		0
13901	M	WI Rework RMM Gate		0
13910	M	WI Fabricate RMM Gate		0
13911	M	WI Rework RMM Gate		0
14301	M	Electric Hoists	1,160	1,231
15000	M	Furnish Mechanical		124,228
15001	M	Pipe Material	2,060	11,537
15869	M	Relief Dampers	40,000	97,767
15900	M	Controls	317,840	301,055
15950	M	Temp Controls	21,020	38,485
16001	M	Drill Ground Rods	1,890	2,160
16010	M	Electrical Manholes		6,081
16620	M	Main Generator	645,560	634,518

PRIME CONTRACTOR   JOB COST STATUS REPORT AS OF 12/31/92

Cost Code		Description	Original Estimate	Cost as of 12/31/92
16621	M	Stanby Generator	32,130	40,147
17800	M	Fringe Benefits	1,000	318
		SUBTOTAL	1,583,705	1,816,748
		GRAND TOTAL	2,743,641	3,691,567
2005	P	Material CRM Rev		845
2008	P	BC Con Rework		3,484
3200	P	Extra Rebar		0
5400	P	Extra Misc Metal		0
13900	P	RMM Equipment Buyout	0	9,350
16010	P	Extra Manholes		0
		GRAND TOTAL	0	13,679
2000	S	Earthwork	340,739	328,628
2250	S	Well	2,810	0
2700	S	Fence	17,340	14,550
2850	S	Work Train	4,000	0
3500	S	Core Drilling	1,380	0
3511	S	Saw Cutting	440	0
5605	S	B/C Railroad-Liner		26,052
7100	S	Waterproofing	5,880	6,185
7500	S	Built up Roof	20,160	7,210
7530	S	Elastomeric Roof	9,790	0
7550	S	Foam Roofing	22,464	36,379
7600	S	Sheet Metal	8,800	3,600
7601	S	Sheet Metal		6,600
7900	S	Caulking	16,480	17,052
8300	S	Telescoping Door	7,070	7,071
8367	S	Vert Lift Door	56,300	52,645
8850	S	Glass and Glazing	350	897
9100	S	Plaster	9,740	30,420
9250	S	Drywall	4,950	0
9300	S	Ceramic Tile	1,590	0
9310	S	Ceramic		2,525
9500	S	Acoustic Ceiling	350	0
9650	S	Resilient Floor	500	1,065
9900	S	Painting	20,000	12,451
9905	S	Gate Equipment Paint		5,106
10200	S	Louver	19,800	19,800
13900	S	Portal Gate	415,000	349,228
13910	S	Millwright	0	605,493
15043	S	Mechanical Contractor	0	1,200

APPENDIX B

PRIME CONTRACTOR   JOB COST STATUS REPORT AS OF 12/31/92

Cost Code		Description	Original Estimate	Cost as of 12/31/92
15180	S	Mech Insulation	12,332	12,414
16000	S	Electrical Contractor	756,150	532,016
		GRAND TOTAL	1,754,415	2,078,587
900	X	Internal Charges	0	132,570
1000	X	Legal Expenses	0	137,996
1100	X	Prepare Claim	0	284,853
13900	X	Engin Mechanical	0	49,375
13901	X	Engin Civil	0	16,303
17900	X	Liability Insurance	0	827
13900	X	Claim	0	0
15000	X	Warranty Work	0	866
		GRAND TOTAL	0	622,790

§ B.16 Consolidated Statements of Operations

PRIME CONTRACTOR

CONSTRUCTION COMPANY AND SUBSIDIARIES

Years ended December 31, 1990 and 1989

	1990	1989
Earnings from construction:		
Revenue earned	$164,911,421	$152,029,537
Cost of construction	156,763,785	146,528,788
Gross earnings	8,147,636	5,500,749
General and administrative expenses	6,154,024	5,256,051
Earnings (loss) from operations	1,993,612	244,698
Other income (expense):		
Gain on sale of property and equipment and investment real estate	102,450	339,304
Interest and dividend income	563,389	379,043
Interest expense	-544,305	-386,911
Other income	55,202	154,853
	176,736	486,289
Earnings (loss) before income taxes and extraordinary item	2,170,348	730,987
Income tax expense (benefit) (note 6)	954,953	322,000
Net earnings (loss)	$1,215,395	$408,987

See accompanying notes to consolidated financial statements.

PRIME CONTRACTOR

CONSTRUCTION COMPANY AND SUBSIDIARIES

Years ended December 31, 1992 and 1991

	1992	1991
Earnings from construction:		
Revenue earned	$153,432,518	$126,808,743
Cost of construction	146,621,441	119,714,217
Gross earnings	6,811,077	7,094,526
General and administrative expenses	5,440,565	5,819,270
Earnings (loss) from operations	1,370,512	1,275,256
Other income (expense):		
Gain on sale of property and equipment and investment real estate	237,405	55,127
Interest and dividend income	579,121	491,281
Interest expense	-289,122	-356,719
Other income	47,450	21,244
	574,854	210,933
Earnings (loss) before income taxes and extraordinary item	1,945,366	1,486,189
Income tax expense (benefit) (note 6)	875,415	668,785
Net earnings (loss)	$1,069,951	$817,404

See accompanying notes to consolidated financial statements.

TABLE OF CASES

237

Case	*Book §*
Camper v. W.J. McDermott, 71 Cal. Rptr. 590 (Ct. App. 1968)	§ 12.4
Capital Elec. Co., GSBCA Nos. 5316, 5317, 83-2 B.C.A. (CCH) ¶ 16,458 (1983), *rev'd on other grounds,* 729 F.2d 743 (Fed. Cir. 1984)	§§ 6.1, 6.2, 6.3, 6.6, 6.8, 6.10, 6.11, 6.15
Capital Sec. Servs., Inc., GSBCA No. 5722, 81-1 B.C.A. (CCH) ¶ 14,923 (1980)	§ 9.7
Carteret Work Uniforms, Inc., ASBCA No. 1647, 6 CCF § 61,651-1951 (1954)	§ 6.15
Carteret Work Uniforms, Inc., ASBCA No. 1647, 6 CCF ¶ 21,501 (1954)	§ 6.15
Carvel Walker, ENGBCA No. 3744, 78-1 B.C.A. (CCH) ¶ 13,005 (1971)	§§ 8.3, 8.4
C.E. Lowther & Son, ASBCA No. 26,760, 85-2 B.C.A. (CCH) ¶ 18,144 (1985)	§ 4.16
C.F.I. Constr. Co., DOT CAB Nos. 1782, 1801, 87-1 B.C.A. (CCH) ¶ 19,547 (1987)	§§ 4.2, 4.9, 8.8
Chaney & James Constr. Co. v. United States, 421 F.2d 728 (Ct. Cl. 1970)	§ 8.3
Charles Burton Builders, Inc. v. L&S Constr. Co., 271 A.2d 534 (Md. 1970)	§ 9.11
Christie-Willamette, VABCA No. 1182-16, 85-1 B.C.A. (CCH) ¶ 17,930 (1985)	§ 9.6
C.L. Fairley Constr. Co., ASBCA No. 32,581, 90-2 B.C.A. (CCH) ¶ 22,665 (1990)	§§ 3.4, 3.7
Clark v. Aenchbacher, 238 S.E.2d 442 (Ga. Ct. App. 1977)	§ 10.1
Clark v. Hirt, IBCA No. 1508-8-81, 84-1 B.C.A. (CCH) ¶ 17,134 (1984)	§ 8.8
Clarke Baridon, Inc. v. Merritt-Chapman & Scott Corp., 311 F.2d 389 (4th Cir. 1962)	§§ 2.6, 2.9, 2.14
Coath & Gross, Inc. v. United States, 101 Ct. Cl. 702 (1944)	§ 6.2
Columbus & S. Ohio Elec. Co. v. J.P. Sand & Gravel Co., 489 N.E.2d 830 (Ohio Ct. App. 1985)	§ 3.23
Commonwealth Dep't of Highways v. Young, 380 S.W.2d 239 (Ky. 1964)	§ 9.10
Consolidated Constr., Inc., GSBCA No. 8871, 88-2 B.C.A. (CCH) ¶ 20,811 (1988)	§ 9.14
Continental Consolidation Corp., ASBCA No. 10,662, 67-1 B.C.A. (CCH) ¶ 6127 (1967)	§ 2.14
Corry Bridge & Supply Co., AGBCA No. 81-149-1, 82-2 B.C.A. (CCH) ¶ 16,008 (1982)	§ 2.14
Cosmic Constr. Co., ASBCA Nos. 24,014, 24,036, 88-2 B.C.A. (CCH) ¶ 20,623 (1988)	§§ 2.19, 2.20
Covington Bros. v. Valley Plastering, Inc., 566 P.2d 814 (Nev. 1977)	§ 8.7
C-Ran Corp., ASBCA No. 37,643, 90-3 B.C.A. (CCH) ¶ 23,201 (1990)	§ 6.1

INDEX